Knight

Noble Warrior of England 1200–1600

OSPREY
PUBLISHING

Dedication

For Jane and Joanna, in recognition of their outstanding patience.

Knight

Noble Warrior of England 1200–1600

CHRISTOPHER GRAVETT

First published in Great Britain in 2008 by Osprey Publishing,
Midland House, West Way, Botley, Oxford OX2 0PH, United Kingdom.
443 Park Avenue South, New York, NY 10016, USA.
Email: info@ospreypublishing.com

Previously published as Warrior 35: *English Medieval Knight 1400–1500*, Warrior 48: *English Medieval Knight 1200–1300*, Warrior 58: *English Medieval Knight 1300–1400*, and Warrior 104: *Tudor Knight*, all by Christopher Gravett

© 2008 Osprey Publishing Ltd

A CIP catalogue record for this book is available from the British Library.

ISBN: 978 1 84603 342 1

Page layout by Myriam Bell
Index by Alan Thatcher
Typeset in Truesdell and Blackmoor LET
Originated by United Graphic Pte Ltd.
Printed in China through Bookbuilders

08 09 10 11 12   10 9 8 7 6 5 4 3 2 1

$39.99

For a catalogue of all books published by Osprey please contact:

NORTH AMERICA
Osprey Direct c/o Random House Distribution Center
400 Hahn Road, Westminster, MD 21157, USA
E-mail: info@ospreydirect.com

ALL OTHER REGIONS
Osprey Direct UK, P.O. Box 140, Wellingborough, Northants, NN8 2FA, UK
E-mail: info@ospreydirect.co.uk

www.ospreypublishing.com

Front cover: Knights in battle, 15th century. (©The British Library/HIP/TopFoto)
Back cover: Armour made c.1515 in the royal workshop at Greenwich for Henry VIII (©The Board of Trustees of the Armouries II.5; VI.1–5 /HIP/TopFoto)
Title page: Window in Tewkesbury Abbey choir, c.1340 (©TopFoto/Woodmansterne)
Pattern and effect used on cover and throughout the book from www.istockphoto.com

Contents

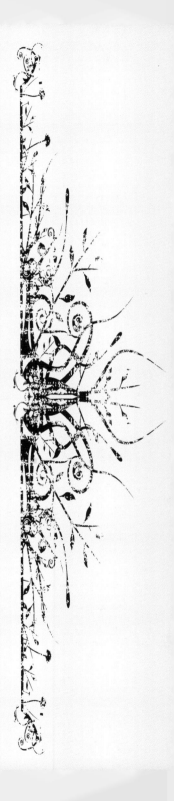

Introduction

The years between 1200 and 1600 saw the flowering of the chivalrous knight and also his ultimate demise. It is the period that embraced both the ideals of chivalry as we think of them today and also the image of the knight in shining armour. Early knights were basically fighting men but during the 12th century this attitude had been somewhat compromised and the modification of 'chivalry' from being a word simply denoting horsemanship, to include the attitude of respect for women and protection of the church and the weak – however idealistic – was underway. The Church had for centuries attempted to rein in the knightly predilection to fight; now it used its influence to direct knightly aggression to its own ends in the crusades. Apart perhaps from the Third Crusade in which Richard I (the Lionheart) had been a leader, England had not notably participated in these adventures. In the 12th century the cult of the Virgin Mary saw a great upsurge in popularity, especially in France, partly because of the writings of theologians such as Bernard of Clairvaux. At the same time the south of France had spawned the troubadours, who sang of unrequited love for high-born ladies. Such sentiments slowly moved north to the slightly less sentimental trouvères, being also adapted by the minnesingers in the German lands. There also arose the great romances of literature, with the magical tales of King Arthur and his Knights of the Round Table being especially popular in England.

Thus, as the 13th century began, English knights were embracing a more civilized regime than perhaps did those who had crossed the sea with William the Conqueror in 1066. Many who had fought under William and been rewarded with estates were joined later by other men who had come over in the wake of the Conquest, eager to find

7

new opportunities in England. Their language was generally French, the language of chivalry; English was the tongue of the conquered, yet it had persisted because of the large number of natives who continued to speak it. English nannies, servants and stewards passed it on as they communicated with their new masters on their country estates, where other French speakers would often be limited in number. Already in the 12th century Orderic Vitalis had noticed that, among freemen, it was difficult to tell French from English in the conquered land. Essentially, as early as Stephen's reign (1135–54), the struggles between the king and Empress Matilda had meant knights had to choose whether to base themselves and their holdings in England or Normandy; the loss of the latter to the French king in 1204 had accelerated such decisions. Growing up in England, the knights were increasingly more likely to acquire French than to have it as their first language. By the end of the century Edward I could charge the king of France with threatening 'to wipe out the English tongue'. As the French spoken in England began to decline in quality, the Hundred Years' War sealed its fate as the main tongue of English lords.

Despite the change in language among knights in England, their very status would form a bond between such warriors from all over Europe, men who shared the same sort of privileged existence, who understood chivalry, armour, weapons and horses, who had learned poetry, romances and good manners, had coats-of-arms and took part in tournaments. They knew they were set apart from others, yet English knighthood was not as elitist as, for example, the French equivalent. At the great battles of the 14th and 15th centuries dismounted knights stood side by side with free-born longbowmen. Their society was dissimilar from that in German lands where initially there were still serf knights called *ministeriales*; it differed too from that in Italy, with its long tradition of urban centres harking back to the Roman past, where knights were more relegated to the countryside. English knights took their place in the shire courts and during the 13th century, in the new parliament in London. Occasionally men from very different backgrounds became knights. Some individuals clever enough to obtain positions in the government or in trade, including some from free peasant backgrounds, attained enough status to be knighted. As the emphasis changed from landed to monetary wealth in the 15th century, so more people were able to enter the ranks of chivalry.

It would be wrong to suppose that England teemed with knights: compared to the population as a whole, or indeed to the other soldiers in any army, their numbers were usually small. The 5,000 of suitable rank under Henry II (1154–1189) had shrunk to about 1,500 by 1300. Knights served in various ways. The feudal system had come to England with the Norman conquerors, hand in hand with the castle and knighthood. Forty days' service to the king or lord each year, in return for land, formed one aspect of the system but some knights also served in their master's households where necessary, being fed and sheltered by him in return for immediate service. The 13th century saw all this begin to change in England with the appearance of contracts, an answer to the problem of providing professional armies to fight abroad; during the next century this became usual.

There were plenty of opportunities to fight in order to gain ransoms and win renown. The struggle between King John and his barons, then between Henry III and Simon de Montfort, provided work for the knight during the 13th century. Henry's son, Edward I, waged war against the Welsh, followed by the Scots. As the century turned, victories were won north of the border but a great defeat was suffered at Bannockburn in 1314 under Edward II. When order was restored under his son, Edward III, English knights found themselves entering the Hundred Years' War from 1337 until 1453, at first winning great victories alongside their archers in France and even Spain. Gradually the French changed their strategy and the victories dried up until, following the English defeat at Castillon in 1453, English forces left France. They would return in the next century under the Tudors, with varying but frequently short-lived success. Meanwhile the knights fell upon one another at home in the Wars of the Roses, where ransoms were often forgotten as families settled old scores, only ending in 1485 when Henry Tudor took the crown after Bosworth.

Fully armed for war, the knight of 1600 was far removed from his predecessor of 1200. The interlinked mail that covered a man from head to toe was gradually replaced during the age of transition – the 14th century – so that by the dawning of the 15th century the knight in shining armour of plates had emerged, his armour designed to furnish a hard, glancing surface against arrows, weapon edges and points. Further fine-tuning of designs would see national styles develop as great centres arose to furnish harnesses of the finest quality. Only in the early 16th century would the royal workshop of Greenwich be founded, to rival the best that could be offered on the Continent. The sword, though now modified from a cutting weapon to one able to thrust through armour, was still the main knightly weapon and never really lost its symbolism. It was a major part of the knighting ceremony, when it was belted around the recipient. Some magnificent blades testified to many hours in the forging process.

Added to the rising cost of armour and weapons, a knight had to have his horse, the 'cheval' from which came 'chivalry'. Increasingly knights owned several mounts, for riding, war and perhaps tournament, as well as pack animals and horses for squires and followers. Warhorses were specially trained and well bred, sometimes extremely expensive animals. Even when knights dismounted for combat their horses were a necessity for the pursuit and, in peacetime, as a badge of rank. Squires or valets were needed to help a man arm, especially when plate armour was worn. The cost of maintaining all these men, animals and equipment was a serious consideration for those wishing to take up knighthood.

The idea of young men serving apprenticeships as pages, then squires, until knighthood was bestowed, was commonplace throughout Europe. Before the 13th century the status of the squire is less clear-cut; many seem to have simply been servants, while others were of noble birth and destined for knighthood. Eligible squires increasingly avoided knighthood because of the expense (not least of the knighting ceremony itself) and the burdens of duties they would be expected to perform. Only knights could lead troops and the situation became so bad in England that, especially in the 13th and 14th centuries, kings forced eligible squires to be knighted by distraint. Some squires never took up the rank, though knighting before a battle, commonest in the 14th and 15th centuries, had several advantages for the recipient, namely a lack of expensive ceremony, better pay and an improved chance of being taken for ransom rather than being killed out of hand.

The adjunct to the knight, his castle, was certainly not something all could afford. A great lord might hold several, one of which would form the centre of his honour – his power base – but others had a more modest stronghold or simply their manor house.

Many knights found that war was a risky business and preferred to live their lives more peaceably, sending others to do their service in the commutation known as 'scutage', first recorded in the 12th century. By contrast some men loved war as a way to make their fortune. If war and ransoms were not available in English armies they hired out their services elsewhere as mercenaries. England was never a noted supplier of hired soldiers, as was for example Brabant, but English knights might be seen in any European hotspot. They assisted the Teutonic Knights in their struggles in Eastern Europe to Christianize the Slav peoples; others journeyed to Italy to seek their fortune in the wars between the despots, such as Sir John Hawkwood who became leader of the White Company in 1364. The theatres of war reeled off by Chaucer in the description of his 'perfect' knight in the *Canterbury Tales* should be remembered. Some knights were naval commanders including, in the 16th century, some of the most famous names in British seafaring history such as Drake and Raleigh.

An alternative to war was the tournament, a useful theatre for battle training. The lists, now becoming an enclosed arena rather than the great tracts of countryside previously allotted, would witness increasing magnificence as the fear of tournaments as potential hotbeds of revolt receded; princes and great lords laid on elaborate spectacles to enhance their own image. In the 12th century, at the earliest tournaments, many knights attended in hope of finding a lord or winning fortunes by capturing opponents for ransom; however over time the spectacle increasingly became the most important part. Rich costumes and imaginative settings brought out the theatrical side of the knight; literary themes increasingly pervaded the scene, as knights entered the lists attired as legendary or mythical heroes. Together with this world of wonderment came more use of the spoken word, as speeches were made to complete the fantasy. By the age of Elizabeth I, lords had suitable images painted on display shields, sported costumes that sent a message to the queen, and declaimed poetry to flatter the royal ego.

The image of an Elizabethan lord, wearing magnificent gilded and blued Greenwich plate armour, running at the tilt or spouting poetry to Elizabeth I in the lists, contrasts with his counterpart of 1200 dressed in mail and sometimes without even a surcoat, still perhaps fighting en masse in tourneys. There had been great change over the centuries but still the knight in armour essentially survived, a man of rank in a shifting society.

Chronology

1199	Death of Richard I. Accession of John.
1203–4	Siege and capture of Château Gaillard by Philip II.
1204	Loss of Normandy.
1214	Battle of Bouvines: Philip II defeats allied Imperial army.
1215	Magna Carta. Siege and capture of Rochester castle by John.
1216	Death of John. Minority of Henry III. Siege of Dover castle by Prince Louis.
1217	Second battle of Lincoln: Marshal defeats rebel army.
1224	Siege and capture of Bedford castle by Henry III.
1227	Henry III assumes reins of government.
1258	Barons' Parliament.
1259	Peace of Paris with France.
1264	Battle of Lewes and capture of Henry III.
1265	Battle of Evesham and death of Simon de Montfort.
1266	Siege and capture of Kenilworth castle by Henry III.
1272	Death of Henry III. Accession of Edward I.
1277	First Welsh War.
1282	Second Welsh War.
1293–4	Third Welsh War.
1296	First Scottish campaign. Scotland annexed to England.
1297	Flanders campaign. Truce with Philip IV of France. Battle of Stirling Bridge: William Wallace defeats the English.
1298	Second Scottish campaign. Battle of Falkirk: Edward I defeats Scots.
1300	Third Scottish campaign. Siege and capture of Caerlaverock castle by Edward I.
1301	Fourth Scottish campaign.
1303–4	Fifth Scottish campaign.
1305	Execution of William Wallace.

1307	Battle of Loudon Hill: Bruce defeats an English army. Death of Edward I. Accession of Edward II.
1314	Battle of Bannockburn: English defeated by Bruce.
1322	Battle of Boroughbridge: Rebel earls defeated by royalist forces.
1327	Murder of Edward II and accession of Edward III.
1332	Battle of Dupplin Muir: Edward Balliol and disinherited Scots defeat Scottish regent.
1333	Battle of Halidon Hill: Edward III defeats supporters of David II of Scotland.
1337	Hundred Years War' begins.
1340	Sea battle off Sluys: English victory over French fleet.
1342	Battle of Morlaix: drawn contest between English and French.
1345	Battle of Auberoche: English victory over the French.
1346	Battle of St Pol de Leon: English victory over the French. Battle of Blanchetaque: English defeat French attempt to hold ford over the river Somme. Battle of Crécy: Edward III defeats French army. Battle of Neville's Cross and capture of David II of Scotland.
1347	Battle of La Roche Derien: English victory over the French.
1348-50	The Black Death reaches England.
1351	Combat of the Thirty. Thirty Frenchmen defeat thirty Englishmen and allies. Battle of Saintes: English victory over the French. Battle of Ardres: English defeated by the French.
1352	Battle of Mauron: English victory over the French.
1356	Battle of Poitiers and capture of King John of France.
1359	Battle of Nogent-sur-Seine: English victory over the French.
1364	Battle of Auray: English victory over the French.
1367	Battle of Najera: the Black Prince helps Peter the Cruel to throne of Castile.
1370	Battle of Lussac: French victory, but lack of horses means they are captured.
1372	Battle of La Rochelle: Castillian fleet defeats English fleet.
1373	Battle of Chiset: French besiegers rout English relief force.
1376	Death of Edward, Prince of Wales, the Black Prince.
1377	Death of Edward III and accession of Richard II.

1381	The Peasants' Revolt.
1385	Battle of Aljubarrota: English troops help Portugal win victory over Castile.
1386	John of Gaunt lands at Galicia with an army to seize crown of Castile.
1387	Battle of Castagnaro: Hawkwood, fighting for Padua, defeats Veronese. Truce between John of Gaunt, John of Portugal and John of Castile. Battle of Radcot Bridge. Lords Appellant defeat royalist force.
1388	Battle of Otterburn: English defeated by Scots.
1399	Henry Bolingbroke lands at Ravenspur. Murder of Richard II. Accession of Henry IV.
1402	Battle of Homildon Hill: English victory over Scots.
1403	Battle of Shrewsbury: Henry IV and Prince Henry defeat Henry 'Hotspur' Percy.
1405	Battle of Mercq: French besiegers defeated by English relief force.
1413	Death of Henry IV. Accession of Henry V.
1415	Battle of Agincourt: English victory over the French.
1416	Battle of Valmont: English victory over the French. Battle of the Seine: English fleet breaks up blockading French and Genoese fleet.
1420	Battle of Fresnay: Franco-Scottish army ambushed and defeated by English force.
1421	Battle of Bauge: Franco-Scottish victory over the English; death of Duke of Clarence.
1422	Death of Henry V. Accession of Henry VI.
1423	Battle of Cravant: Anglo-Burgundian victory over a Franco-Scottish army.
1424	Battle of Verneuil: English victory over Franco-Scottish army.
1428–29	Siege of Orleans by English forces.
1429	Battle of the Herrings (Rouvray): French beaten back from English supply wagon laager. Battle of Patay: French victory over English. Confrontation at Mont Epiloy: inconclusive skirmishes between English and French armies.
1430	Battle of Clermont-en-Beauvoisis: English garrison of Gournay defeats French force. Battle of Guerbigny: Anglo-Burgundian army routed by French force.

1431	Joan of Arc burned at the stake in Rouen.
1435	Battle of Gerberoi: French defeat English besiegers by sallying out; death of Earl of Arundel.
1450	Battle of Formigny: French victory over the English. Battle of Blanquefort: French victory over English force sallying from Bordeaux.
1453	Battle of Castillon: English relief forces defeated at French entrenchments. End of Hundred Years' War; English forces leave France.
1455	First Battle of St Albans: Yorkist victory heralds first battle of the Wars of the Roses.
1459	Battle of Blore Heath: Yorkist victory.
1460	Battle of Northampton: capture of Henry VI; Richard of York proclaimed Protector of England. Battle of Wakefield: Lancastrian victory.
1461	Battle of Mortimer's Cross: Yorkist victory. Second Battle of St Albans: Lancastrian victory. Henry VI recovered by Lancastrians. Accession of Edward IV. Battle of Towton. Yorkist victory.
1464	Battle of Hedgeley Moor: Yorkists beat off Lancastrian attempt to seize Scottish ambassadors. Battle of Hexham: Yorkist victory.
1469	Battle of Edgecote: Lancastrian 'Robin of Redesdale' defeats Yorkists. Capture of Edward IV.
1470	Battle of Losecoat Field: Yorkist victory over Lincolnshire rebels. Restoration of Henry VI.
1471	Battle of Barnet: Yorkist victory; death of Richard Neville, Earl of Warwick, the 'Kingmaker'. Battle of Tewkesbury: Yorkist victory, death of Prince Edward. Murder of Henry VI in the Tower of London and restoration of Edward IV.
1483	Death of Edward IV. Accession and murder of Edward V. Accession of Richard III.
1485	Battle of Bosworth: Lancastrian/Tudor victory; death of Richard III. Accession of Henry Tudor as Henry VII.

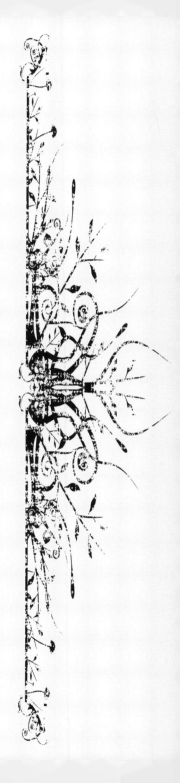

1487	Coronation of Lambert Simnel as 'Edward VI'. Battle of Stoke Field. Defeat of rebel force and capture of Simnel.
1499	Execution of Perkin Warbeck ('Richard, Duke of York'). Execution of Edward, Earl of Warwick.
1509	Death of Henry VII. Accession of Henry VIII.
1511	English archers sent to Low Countries to assist Margaret of Savoy against Duke of Guelders.
1511–12	English forces sent to Spain to assist Ferdinand of Aragon.
1513	First invasion of France and siege of Thérouanne. Battle of the Spurs: French attack rebuffed. Battle of Flodden Field and death of James IV of Scotland.
1520	Field of Cloth of Gold.
1522–23	Second invasion of France.
1523	Capture of Bray, Roye and Mondidier.
1536–37	Pilgrimage of Grace.
1541	Henry VIII proclaimed King of Ireland.
1542	Capture of English raiders in Scotland at Haddon Rig. Battle of Solway Moss: French defeated by English.
1543–44	Third invasion of France.
1544	Siege of Montreil. Siege of Boulogne.
1545	Scots defeat English at Ancrum Moor.
1546	Surrey defeated outside Boulogne.
1547	Death of Henry VIII. Accession of Edward VI. Battle of Pinkie Cleuch: English defeat Scots.
1549	Uprisings in southern England. Kett's Rebellion defeated at Dussindale.
1553	Death of Edward VI. Accession of Mary I.
1554	Execution of Lady Jane Grey.
1557	Battle of St Quentin: Spanish victory over the French. English troops under Pembroke assist in siege of the city that followed.
1558	Death of Mary I. Accession of Elizabeth I.
1559	Campaign to Normandy.

1560	Expedition to Scotland.
1561	Attacks by O'Neills of Tyrone defeated.
1567	Uprising of Shane O'Neill ends with his death. Abdication of Mary, Queen of Scots.
1569–70	Northern Rebellions.
1569–73	First Desmond War in Ireland.
1572	Three hundred volunteers cross to the Low Countries.
1575	Revolt by Fitzgeralds of Ireland.
1579–83	Second Desmond War in Ireland.
1585	Expedition to the Low Countries.
1586	Battle of Zutphen: death of Sir Philip Sidney.
1587	Execution of Mary, Queen of Scots.
1588	Defeat of Spanish Armada.
1589	Expedition to France to assist the Protestant Henry IV. Expedition to Portugal.
1591	Expeditions to Brittany and Normandy.
1594	The Nine Years War breaks out in Ireland. Battle at the Ford of the Biscuits, near Enniskillen: English relieving force defeated.
1595	Gaelic uprising in Ireland. Hugh O'Neill ambushes English army at Clontibret. Battle in the Curlew Hills: English defeated.
1596	Expedition to Spain. Essex captures Cadiz.
1598	English force attacked at Yellow Ford, Ireland.
1599	Essex arrives in Ireland with large force.
1600	Battle of Moyry Pass: Mountjoy defeated by O'Neill. Battle of Nieuport: Francis Vere assists Dutch to defeat Spanish.
1601	Spanish forces blockaded in Kinsale. Mountjoy defeats O'Neill's relief force.
1602	O'Neill defeated at Omagh.
1603	Death of Elizabeth I. Accession of James I (House of Stuart). Treaty of Mellifont ends Nine Years War.

Part I

English Medieval Knight 1200–1300

Introduction

The 13th-century knight was faced with rising costs and increasing demands on his time for local government because of his very status in society, until knighthood itself was sometimes avoided. Feudal service would be increasingly supplemented by pay especially for duty beyond the borders of England.

Since 1199 England had been ruled by John. His co-ordinated plan to raise the siege of Château Gaillard in 1203 went wrong, and Normandy was lost to Philip II of France the following year. There was still an English presence in Gascony, but John's efforts to assist the German Emperor, Otto IV, against Philip II of France failed and the Emperor's forces were beaten at Bouvines in 1214. This was the final straw as far as some barons were concerned. The following year, numbers of English barons met together, partly under cover of tournaments and, having seized London, representatives came to the king on 10 June. Agreements were reached, and on 15 June the armed rebels appeared to meet the king at Runnymede, a small island in the river Thames. Having learned the rebel terms, John reluctantly agreed to the Articles of the Barons, which would later be set down as the Magna Carta, or 'Great Charter'. It was actually a document largely designed to voice the complaints of the barons rather than being set out to benefit the common man as many have since come to believe, though among the many feudal issues it addresses, it does specify that no free man is to be unlawfully imprisoned and no one denied the right of justice. As soon as John felt strong enough he repudiated Magna Carta, and civil war broke out, continuing after his death in 1216 during the minority of his son, Henry III. Prince Louis of France and his allies besieged Dover and Lincoln but were foiled and withdrew.

In 1227 Henry declared himself fit to govern, but not until 1232 did he feel strong enough to challenge the rule of Hubert de Burgh, his justiciar or chief minister. A king who was happiest with the arts, his expeditions against Llywelyn ap Iorweth of Wales failed miserably and he vainly campaigned in France to seize lost territories. He upset many barons by his demands for various taxes, known as aids and scutages, by the extortion allowed the sheriffs, and by royal generosity to foreigners such as his own Poitevin half-brothers, the Lusignans, William de Valence, lord of Pembroke, and Aymer, bishop elect of Winchester. Richard Marshal, whom Henry eventually disgraced, in alliance with Llywelyn carried on a civil war against the Poitevins.

In 1254 Henry accepted the crown of Sicily for his son, Edmund, as the Pope strove to break the power of the Hohenstaufen German emperors there. Expected to send English troops, Henry faced baronial opposition though a German victory made further moves more unlikely. Three years later Henry's brother, Richard, Earl of Cornwall, was elected King of the Romans (the title for the heir to the Holy Roman Empire), a hope that never materialized. Baronial discontent came to a head in the parliament of London, in 1258; a rising force, 'the community of the bachelry of England', came increasingly to prominence. Their leader was Simon de Montfort, Earl of Leicester, son of a noted Albigensian crusader and Henry's brother-in-law. A number of magnates were jealous of this Gascon who now virtually ruled England and once again civil war erupted, known as the Barons' War. Henry, freed from the French war by the Peace of Paris in 1259, now

A wall painting from All Saints Church, Claverley, Shropshire, probably executed around the turn of the 13th century and probably depicting the battle between vices and virtues. The knights, some in surcoats, wear flat-topped, round or conical helmets, with rather crudely painted face-masks. (Author's collection)

21

A copper-alloy moulded mace-head, probably of later 12th- or early 13th-century date. (By courtesy of the Trustees of the Armouries, VIII.250)

challenged Simon. At the battle at Lewes (1264) Henry was himself captured but Simon's government was short lived, and he was killed at Evesham the following year. In 1266 the siege of Kenilworth ended the campaign.

When Henry died in 1272 he left the crown to his able son, the tall and warlike Edward I. Prince Edward had led a small English contingent to the Holy Land before his coronation, and English knights were present in other crusading bodies. He is perhaps best known as the 'Hammer of the Scots', but it was the Welsh who first encountered him when Prince Llywelyn ap Gruffydd refused homage in 1272. Edward seized the corn supplies in Anglesey with a fleet and forced the prince, trapped in Snowdonia, to surrender in 1277. He rebelled again in 1282, prompting a full invasion and Llywelyn's death in a skirmish. Edward was a prolific castle builder and a serious Welsh uprising in 1294, the same year that war with France broke out over Gascony, saw Edward's castles prove their worth. In 1297 he took a large army across to Flanders to block the expansion of Philip IV but was hampered partly by recalcitrance at the huge scale of military aid he tried to enlist, and a truce was arranged. With John Balliol's revolt in 1296 the Scottish Wars of Independence began. Despite a setback with William Wallace's success at Stirling Bridge in 1297, the now ageing King Edward won victory at Falkirk in 1298, but the wars would drag on beyond the king's death in 1307.

Organization

The forces of English kings and magnates in the 13th century were made up from several elements. Household 'knights' formed the core of fighting men, a group made up of bannerets, knights and squires directly serving their lord or king, whose numbers could be augmented by several means. The old idea of military service as a feudal obligation, though still alive, was diminishing in importance, increasingly being supplemented or replaced by service in return for pay. The idea of using wages was not new, but the extent to which this method would be employed, and the idea of military contracts that also developed, was different. In contrast to this new type of military–financial arrangement we also still find magnates who followed the king for nothing but honour and sometimes a desire to avenge themselves on their enemies.

There were several ways a knight could join a retinue, the usual avenues being as a family member, as a household knight, or as a military tenant. Kinsmen provided an obvious source of warriors for a lord. In 1297, for the Flanders and Falkirk

The early 13th-century silver seal die of Robert FitzWalter showing what appears to be a padded testier on the horse's head and neck. (The British Museum/HIP/ TopFoto)

campaigns, Aymer de Valence contracted with Thomas and Maurice Berkeley for knights and troopers for a fixed fee in peace, to serve at the usual wages in war, themselves serving as bannerets with two squires each, the knights with one each besides troopers.

The Familia

Harking back to the Germanic hearth troop, lords had their *familia* ('family') of paid household knights. This provided fighting men at short notice and was especially valuable in conquered or turbulent regions such as the Marches on the borders with Wales or Scotland. The knights and squires who composed a familia might become close to their lord. When near death in 1219, for example, William Marshal refused to allow the sale of his furs and robes to raise money for alms, since he wanted them to go to his household knights.

The king's familia similarly made up the nucleus of the royal army, with as many soldiers as the feudal contingents, and this important body grew in size. The bannerets, knights bachelor and troopers in the royal familia drew rations and daily pay (4 shillings a banneret and 2 shillings a knight) but when on active service the knights received 3 shillings, perhaps to pay for extra rations or to pay the orderly who accompanied them. The household knights did a variety of jobs, ferrying prisoners, bringing up infantry or workmen, overseeing castles, or helping to govern conquered areas. Some stayed close to the king. Henry III had 30 or more knights receiving fees from the exchequer, while others seem to have been summoned. A muster list for the military household from 1225–26 reveals a total force of 97 knights (about 200 when their own retainers were added). Pay accounts

One of a pair of early 13th-century prick spurs, with slotted arms for the leathers. (By courtesy of the Trustees of the Armouries, VI.331)

Knight c.1210

The central figure wears a mail coat as a main body-defence. It reaches his knees, while the arms extend to form mail mittens. Beneath can be seen a vertically quilted aketon. The surcoat is here without a waist belt. At the beginning of the century, and increasingly rarely thereafter, some shields were still fitted with a metal domed boss, secured by rivets through a flange. This was a relic from the days of circular shields, when a hole was cut out of the board to accommodate the hand grasping the grip, and the boss covered it. Circular infantry bucklers continued to use a central grip.

1 Mail coat worn without covering and lacking mittens.

2 Mail mufflers or mittens. To aid grip, the palm of the hand is covered by leather or a glove stitched inside; a slit allows the hand to protrude. A thong threaded through the links at the wrist prevents them bunching over the hand.

3 Interlinked riveted mail rings.

4 Iron scale armour.

5 Helmet fitted with face mask.

6 Rounded style of helmet that would supersede the conical form in popularity, here with a nasal.

7 Cylindrical style, here with a nasal; it occasionally tapered gently to the brim and was sometimes drawn up to a very slight apex. The top section is secured by overlapping the side and riveting all around.

8 The controversial chin-defence.

9 Conical helmet with conjectural padded lining, scalloped at the top and with draw string.

10 Mail coif thrown back to show padded arming cap and lined aventail, and with the latter laced in place.

11 Strip of mail to guard leg.

12 Mail chausses over hose, and tied to waist belt.

13 Iron prick spur; the leather is bolted to the terminal c.1200–1300.

14 Surcoat worn as a super-tunic.

15 Long tunic with magyar sleeves; cross-gartering sometimes worn by the rich at this date. Stalked hat.

16 Sword, c.1200 or earlier.

17 Sword, c.1200–1300

18 Sword, c.1200–1300.

19 Exploded view of sword hilt to show wooden two-part grip.

20 Mace with moulded copper-alloy head, c.1200.

(Graham Turner © Osprey Publishing)

mention that 527 out of 895 men bound for the Flanders campaign of 1297 were members of the household. Gascons and Spaniards were included in the royal familia.

Household knights and retinues varied in number, but Henry could probably raise 100 or more knights quickly. Such figures varied depending on royal requirements and money, and generally fell between 40 and 80 knights and bannerets. To this figure must be added squires and sergeants of the household, some 170 in about 1285, plus the retinues of the knights themselves. Each knight had to keep two squires and three horses. The king provided horses and sometimes gave armours or pieces of armour.

Permanent units of mercenary knights and crossbowmen were also attached to the royal forces. John employed large numbers under such men as Fawkes de Bréauté, honourably mentioned at the second battle of Lincoln in 1217. Magna Carta attempted to expel all foreign mercenaries from the country and numbers diminished after this, but in 1230 Henry III may have hired as many as 500 knights and 1,000 sergeants in Poitou. In 1242 some 700 mercenary crossbowmen were in the English army campaigning in France and Edward I hired 1,523 crossbowmen from Gascony in 1282, compared to 173 household knights and bannerets and 72 squires. Mercenaries were usually arranged in constabularies of 100 men, the individual troops composing these averaging ten to 15 men, and 25 to 35 for the commander of the unit. The usual period of paid service was 40 days at a time, reflecting feudal duty.

At Falkirk in 1298 the total strength of the household troops plus associated mercenaries was slightly less than 800 men, compared to only 564 supplied by the nobles. In 1300 the household cavalry and mercenaries came to 522, as opposed to 40 knights and 366 sergeants from the feudal summons. From 1277 Welsh footsoldiers were recruited into the royal forces.

The Feudal System

Feudal society had come to England with William the Conqueror in 1066. Magnates received land, often scattered over a number of areas, in return for military service. Lesser lords might in turn be enfeoffed of the magnates, though some held directly from the king. Some knights held land from several lords, in which case the most powerful usually became their liege lord, the one they followed above all others excepting the king himself. Such sub-infeudation weakened a lord's hold on his men, and could lead to court cases. Homage was a formal ceremony in front of witnesses when the man knelt before his prospective lord and

Opposite:
The effigy of William Longespée in Salisbury Cathedral, dated around 1230–40, is the earliest surviving English military effigy, though restored in the 19th century. Note the lace threaded through the mail links to keep the coif in place; the shape of the latter suggests a padded arming cap beneath designed for a helm. The square end of the laced ventail is also visible as are the laces threaded through the mail below the knees. (Topham Picturepoint/ TopFoto)

placed his hands between those of the latter, then swore to be his man and to follow him. The oath of fealty was also taken. The new vassal, or tenant, was then given some token to signify the agreement, such as a glove or flag. By the 13th century the knight's fee was assessed on property rather than on land held, so that men could be summoned who could afford the costs involved.

Tenure by Knight Service

Initially magnates were expected to serve in person with their full agreed quota of knights, which included two or more troopers in each knight's retinue. Lesser barons could make up their quota of knights using the notion that one knight was worth two retainers; thus a requirement of six might be made up of three knights and six retainers. Unlike the richer bannerets, many knights brought perhaps a single squire and one or two other followers. A few tenants-in-chief did feudal service under an earl rather than bring several horsemen to the larger muster. Service required beyond 40 days was usually paid, though some, out of pride or hatred for the enemy, refused to take payment.

As soon as scutage ('shield money': a tax paid by knights in lieu of performing military service) was accepted in the 12th century, knight's fees could be held by people with no intention of becoming knights. By the early 13th century some 80 per cent of the 5,000 knights in the country paid scutage or fines, rather than serve in person. At this time the feudal knights of William Marshal composed only about one third of his men, though other evidence shows a lord's retinue could often be composed largely of his tenants. Records surviving from Edward I's reign show that many magnates rarely served in person. After the First Welsh War in 1277 sheriffs were ordered to collect scutage at 40 shillings per knight's fee.

Feudal troops serving their tenant-in-chief seem to have been paid, but when serving to fulfil the tenant's obligation to the king, the service was at their own expense. Sometimes the service was performed without a summons being issued, and by the end of the century this type of service was often performed for pay.

Some men saw the opportunity of obtaining land or privileges by offering the king knight service. John was in need of men for his projected French campaign in 1205, and was especially likely to respond at this time. In that year he ordered that all knights in every shire should be constrained by the sheriffs to send one from every ten knights of the shire

Two statues from the west front of Wells Cathedral, c.1230. The helm of the left-hand figure has a single vision-slit. Note too the stiff upstanding shoulders of the surcoat and the lack of a waist belt. The other figure wears a padded arming coif with a roll around the brim to support a helm, and a stiff throat-defence, all worn over the mail coif. The surcoat has a dagged lower edge. (© Crown Copyright, National Monuments Record)

The Hunt

Hunting provided exercise for knights and squires, and the prospect of additional fresh meat. Deer hunting could take two forms. Sometimes the animals were hunted from horseback. Later medieval evidence suggests that a single deer was picked out (harboured), then relays of hounds were set along paths the quarry would likely take. Once the deer and half the pursuing hounds had passed, the huntsman slipped his dogs to join the chase. Knights and ladies rode after them, blowing their horns to signal what was happening. When the beast was brought to bay, it was usual to wait for the lord to kill the animal by a sword-thrust through the shoulder into the heart. The other form of deer hunt was the bow and stable, with a line of men driving the game towards the waiting bowmen. (Graham Turner © Osprey Publishing)

to the royal host, to be armed and paid by the other nine at a rate of 2 shillings a day. It seems the king expected these knights to stay with him as long as he needed them, and no length of service was specified. The army was gathered but did not cross the Channel.

On occasion two knights came to a mutual agreement called brotherhood in arms. A brotherhood agreement from 1298 is a rare survivor of a common practice, by which gains were shared as well as losses, and the two knights mutually supported one another.

As well as military service in the field, knights were expected to perform castle-guard at the tenant-in-chief's castle or a local royal fortress. Service varied, from 15 days a year to four months in every 12. Some knights were expected to do the service only in wartime; some were exempted from service in the army, others had to do both. By the 13th century castle-guard service was commonly commuted for money to pay for mercenaries. Marcher lords held strongholds along the borders with Wales, which they helped to subjugate. Marcher lords on the Scottish borders were constantly called out to repel raids.

A Time of Change

At the beginning of the 13th century the nature of feudal service began to change. The system that had been in use for several centuries could not supply the requirements of a modern fighting force. One pressing problem was the need for men to fight in long campaigns outside England, something for which the traditional 40-day feudal service limit was not well designed. Another was the rising cost of knighthood, of equipping horsemen. Paying knights at 2 shillings per man per day meant that it would be extremely expensive for a magnate to provide as many fully armoured cavalry as had been expected in the previous century, when prices were much lower. New royal feudal bargains reflected this, with much lower demands for men. Some magnates simply did not bring their full quotas when summoned. In 1214 the Earl of Devon brought 20 knights, rather than the 89 he actually owed. According to the Unknown Charter, issued before Magna Carta, the barons believed that anyone owing over ten knights should have their service reduced. As well as magnates and their large retinues, John summoned individual knights from great honours such as Tickhill, who often came alone or with one knight. Unusually, John gave repayable prests (cash advances) to those performing feudal service, as in the Irish expedition of 1210 and that in Poitou in 1214.

Magna Carta did not reduce quotas, only prevented further burdens. Individual bargains, however, did result in a large decrease in the size of the feudal call-up for magnates, though lesser lords did not feel anything like so great a benefit. The occasional inclusion of countesses in the lists indicates that personal service was not demanded, however. In 1229 about 500–600 knights were collected. Courtenay had owed 92 knights but now only had to provide three; Robert of St John sent five instead of 55, and actually owed only three. Robert of Newborough's quota had been reduced from 15 to 12 but he still only supplied two knights. Nor were knights' fees greatly enlarged to go with the reduced quotas. Magnates who had owed large numbers of men would have incurred huge expenses to bring them all, and a large number in reserve ensured a supply for a long campaign. It was perhaps also safer for the crown that such lords did not get into the habit of raising impressive forces, which could be dangerous. In 1282 the Earls of Norfolk and Hereford withdrew with their quotas after their 40-day service, highlighting the dangerous gap that would have been left had their whole retinues been present.

'The just man', a virtuous mounted English knight facing evils, from the *Summa de Vitiis* of Peraldus, made c.1240. (akg-images/ British Library)

These new quotas were too small to be practical, and it is significant that the crown (and lords in their turn) still demanded scutage at the old rate. Fines were levied for underpayment of scutage or refusal to send adequate numbers of men, but there were many occasions when the fines were carried over and large sums remained owing. In 1263 the tenants-in-chief were mustered with these new quotas, but the sheriffs were also charged to muster all those holding at least a knight's fee. Feudal service was thus still used to summon men, complete with references to fealty and homage, or in some cases one or the other. The Barons' Wars of the mid-century were still feudal in character. Churchmen whose landholdings made them liable to military duties usually contracted with a professional to provide the necessary men for feudal service.

Although it might have been simpler for the kings to move to an entirely money-based military system, objections from the nobles to their feudal duties being replaced by wages caused the continuation of the summons. When Edward I tried to raise troops for Gascony in 1294 the muster had to be postponed because of poor attendance. However, campaigns such as Flanders (1297) and Falkirk (1298) were conducted without a feudal summons.

Paid Service

By Edward I's reign greater finances were available especially from taxation, customs duties and credit obtained from Italian merchants. Edward was thus able to recruit much larger armies than previously, and paid troops were useful in campaigns such as those in Wales and Scotland. In 1277 and 1282 some retainers were taken into pay after their 40-day feudal service, for periods of 40 days at a time. In 1282 Edward offered pay to six earls and many tenants-in-chief but six weeks later there was a full feudal levy. Many magnates, perhaps not wishing to be equated with mercenaries, served voluntarily and did not accept royal pay. However, such voluntary service could not go on indefinitely, and almost all barons served for pay at some time. The first surviving contract for pay dates from 1270, for Prince Edward's projected crusading enterprise; as king he first used them in the 1290s for campaigning in Gascony. In 1294 writs were served to 54 tenants-in-chief for paid duty in Gascony. For an expedition such as that of 1298 – the largest force raised by contract in Edward's reign – the paid troops appear to have composed between a quarter and a third of the forces. Horsemen in the king's pay were provided with their own arms, armour, and horses. The king often gave favourite

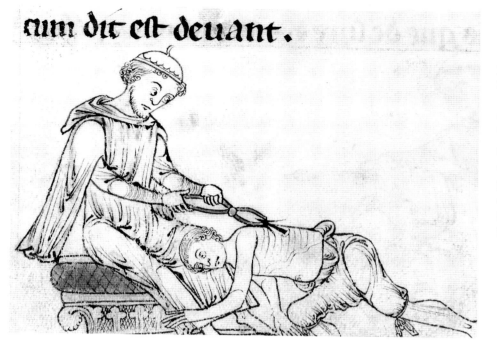

cum dit eſt deuant.

In order to extract a barbed arrow, it was necessary to first flatten the barbs with pliers, as demonstrated in an English version (c.1230–50) of Roger of Salerno's *Chirurgia*. The seated surgeon wears clothing suitable to his station. (Reproduced by permission of the Master and Fellows of Trinity College, Cambridge, MS 0.1.20, f.248v.)

bannerets valuable animals, as well as armours or pieces of armour and horses lost in service were replaced. A document of 1283 directed that arms and armour lost in royal service in war were to be made good, and mentions 200 shields, 140 headless lances and 120 lance-heads. In the unpaid feudal host such losses fell to the baron or retainer.

The horse valuation lists provide a figure of about 1,300 men receiving pay at this time, which Michael Prestwich suggests gives a total figure of perhaps 4,000 knights, squires and sergeants. The Earl of Surrey had six squadrons in pay, a total of 500 horse, and could raise another 200. Roger Bigod, Earl of Norfolk, commanded five bannerets, nine knights and 17 men-at-arms. Financial accounts do not take note of non-combatants such as grooms or valets. However, the majority of cavalry were probably not generally in receipt of wages from the king.

By late century there was a rapid turnover of membership of retinues, men serving a different lord on each campaign, and personal loyalty was rare, one exception being Robert Clifford. Many knights came with only one or two followers, and were paid independently. It is uncertain whether they were placed in informal groups or perhaps, more likely, were given some independence within larger divisions. In the 1300 campaign John de St John had 65 followers, by far the largest single group, but there were many small ones.

Opposite:
A praying crusader, drawn
by Matthew Paris in about
1250. The unarmoured
palms, and the ventail
pulled across and tied at
the temple, are clearly
visible. The small crosses
rising from his shoulders
may be attached to some
form of cuirie, or an upper
chest and throat-defence,
perhaps an explanation
for some surcoats with
upturned shoulders. The
thighs have mail chausses
but the lower legs,
unusually, are protected
by strips of something very
like the later 'penny plate'
armour which consists of
small discs held by a rivet
through the centre. (akg-
images/British Library)

Composition of Troops

The captain of a paid squadron was normally of rank. Bannerets were usually tenants-in-chief but often with small feudal obligations, with perhaps 13 to 15 followers; some were themselves part of a large retinue. Bannerets could also be promoted from knights-bachelor, a change signified by cutting the end off the knightly pennon to make the square or rectangular banner. These were often landowners living near to each other and their captain. Even when tenants-in-chief were present, it was rare for them actually to serve in person, most instead using a substitute.

In the early 13th century knights, squires and sergeants appear roughly equal on pay rolls. By the time of Edward I the squire received the same as the mounted sergeant. In the Welsh wars, squires riding armoured horses were paid 1 shilling per day, but those on unprotected horses received only 6d or 8d. Military pay records show that, under Edward I, between a quarter and a third of cavalry were knights, the rest being squires, sergeants and other men-at-arms. In the second Welsh war of 1282–83, of those mustered at Chester, 28 per cent were knights or bannerets, while at Gloucester it was 24 per cent.

Hobilars were light cavalry of Irish origin first used in Scotland in 1296; other types of light-armed horsemen had been in use on the Welsh march for over a century.

In the early part of the century, knights often out-numbered sergeants, but the ratio was changing. For the Welsh war of 1277, 228 knights and 294 sergeants served for 40 days without pay, with two sergeants equated to one knight in discharging their obligations. Only 40 knights were on the Caerlaverock campaign in 1300, but the number of sergeants had increased to 366. By this date sergeant (*serviens*) was the rank below a knight, as was squire (*scutifer*) and valet (*valletti*), which appears to be another term for squire (as was *armiger*).

During the 13th century the organization of cavalry units seems to have undergone a change. At the beginning of the century they were usually divided into units or multiples of ten, called *conrois*, as had been used in Norman England. A unit of ten men seems to make up the *constabularia*.

A document from late in Edward's reign suggests royal household cavalry were still organized into constabularia. Most cavalry by this time, however, was divided into the retinues of bannerets and knights. Unlike in France, the decimal system of organizing units in tens, hundreds and thousands seems to have gradually dropped out of use. The loss of such systematic organization may have something to do with the reduction of

A battle scene from *Lives of the Two Offas*. (By permission of the British Library, MS Cotton Nero D I, f.4)

effectiveness of horsemen in a co-ordinated charge, and possibly has a bearing on the failure of cavalry in the Scottish conflicts. By 1300 the decimal system had disappeared in England.

Already in the 'Assize of Arms' of 1181, Henry II expected every baron who had a number of knights' fees on his *demesne* to supply as many sets of *hauberks*, helmets, shields and lances for them. Henry III's 'Assize' raised the limit to £15 and added a horse to the requirements. Henry III's Assize of 1242 and Edward I's Statute of Winchester in 1285 confirmed the obligation of freemen between the ages of 16 and 60 to perform military service. In 1205, when a French invasion seemed imminent, John called up all freemen over the age of 12, to be organized under constables in their respective hundreds, towns or boroughs. By 1225 even unfree villeins were liable to call up in an emergency, usually being organized by the sheriffs. In the late 13th century, commissioners of array took over. The service, normally paid except within the shire, was usually for 40 days. Infantry were usually divided into units of 100 under a mounted constable. Each unit was subdivided into five units of 20 under an officer called a *vintenar*; by the end of the century the millenar (who might be a knight, and possibly of the Royal Household) looked after bodies of 1,000 men. Towns also raised militias, that of London suffering particularly on the rebel side at the battle of Lewes.

Training

A candidate for knighthood might well be the son of a knight, though it was possible for a burgess to place an aspiring child. Training began when about ten years old, though in some cases it could be when as young as seven (reflecting the medieval love of counting in sevens). Often the boy would be sent away to learn his trade, commonly to the household of a relative such as an uncle, though the sons of noble houses might well find themselves at the king's court. As a page, the new recruit would be taught how to behave in polite society, how to keep ladies company, how to sing and dance and recite poetry. However, the boy also needed to begin the tough training that would enable him to survive on the battlefield, and he would start to handle practice weapons and learn about horses. When about 14 years old he graduated to the role of squire, the word being derived from the French *ecuyer*, meaning a shield bearer. The youth now trained in earnest with weapons. He cut at the pell or wooden post, wrestled and practised against other squires or knights. When pulled on a wooden horse by comrades, or mounted on a real horse, he tried to keep his seat when his lance rammed the quintain, a post on which was fixed a shield. Some had a pivoting arm, with a shield at one end and a weighted sack at the other; if a strike was made the rider had to pass swiftly by in order to avoid the swinging weight.

Roger of Hoveden, who died about 1201, wrote:

No athlete can fight tenaciously who has never received any blows: he must see his blood flow and hear his teeth crack under the fist of his adversary, and when he is thrown to the ground he must fight on with all his might and not lose courage ... Anyone who can do that can engage in battle confidently.

The youth came to know how to control the high-spirited stallions that knights rode. He learned to control the horse with his feet and knees when the reins were dropped so he could slip his arm through the enarmes of the shield for close combat. He became used to the weight of the mail coat and to the sensation of wearing a helm over mail and padding. He learned to swing up over the high-backed cantle of the saddle while wearing all his equipment. As well as acquiring these skills, he was now apprenticed to a knight, who might have several squires depending on his status. He had to look after the armour, cleaning mail by kicking it round in a barrel containing sand and vinegar, to scour between the links. Helmets needed polishing and oiling if they were in store. He helped look after the horses, and ordered the knight's baggage.

Making a knight, from *Lives of the Two Offas.* The new knight has spurs buckled to his feet, and is belted with his sword, then a mail coat is pulled on while his shield and banner await him. (By permission of the British Library, MS Cotton Nero D 1, f.3)

As he grew older he also had to follow his lord into battle. In many cases this duty was probably carried out as described in the 13th-century *Rule of the Templars*, where each knight had two squires. On the march they went ahead of the knight, weighed down with equipment and with the led horses. As the knights drew up for battle, one squire stood in front of his master with his lance and shield, the other in the rear with the horses. When battle was imminent the first squire passed the lance and shield to his master. The second withdrew with the horses. When the knights charged, the squire riding the spare warhorse

Magna Carta

The strong government machinery and laws of John's father, Henry II, had kept working after the latter's death in 1189. When John came to the throne in 1199 many barons were tired of the restraints, and the loss of Normandy in 1204 was compounded by the failure of the Anglo-German allies at the battle of Bouvines in 1214. In June 1215 the barons seized London, and then sent a representative to the king. Later that month the king agreed to meet the barons, and reluctantly agreed to the Articles of the Barons which would later be set down as the Magna Carta. Here rebel leader Robert FitzWalter points at the document with his comrade, Saher de Quency, Earl of Winchester. The seal press stands ready to impress the royal seal on the wax. (Graham Turner © Osprey Publishing)

In this scene from *Lives of the Two Offas*, not only are plate schynbalds and poleyns visible, but a representation of a face plate without any helmet. (By permission of the British Library, MS Cotton Nero D 1, f.7)

followed after his master, to remount him if the first horse was killed or blown. The squire's job was also to extricate his master from the press if wounded.

Some squires were required to care for their lord as a manservant would. The squire learned how to bring in the more important dishes at dinner and to carve them in public. He was taught to hunt in the field, a good exercise, and the arts of falconry and venery, including how to 'break' a kill. To kill deer a squire or knight sometimes handled a bow or, less likely, a crossbow, though he would not use these on the battlefield. Some might be given lessons by a clerk or priest, though many were still illiterate.

Somewhere between the ages of 18 and 21 (the magical multiple of seven again), the successful squire was initiated into the ranks of knighthood. Any knight could bestow this honour but it usually fell to the lord of the squire's household or even the king if the boy was at court. Sometimes knights were made on the battlefield before action, being expected to fight hard but also able to lead men. Simon de Montfort knighted the young Earl of Leicester and his companions before the battle of Lewes in 1264. Sometimes a squire might be knighted after a battle, a reward for valiant deeds. Usually, however, the process entailed a costly ceremony with all the trimmings, an increasingly onerous burden on many families, since a feast would be expected and perhaps a tournament as well. The Church had by now become inextricably involved with the ideas of chivalry and knighthood, though it could never achieve such a hold over the creation of knights as it had with the crowning of kings, simply because too many knights were of only modest means and could not afford any great proceedings.

A full-blown ceremony would often include many or all of the following elements. The hair and beard (if worn) were trimmed. The day before the ceremony the candidate had a bath, from which he arose clean, a reflection on baptism. He might stand vigil in the chapel all night, his sword laid on the altar, so that he could spend the time in prayer and thoughtful meditation. A bed foreshadowed the place in paradise each knight hoped to win. The young man was then clothed, the meaning of the symbolic colours and accoutrements being explained in a French poem written between 1220 and 1225: a white tunic for purity; a scarlet cloak to represent the blood he is ready to spill in defence of the Church; brown stockings, representing the earth that he will return to in time, an eventuality for which he must always be prepared; a white belt symbolizing purity; gilded spurs showing that he would be as swift as a spurred horse in obeying God's commands; the two edges of his sword symbolizing justice and loyalty, and the obligation to defend the weak; the cross-guard echoing the cross of Christ. The candidate progressed to the assembled throng, for with no written certificate, even low-key ceremonies needed witnesses. His sword was belted on and spurs set on his feet.

The aspirant was then knighted by a tap on the shoulders with a sword, or perhaps still by the buffet often given previously, a symbolic blow that was the only one the new knight had to receive without retaliation. On the other hand it may have symbolized the awakening from evil dreams and henceforth the necessity to keep the faith (as mentioned in a prayer book of 1295). Alternatively it might have been to remember the knight who delivered it. It may even have derived from the habit of boxing the ears of young witnesses to charters to make sure they remembered the occasion, but it is not certain. Words of encouragement and wisdom were exchanged, along the lines of protecting the Church, the poor, the weak and women, and refraining from treason. The new knight then displayed his prowess, sometimes in a tournament, and there was celebrating. A number of squires were sometimes knighted together.

The Magna Carta has a clause confirming that the king and magnates could ask their tenants for a sum to defray the costs of knighting their eldest sons. It was these expenses, plus the rights and services expected of knights, that drove many to avoid knighthood altogether and led to its subsequent enforcement through laws of distraint. In 1204,

A gilt copper-alloy prick spur of the first half of the 13th century, found in London. The arms are damaged. (By courtesy of the Trustees of the Armouries, VI.380)

A battle scene from *L'estoire de Seint Aedward le Rei* of c.1245. One knight wears a circlet of peacock feathers round his helm, while the king has a simple cervellière. A rather large horseman's spiked axe is also carried. The decorated arçons protrude through slits in the saddle cloths. (Syndics of Cambridge University Library MS EE3.59, f.32v)

for example, King John spent £33 on 'three robes of scarlet and three of green, two baldekins, one mattress and other necessities for making one knight'. He also knighted one of his valets, Thomas Esturmi, that same year but spent only £6 10s on the latter's robes: 'A scarlet robe and a hood of deerskin, another green or brown robe, a saddle, a harness, a rain-cape, a mattress and a pair of linen sheets'. In 1248 William de Plessetis is told to send 'one silk robe, two linen robes, a cape and a bed and other things necessary to the making of a knight'.

New knights continued their training in the same way as they had when squires, since they were expected to be able to fight well when required.

Armour and Weapons

The commonest body armour of the 13th-century knight was mail, consisting of interlinked iron rings made up into garments. Despite the amount of mail that was undoubtedly in use, little has survived in any quantity dating from before the late 14th or early 15th centuries and none of that which does survive is of English manufacture. For the most part we are thrown back on manuscript illustrations and sculpted figures to reconstruct the knight of the period.

The process by which mail was made has largely been lost but certain procedures must have been necessary. First wire would be drawn through a board with holes of varying diameter to arrive at the correct thickness. The wire was then wound round a rod and cut down one side to produce individual rings. Each was flattened at the ends to allow a tiny hole to be pierced, before being interlinked with four other rings. The open ends were overlapped and secured by hammering a tiny rivet cut from a sheet. This process had to be done thousands of times to produce a single coat. It is likely that a workshop included men who drew wire and cut out the rings ready for assembly, this being done by the mailmaker. It required a knowledge of how to add or subtract rings to expand or narrow a garment and to allow an arm to be lowered without bunching in the armpit. The finished garment might be case-hardened by packing charcoal around it in a charcoal fire. Whether special tools were produced to speed up the process is not known for certain. In some cases alternate lines of riveted and welded rings may have been used, but this form was rare by the 15th century and it was far more usual for all rings to be riveted.

The mail coat was called a hauberk. This was usually about knee-length or a little shorter, split up the fork a short distance to facilitate riding, with wrist-length sleeves extended over the hands to form mail mufflers, or mittens. The neck was extended up to form a hood. To guard the throat the slit below the chin, which facilitated putting on the coat, might be laced shut. However, it was more common to extend one side of the lower edge of the hood as a flap of mail that could be drawn up across the chin and often the mouth when action was expected. This was called a *ventail*, and was probably usually lined or padded for comfort. In order to secure it in place a lace, threaded through the rings at the temple to keep the hood in place, was tied through the rings on the ventail. Some were fitted instead with a buckle to secure through a strap, or possibly a hook. A padded and quilted *coif* or cap was worn under the mail, tied under the chin with laces. By about 1275 some knights had begun to wear a separate coif but integral coifs remained equally if not more popular throughout the rest of the century.

A mail coat weighed roughly 30 pounds (13.6kg), depending on its length and the thickness of the rings. Some slightly shorter versions were also seen, with three-quarter or elbow-length sleeves, and are very probably the form known as a *haubergeon*.

In about 1250 Matthew Paris depicts a cuffed gauntlet made separately from the sleeve of the mail coat, but such an item was rare until the following century. At this date it appears to have been a form of bag gauntlet of leather with a flaring cuff, or a form reinforced by whalebone or metal plates inside or outside a leather or canvas mitten.

The legs were covered by *chausses* (mail stockings), fitted with leather soles to aid grip and braced up to a belt at the waist, rather like the cloth stockings worn underneath. A leather belt was probably used to anchor them with ties, rather than bracing them to the girdle of the *braies* (drawers). A further tie laced through the links below the knee might be used to prevent sagging. Sometimes a strip of mail was worn over the front of

Hugh de Boves flees at the battle of Bouvines in 1214, from the *Chronica Majora* of Matthew Paris, c.1250. (The Master and Fellows of Corpus Christi College, Cambridge, MS 16, f.37r)

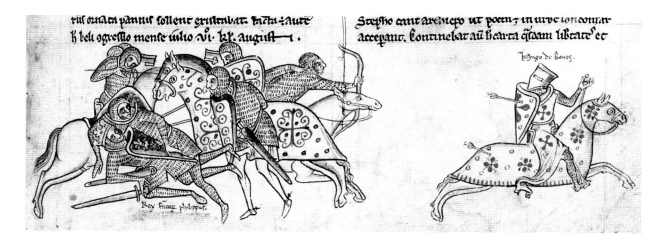

the leg and foot instead, this being secured with lacing and presumably held up in a similar fashion to a waist belt.

By about 1225 the *gamboised cuisse* appeared to protect the thigh and knee, and took the form of a quilted padded tube, presumably tied to the same belt as the chausses. By mid-century small cup-shaped pieces called *genouilliers* (also known as *poleyns*) were occasionally worn over the knees, either attached directly to the mail chausses or else over the gamboised cuisses. At first they were small but soon larger versions appeared that wrapped around the sides of the knee as well. Some may have been made from *cuir bouilli* (a hard but light material made by moulding leather that has been boiled or soaked in water or oil) and they may have been laced or stitched in place or else riveted through the mail. Very rarely, a similar small cup-shaped piece was seen at the elbow. Shin-defences, called *schynbalds*, were simple gutter-shaped plates strapped around the leg over the mail.

It is likely that a padded tunic, known as the *aketon* (from the Arabic *al-qutun* for 'cotton'), *wambais*, *pourpoint* or *gambeson*, was worn under the mail. Though mail moves easily, its very flexibility means that a powerful blow can result in bruising or even broken bones without the links being torn. If mail links were cut, they could be driven back into the wound, increasing the likelihood of septicaemia. In the early 13th century Guillaume le Breton, writing of a fight some years before between William de Barres and the future Richard I, describes the lances piercing shield, hauberk and aketon. Gerald de Barri, writing in the late 12th century, mentions a leather tunic worn under mail, which may have been an alternative to an aketon. Padded aketons seem to have consisted of two layers of cotton stuffed with wool, cotton, old rags or similar, and held

The siege of Damietta in 1219, showing a staff sling in use, from the *Chronica Majora*, c.1250. William Longespée was present with the other crusaders. (The Master and Fellows of Corpus Christi College, Cambridge, MS 16, f.55v)

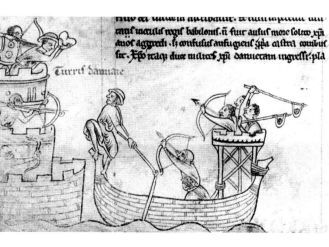

in place by vertical, or occasionally trellis, stitching. Later versions are known to have been made from numerous thicknesses of linen, and this may have been an alternative style. Some examples worn by infantry in illustrations in the mid-13th century French *Maciejowski Bible* seem to have inset sleeves, since nowhere do they vary in colour to suggest a sleeved coat under a sleeveless version (although gambesons are sometimes referred to as being worn over an aketon). However, it is not known if examples worn beneath mail were similar. Some gambesons, perhaps those mentioned as made of silks and other rich materials, were occasionally worn over mail and, at the end of the century, over the coat of plates.

In a few instances a mail coat is shown with a long flowing garment issuing from below the hem, in much the same way as was seen in the 12th century. This is far too fluid to be a padded coat, and in any case is also occasionally seen under civilian tunics.

The description by Guillaume le Breton also mentions a plate of worked iron worn under the aketon, presumably over the heart. No illustration of such a defence is known. However, by mid-century, glimpses of additional body defences begin to appear. An effigy at Pershore Abbey in Worcestershire and another in the Temple Church, London, show that some form of breast and backplates are buckled over the mail but under the surcoat. It is not known whether iron, steel or *cuir bouilli* is intended. Examples of some form of leather body armour, the *cuirie*, with or without additional metal pieces, appear to be worn by infantrymen in several 13th-century manuscripts, laced at about two points down the side.

It is possible that the upwardly curved shoulders seen in the *Maciejowski Bible* example and some instances of surcoats with similar shoulders may be explained by some form

Crusaders attacked by Muslims, from the *Chronica Majora*, c.1250. Longespée called for restraint but the Templars ignored this advice. (The Masters and Fellows of Corpus Christi College, Cambridge, MS 16, f.170v)

Knight c.1250

This knight still wears the mail coat as his main body-defence, but in addition solid schynbalds over the mail chausses protect the shins and poleyns guard the knees.

1 Helms, from statues on Wells Cathedral, c.1230–40.

2 The kettle hat had been known from the mid-12th century. It was usually worn by those below the rank of knight, but already in the mid-13th century we hear of King Louis of France exchanging his helm for the lighter kettle hat, which allowed more air to the face, especially useful when crusading. Two forms, shown here, seem to have been used in this period. The skull was made from two or four pieces, the joints covered by applied riveted bands, and the brim riveted on.

3 Shaped arming cap for a helm worn under the mail coif, held in position by a lace through the links.

4 Arming cap with padded roll and a solid collar, from Wells, c.1230–40.

5 Buckled padded ventail, covered collar, and cervellière worn over arming cap but under coif.

6 Sleeved surcoat with dagged edges.

7 Gamboised cuisse, which would be tied to a waist belt.

8 Poleyn attached to mail.

9 Poleyn attached to gamboised cuisse.

10 Sword from the Ouse at Ely, Museum of Archaeology, Cambridge, c.1150–1250.

11 Great sword, c.1250–1300.

12 Scabbard detail.

13 Flanged mace.

14 Knobbed mace.

15 Various styles of dagger.

16 Horseman's axe.

17 Long axe.

18 Short glaive.

(Graham Turner © Osprey Publishing)

The left-hand sword dates to the first half of the 13th century. The middle sword is probably of the 12th century but might still have been worn in the 13th. The right-hand weapon dates to the second half of the 13th century and is similar to the type seen on the great seal of Edward I. (By courtesy of the Trustees of the Armouries, IX.1027, 1082, 1107)

of leather armour, though this shape could equally be achieved by stiffening the surcoat material. The inventory of Fawkes de Bréauté of 1224 mentions 'an espaulier' of black cendal silk (a silk textile resembling coarse sarsenet), perhaps a padded shoulder piece of some kind. It is also possible that a large upper chest piece or collar produced the shaped shoulder. However, collars of a certain form do appear on a number of illustrations, worn over the mail or else beneath, visible when the ventail is loosed and the coif is flung back on the shoulders. They appear to be covered in cloth but it is not clear if they are of iron or whalebone, as sometimes mentioned; a few may simply be quilted. Equally it is not clear if they are all separate or whether some were attached to the aketon, as shown when worn by footsoldiers. It is not known how they articulated, but it seems that they either fastened at both sides or hinged on the wearer's left and were laced on the right side. At the end of the century a plate defence for the chin and neck, the *gorget* or *bevor*, was known in France and possibly England.

The surcoat was a cloth garment worn over armour. It appears to have been introduced in the second quarter of the 12th century and was increasingly popular by the early 13th century, though even towards mid-century by no means all knights wore one. The length varied from above the knee down to the ankles, and the skirts were split front and rear almost up to the waist for ease in riding. Its main purpose is not clear, suggestions varying from keeping the armour dry or out of sunlight, to copying Muslim fashion or for displaying heraldry. The latter is the least persuasive: the surcoat was frequently left in a single colour which appears to bear little relation to a family's coat-of-arms. As for other aspects of their design, most appear to have been lined in a contrasting colour. They were usually secured at the waist by a plaited cord or decorative belt, which also helped to hitch up the mail beneath and ease the weight on the shoulders. A few surcoats may have been lined over the chest with plates.

A new item of equipment evolved in mid-century. The coat of plates was a poncho-style garment pulled on over the head, with side panels that wrapped over the back flap where they were tied or buckled. The front and sides were lined with large rectangular plates, presumably either of iron or whalebone, the rivet heads visible on the outside. By the end of the century many English documents mention the coat of plates, or plates as it is often called, over the mail but under the surcoat. It is not known if variants seen in the following century, such as those opening at the sides or shoulder, or constructed with smaller plates, were used at this time.

Scale armour was still worn occasionally, though was by no means as popular as mail. It is sometimes represented in art, but when it does appear it is commonly allocated to Saracens or other groups, as though to distinguish them from the Western knights. It was constructed from small scales of iron, copper-alloy, whalebone or leather, attached to a cloth or leather backing so that the scales overlapped downwards, like those of a fish.

Several varieties of helmet were in use. The conical form was either raised from a single piece of iron or steel, sometimes with reinforcing bands, or else made in the form of the old Germanic *spangenhelm*, from four segments riveted inside a framework of iron bands, usually four springing from a brow band. Such helmets would still be seen in mid-century, but in art they are sometimes ascribed to the 'baddies', emphasizing the more up-to-date equipment of the 'good guys'. By 1200 round and cylindrical variants were already popular. All three forms might have a nasal, but are sometimes provided with a face mask. A few had a neck-guard, and in the late 12th century the two were joined to produce a rudimentary form of the great helm. This form, rare in 1200, was usually shallower at the rear than at the front, though the second seal of Richard I suggests that helms reaching the same depth all round were known before 1200.

The penalty of rebellion. Prisoners hang outside Bedford castle after the siege of 1224, from the *Chronica Majora*, c.1250. They have been stripped to their braies. (The Masters and Fellows of Corpus Christi College, Cambridge, MS 16, f.60r)

The all-enclosing helm became increasingly popular through the 13th century. Some had a single vision-slit across the front, and gradually reinforcing bars were added to strengthen the metal around the slits and down the medial line at the front. The front plates overlapped those in the rear to afford a smoother surface against a weapon point. The flat top was riveted over the upper edges. This form of top surface was much less protective than conical or even round-topped helmets, but nevertheless remained the usual form until later in the century. After about 1250 the upper sides began to taper, though the top usually remained flat. From about 1275 a few tapered to a point and by the end of the century round-topped examples were also seen. The lower edges had also deepened and by 1300 the first visors may have appeared.

By mid-century the *cervellière* (also known at this date as a *basinet*), a small, hemispherical skull cap of iron, had become popular and increasingly supplanted the conical and round-topped helmets. Sometimes worn over the mail hood but under the helm, illustrations reveal that it could also be worn under the hood but over the padded coif, and would account for a number of pictures showing warriors apparently wearing very rounded coifs and seemingly no other head-defence. Such hoods often show a lace around the temples, either to keep the mail in place or also to help secure the cervellière.

All helmets were fitted with a padded lining, though representations at this date are virtually non-existent. Surviving 14th-century linings and representations in art suggest linings were typically of canvas padded with horsehair, tow, wool, grass or something similar, either glued inside the helmet, or else secured by stitching to a line of small holes along the helmet rim, or else to a leather or canvas band riveted inside the brim, the band held by crude square or rectangular washers. The upper part was probably scalloped and a draw string threaded through the top ends of each scallop to adjust for fit. This was particularly important once the face was covered, since the vision-slits needed to align with the eyes whenever the helmet was donned. The lining of a great helm did not extend down over the face plates, as this would cover the ventilation holes. Helmets were laced or occasionally buckled in place under the chin; laces (some probably bifurcated) were secured either to one of the rivets or else to a flattened hook or loop inside the brim. Manuscript illustrations and references show that some helmets were painted.

In the later 12th century helmet crests had appeared, usually on the helm – Richard I is shown with one on his second seal. The fan crest was sometimes made from thin metal, though wood and parchment were also used, especially for tournament versions. The fan could be painted with the coat-of-arms or some part of it. Three-dimensional crests were also sometimes used, made from whalebone or, more commonly, wood, parchment or leather.

A shield was carried since this provided a solid defence as opposed to the flexible defence of the mail coat. Made from wooden planks and faced with leather or parchment, most were probably lined with parchment, cloth or leather as well. No English shield from this period survives, and Continental examples come from churches, perhaps being specially made for this purpose, so it is not certain that coverings such as gesso and moulding would usually have been used on warshields. The wood tends to be about ⅗ inches (1.5cm) thick. There are usually three brases or enarmes (carrying straps) riveted through to the front; illustrations sometimes show buckles to adjust their length. In order to prevent bruising to the forearm a pad was nailed between the straps. In addition, a guige strap allowed the shield to hang from the neck (or with only the forearm through the brases) in the charge or to prevent loss in battle, or allowed the shield to be strapped to the back or hung up when not in use. Rarely a buckler, a small circular wooden shield with a central metal boss over a hand grip, may have been used.

An indenture for the hire of a suit of armour, dated 1282, mentions an aketon, haubergeon, collar, basinet, a pair of whalebone gauntlets, a pair of *mustiliers* and of cuisses, and a cendal silk tunic of arms. Valued at 6 marks, this expensive equipment was probably for the Welsh wars but the indenture also noted that the armour was to be returned in good condition!

Tournament armour was also starting to evolve at this time, though in a much less noticeable form than later. The Purchase Roll for the Windsor Tournament of 1278 mentions leather cuirasses with buckram sleeves, cuir-bouilli helms painted silver, with

Richard Marshal unhorses Baldwin of Gynes at Monmouth in 1233, from the *Chronica Majora*, c.1250. (The Masters and Fellows of Corpus Christi College, Cambridge, MS 16, f.85r)

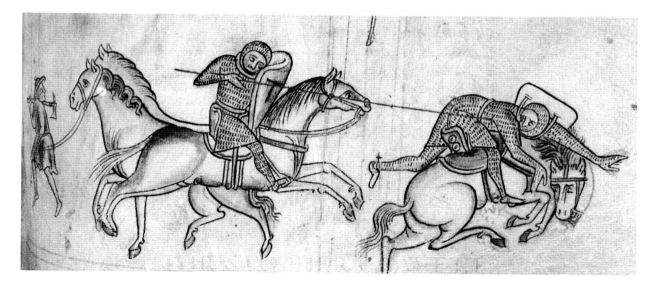

similar *shaffrons* for the horses. *Ailettes* are tied with silken cords. Cendal silk surcoats were worn. Whalebone swords were covered in parchment and silvered and their hilts gilded. There is no mention of lances, so this was presumably a form of *behourd* with blunt weapons. Another reference in 1204 mentions linen armour but with lances, suggesting the use of a form of thickly padded aketon, perhaps of numerous layers of linen.

Weapons

As in other centuries, the prized weapon was the sword. In the early years of the century the sword was essentially a cutting weapon, divided into five major types. Some blades had straight, razor-sharp edges running almost parallel to a sharp point, with a fuller (or channel) down the centre of each side of the blade, to lighten it. Another form was more tapered, the fuller running perhaps three-quarters of the way down; this would become the commonest form of sword until the third quarter of the 13th century, and some were large specimens. In about 1240 a new type of sword appeared, broad-bladed, often widening slightly towards the grip, which was often about 6 inches (16.25cm) long, though narrower blades and shorter grips were also seen in the second half of the century. The fuller usually reached about halfway down the blade. Larger versions of this form had blades from about 37 to 40 inches (94–104.6cm) in length, the grip rising to perhaps 9 inches (23cm). These, like the larger swords mentioned previously, were great swords or swords of war, also later known as bastard or hand-and-a-half swords. It may be that the gradual increase in solid body armour and limb-defences was the reason

Prisoners at Damascus in 1240, from the *Chronica Majora*, c.1250. Note the flowing garment issuing from below several of the surcoats. (The Masters and Fellows of Corpus Christi College, Cambridge, MS 16, f.133v)

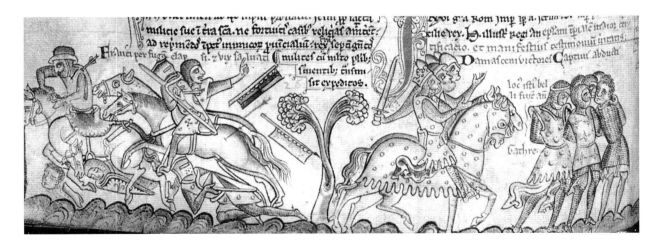

for the development of a short, wide-bladed slashing sword that nevertheless tapered to a sharp point. The fuller on these ran about halfway, and it always seems to be provided with some form of wheel pommel at the end of a usually short grip. In about 1280 a strongly tapered acutely pointed sword of flattened diamond section made its appearance

Pommel forms varied. The plain or chamfered variety of disc pommels were perhaps the commonest forms, though a wheel type with a pronounced form of centre was known but not particularly common until the second half of the century. A rare type, shaped like a petalled flower, was in use from about 1280. A version of the old 'cocked hat' Viking pommel was in use mainly in the middle 50 years of the century, and a diamond version was also seen until about 1275. Another throwback had indented top edges and is found largely on northern English and southern Scottish monuments dating from about 1250 onwards. Rarely, spherical pommels were seen, or perhaps a low boat-shaped type.

Horsemen lay about them, from the *Douce Apocalypse* of about 1250. Note the mail mittens pushed back from the hand of the central figure who wears a kettle hat. Two riders wield falchions, that on the left rather fanciful. (The Bodleian Library, University of Oxford, MS Douce 180, f.31)

The cross-guard was often fairly simple, sometimes curving slightly towards the blade. The tang was covered by a wooden grip formed from two halves carved out for the tang and glued together, usually further bound with leather and sometimes by leather or silk cords, perhaps mixed with silver or gold wire. Scabbards were made from wooden boards, covered in leather and fitted with an iron or copper-alloy chape at the tip. Some had a metal locket at the mouth. The sword belt became an ingenious arrangement of cut and interlaced straps designed to hold the sword at a convenient angle for drawing and to prevent the owner tripping over it. At the beginning of the century belts were forked at one end and tied by passing these through two slots cut in the side attached to the scabbard, before knotting them together. By mid-century a strap and buckle arrangement had become usual, the strap ending in a metal finial. Belts were often decorated, perhaps with gilt eyelets and bars.

An unusual form of sword that appeared in the 13th century was the falchion, in shape not unlike a butcher's cleaver. Instead of being designed to balance as close to the hand as possible, it had a short blade that was wider and heavier towards the point, to produce a powerful cutting weapon.

Daggers were sometimes worn, though seldom are the sheaths shown in art, even when knights are holding the weapon. The blades tapered to a point but otherwise the hilt tended to resemble that of a small sword; the short cross-guard seems in some cases to have curled in tightly towards the blade. Surviving leather knife sheaths are often embossed with designs.

The lance was carried by horsemen, a straight wooden staff, often of ash, tipped with a socketed iron or steel head nailed on to the shaft. There does not appear to have been any form of vamplate to defend the hand until the 14th century. Already for jousts of peace in the tournament some blunted heads were in use, and some form of coronel, a head formed of three or more points to spread the force of a blow, may have been used.

The mace was sometimes carried, though it was not as popular as it would be when plate armour began to proliferate. The haft was made of wood, and in the early years the head tended to be a moulded copper-alloy knob covered in projections. By mid-century flanged forms were also in use, usually with parallel sides. A wrist strap might be bound round the haft. The military flail for horsemen appeared by the end of the 13th century, a spiked ball chained to a haft, but was not common.

Other weapons were sometimes carried. A long-handled axe with a trumpet-shaped head could be used on foot and, surprisingly, is also sometimes seen being wielded by horsemen, occasionally fitted with a rear spike. A more convenient form for the rider was

a short horseman's axe with a rear spike, in form rather like a tomahawk or modern fireman's axe. Another two-handed weapon also occasionally shown in use on horseback is the glaive, consisting of a long convex blade mounted on a haft.

Flags took several forms. The pennon or pennoncelle was a small triangular flag nailed to the lance behind the head, and was painted with the owner's arms. Bannerets had a banner, at this time usually a slim rectangular flag with the longest side against the staff, where it was nailed or tied in place. Banners bore their owner's arms and were carried by banner bearers whose duty was to stay close to their lord.

The lord's arms at this period could also be carried by all his followers. In 1218 a robber is recorded buying 100 marks' worth of cloth for his band as though he were a baron or earl, suggesting that followers could be equipped in coats of the same colour at least. Barons and knights had the right to have their knights and squires wear a badge or uniform.

Warriors on foot, that on the right with a stiffened collar. A number wear gamboised cuisses and poleyns. The squatting demon at left seems to have a reinforced cuirie. (The Bodleian Library, University of Oxford, MS Douce 180, f.87)

Horse Furniture

Horses were sometimes covered in a trapper or caparison, a cloth housing coming down to the hocks and sometimes covering the tail. These were often divided into two parts at the saddle, but illustrations occasionally show trappers that appear to be made in one piece. They were usually extended to form a head covering, sometimes with shaped ear coverings. In some instances the whole trapper was probably quilted. It was increasingly used to display the arms of the rider, although many were plain. By the end of the century illustrations often show the shield and trapper carrying the coat-of-arms, while the surcoat is plain. Trappers appear to have had linings, perhaps as separate items to absorb the horse's sweat, though illustrations suggest they were integral. By mid-century some illustrations show trappers made from mail, which must have been supported by a quilted trapper beneath or else a linen lining, as probably described in the inventory of Fawkes de Bréauté of 1224, where mail and linen are mentioned together. In 1277, 16 shillings was paid for two linen coverings to go under the mail. Such trappers covered the whole horse except the ears. Squires in Edward I's army were expected to ride 'covered' horses, and if they did not, their wages fell to 6d or 8d. Since their animals were *rounceys* worth about £5–£8, rather than powerful warhorses, does 'covered' refer to cloth or quilted trappers, or even perhaps those made from cuir bouilli?

Armourers at work, hammering a helm and checking a sword, watched by a mailed horse, from the *Roman de toute chevalerie* of Thomas of Kent, c.1250. (Reproduced by permission of the Master and Fellows of Trinity College, Cambridge, MS 0.9.34, f.24r)

horses

Horses were essential to a knight, and included a warhorse, the destrier or courser, a good riding horse, the palfrey, and rounceys for squires or servants. Sumpters for baggage, or wagon horses, were also needed. Replacements were necessary, too; in 1266, 38 men took 64 horses when they went to garrison Nottingham castle. By the early 13th century prices were rising fast. An average warhorse could cost up to £50, and by the end of the century well over £60 (for barons and bannerets between 60–120 marks). Some lords offered horses to the king in lieu of some other payment. Horses were brought in from foreign areas such as Spain, Lombardy and France, but royal studs were also known. By Edward I's reign they were dotted about the country. Edward also imported horses, especially Spanish stock, to improve the mounts of his cavalry. Knights bachelor rode horses of 20–40 marks (£15–£30), while rounceys for squires and sergeants cost £5–£8, or £12–£15 for the best examples, such as for troopers in the king's familia. In 1295 the horses of stipendiary troops were valued in case replacement was necessary.

1 The warhorse is shown in a full caparison. The tail was often enclosed under the cloth. Solid shaffrons for the horse's head were certainly in use during the 13th century, but English illustrations are virtually non-existent. This depiction is based on a mid-13th century Spanish manuscript and has been interpreted as cuir bouilli, described in the Windsor Tournament Roll of 1278. A fan crest was occasionally worn. The war saddle has a high cantle that curves slightly round the rider's body, while the bow usually curved slightly forward. The long stirrups produced a military riding posture, giving a secure seat but preventing the knight from standing in his stirrups. There were often two girths, and usually a breast band, sometimes fastened around the cantle for added support. Crupper bands might also be used.

2 A mail trapper and chain reins to prevent cutting.
3 Palfrey with harness decorated with pendants and bells.
4 Harness pendant with backplate secured by a rivet at each corner, shown with suggested coloured insert, Museum of London.
5 Snaffle bit.
6 Curb bit, Museum of London.
7 Stirrup.
8 Bridle with snaffle.
9–11 Bridle styles with curb bits, c.1250.
(Graham Turner © Osprey Publishing)

The seal of Robert FitzWalter shows the neck and head of a horse covered with trellis patterning, as though this area is quilted. Separate versions of these hoods, probably those referred to as *testiers*, are sometimes seen towards the end of the century. Shaffrons are not illustrated although leather forms are mentioned in the Windsor Tournament Roll of 1278, and they appear on some Continental illustrations.

Civilian Dress

Basic dress was much the same at all levels of society, but the cut and materials varied with the rank of the wearer. Undergarments consisted of a linen shirt with wrist-length sleeves, and a pair of linen drawers or braies. The braies came down to the knee or below, the loose ends sometimes being turned back and tied to the draw-string at the waist, which emerged at intervals. Over the shirt came a *tunic*, again with wrist-length sleeves, that virtually hid the shirt. Knee-length tunics were common, but ankle-length versions might be worn by men of rank and on formal occasions. Both types were usually slit up to the girdle at front and rear. Tunics were provided with a short vertical slit at the neck closed with a brooch or pin, or sometimes with a low neck, to allow them to be pulled on. Less commonly diagonal slits from neck to chest, or horizontally to the shoulder, were seen. More rarely than in previous centuries, embroidered bands of woven or appliqué decoration might be added at neck, wrist, hem or occasionally the upper arm, or an all-over pattern used, more likely on long tunics. Many, however, were of a single colour, though the cloth might be lined in an alternate colour. The sleeves in this century were often of magyar form, that is, made in one with the body with a wide armhole often reaching the waist, tapering to a tight cuff.

Over the tunic might be worn a variety of *super-tunics*, also called *surcoats*. Some were similar to those worn the previous century, either the same length as the tunic or a little shorter, with either tight or loose sleeves, the latter sometimes elbow-length or, rarely, with pendulous cuffs. Some were worn with a girdle. The *pelisson* was a super-tunic lined with fur. Fashion-conscious males, however, wore a variety of new super-tunics. The *tabard* was rather like a poncho put on over the head, the sides either stitched at waist level or clasped. The front was often slit up to match the side openings, but no belt was worn. The *garde-corps* or *berygoud* was a bulky coat reaching shins or ankles, with wide tubular sleeves gathered at the shoulders and reaching beyond the hands; long slits in the front of the sleeve allowed the arm to pass through. The garde-corps was usually hooded, and worn without a belt. From about 1260 a loose super-tunic with wide sleeves reaching just below the elbows might be worn, sometimes with a belt. At about the same time the *garnache* appeared, rather like the tabard but with very wide shoulders, while the sides could be stitched below waist level, or from waist to hem, or simply left open. It, too, was beltless. Some wore a belted sleeveless surcoat similar to that worn over armour. From c.1250 those super-tunics with no side opening were provided with vertical slits called fitchets, allowing access to the purse or keys if carried on the tunic girdle.

The legs were covered by stockings. Short ones reached the knee and might have an ornamental border. Longer versions reached mid-thigh and were pulled over the drawers. They ended in a tongue and were secured by a tie to the girdle of the drawers. Some had a stirrup instead of feet, while others were footed with a leather sole, this type being made of wool or occasionally of thin leather. Some were gartered below the knee, and for a short period around 1200 cross-gartering over the whole leg was sometimes

A good representation of a mail coat complete with integral hood and mittens, from the *Roman de toute chevalerie* of Thomas of Kent, c.1250. Note there is no evidence of an aketon underneath though the hatched lining could just represent a quilted lining. One horse wears a mail trapper. (Reproduced by permission of the Master and Fellows of Trinity College, Cambridge, MS O.9.34, f.17v)

Comenw le chiualer defornfe fori alīfadan ar.

The Battle of Lewes 14 May 1264

The charge of Prince Edward's cavalry routs the Londoners at the battle of Lewes. Henry III faced Simon de Montfort with perhaps 10,000 men; Simon had about half that number. Apparently the rebels made small white cloth crosses which were sewn on to their breasts and backs. The prince's coat-of-arms is reversed on the horse's right side, so that heraldic animals are facing towards the horse's head. Edward's royalists chased the Londoners off the field, and did not return for some time. Simon probably now launched his own attack, which crumpled the royalist centre. Despite gallant resistance by the king, Simon swung in his reserve. Scattered fighting took place around the river and town, seized by the rebels before Edward returned. (Graham Turner © Osprey Publishing)

used by noblemen. Shoes were often plain and shaped to the ankle, with inner lacing or buckles. Others were open over the foot and cut high behind the ankle, or open over the foot and closed by an ankle or instep strap. Loose boots (buskins) were sometimes worn, often being quite short.

Cloaks were sometimes worn, being rectangular or semicircular and reaching anywhere from the knee to the ankle; some were hooded. They were fastened in the centre or on the left shoulder to allow free movement of the right arm and secured by an ornamental brooch or clasp, or else by drawing one top corner of the cloak through a ring sewn to the other corner, then knotting the end. They were made from various materials, richer cloth being used by the nobility, who tended to wear longer versions. Cloaks were often lined with fur, one such version being quite small.

As well as hoods, which might be buttoned, other forms of headgear were worn. There was a cap called a *hure*, stalked round caps, and large brimmed hats for travelling, sometimes with the brim turned up at the back or worn reversed with the turned-up brim to the front. Some round-crowned hats (that might have a knob on top) had down-turned brims, rolled brims or those like bowler hats. The coif was similar to that used with armour, though unpadded. Hair was worn with a fringe or centre parting and was waved to the nape of the neck; beards and moustaches were not overly long. Young men tended to be clean-shaven, and bobbed their hair, with a fringe or roll curl across the forehead and at the nape, which appeared below the coif when one was worn.

Gloves were sometimes worn by the nobility, some almost elbow-length, and often decorated with a broad band of gold embroidery down the back to the knuckles. Buttons were used for ornamentation. The rich used expensive materials such as silks; baudekin or siclaton was a silk cloth with a warp of gold thread. Byssine was a fine cotton or flax material, burnet a brown cloth. Cotton was at this time a woollen imitation of Continental cotton cloths.

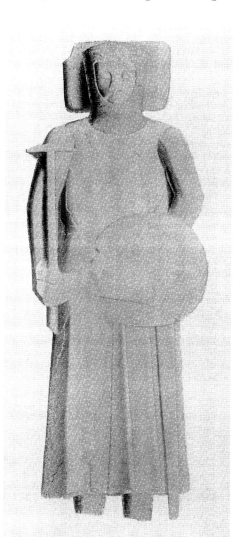

Stothard's drawing of an unusual effigy from Great Malvern Priory, Worcestershire. The pick-axe and circular shield may denote a champion in trial by battle but equally may suggest a man kitted for lighter work on the Welsh borders. (Author's collection)

Ideals and Customs

Chivalry

Binding knights together was chivalry, from *cheval*, the French word for a horse. By the 13th century the connection with riding had expanded to include a whole range of other ideas. The Church had done its best to harness the violence of the warrior class, by imposing the Peace and then the Truce of God from the 11th century, but this had only met with marginal success. Nevertheless it steered knights into crusades for the glory of God and invoked their protection for the weak and for women. The cult of the Virgin had grown in France during the 12th century, as had the love poetry of the southern French troubadours, which then moved north to find a less heady form among the trouvères of northern France. Also in the 12th century tales of King Arthur grew more widely known, supported by the English kings who, as foreigners themselves, were keen to associate with a native English hero. These romances were a blend of adventure, love, monsters and magic. The sub-Roman Arthur became a medieval knight, his court echoed in the social gatherings called Round Tables held by English kings. The romances showed how knights should behave, as brave and bold adventurers, seeking the Holy Grail that only the purest would attain.

Reality, of course, was often far different. Marriages were usually hard bargains, a matter of lands, dowries and marriage portions, and girls were often betrothed when only ten years old or less. Not a few knights were quite happy to let someone else do the fighting.

Effigies of c.1250–60 in the Temple Church, London. The left figure is sometimes attributed to Geoffrey de Mandeville. The presumed difficulty of removing such a helmet has led to suggestions that the chin-defence is simply a pad, or a thick lace tie (unlikely on a detailed effigy) or else a padded arming cap with chin pad. The latter is unlikely since reinforcing bands are in evidence around the helmet, Stothard shows it as grey, and similar helmets are also seen on a late 12th/13th-century scene of the murder of Becket. The right figure wears a tight arming cap over his mail with a rolled pad to support a helm. Another figure of the second quarter of the century has a 'balaclava-like' form also covering the neck. (Author's collection)

Tiles of about 1255–60, from Chertsey Abbey in Surrey, depicting Richard I jousting against Saladin. Note the crown around Richard's helm. (World History Archive/TopFoto)

But chivalry bound this stratum of society together, and the exclusivity attached to it seems to have increased during the 13th century, perhaps reflected in the appearance of knightly effigies. The social divisions in England after the Norman Conquest had been diluted by intermarriage, enough for Orderic Vitalis in the 12th century to remark that it was difficult to tell apart freemen of the different races. Despite the sons of knights increasingly having to learn French as a second language, the court language would remain French until at least the 14th century, and the more cultured could read Latin, though most were still illiterate, and proud of it. They ate few green vegetables (considered food for peasants) but large amounts of meat, with fish on Fridays. Men of standing validated documents with their personal seals, usually depicting them in armour on their warhorses.

The poetry and romances often depict the heroes as men of matchless courage, slaying left and right. It has been pointed out, however, that knights in real war reacted to combat as most men will in any age. They felt braver than others might do because they were well armoured (though this was by no means proof against all weapons). They advanced in close formation partly because there was safety in numbers and it was reassuring to be pressed up close with comrades. The ideals of honour and steadfastness under the eyes of friends kept men at their station, but such bravery might evaporate and knights slip away or be involved in the infectious panic that turned into flight.

England was a Catholic country and, where possible, knights heard Mass daily. All castles were equipped with a chapel of some description, from small workmanlike structures to beautifully decorated affairs. The Church always tried to take its part in everyday life, and it was useful for fighting men to have God's ear; those in peril of death were often keen to make confession before risking their life. In the field a sword's cross-guard made a suitable crucifix, especially if the sword had been blessed on the altar.

All the same it is hard to accept that some of the more brutal mercenaries had much care for Christian beliefs. The Flemish mercenaries of King John were hated for their cold callousness. The Scots who raided into Cumbria and Northumberland after Wallace's victory at Stirling Bridge killed men, women and children, causing an outcry that suggests this was not considered normal practice in England. The *Chronicon de Lanercost* relates that Hugh de Cressingham, killed at Stirling Bridge, had his skin stripped off to make a sword belt for Wallace.

Inheritance and Tax

The rule of primogeniture meant that a man's inheritance usually passed to his eldest son, thus leaving large numbers of landless younger sons, some of whom went into the Church. Many, however, went off to seek their fortune, hoping for employment in the retinues of other lords. When an eldest son came into his inheritance he had to pay his lord a relief, a sort of death duty or fine for permission to receive his father's lands. Magna Carta laid down that this should be £100 for a barony and 100 shillings for a knight's fee. If a lord had no son, his inheritance was split between his daughters. If they were not heiresses, a lord's daughters were sometimes married off to his knights, but the latter, when marriage was the easiest way to advancement and wealth, might well need an incentive such as a cash payment, land or a reduction in their knight service. Under-age heirs who became orphans were made the wards of their lord or king, who usually milked their estates for every financial gain possible.

A late 13th-century copper-alloy aquamanile, designed to carry water, found in the River Tyne near Hexham. It is cast in the shape of a mounted knight, filled via the helm and emptied through a spout on the horse's head. The knight is dressed in a surcoat, but his shield and couched lance are missing, as is the hinged lid, which formed the top of his helm. Rosettes decorate the bridle and breast band of his mount. (The British Museum/HIP/TopFoto)

There were certain occasions when a lord could demand an 'aid' from his free tenants to meet some very heavy expenditure. Magna Carta limited this burden to ransoming the lord himself, knighting his eldest son or marrying his eldest daughter for the first time. Not until the Statute of Westminster in 1275 was a financial limit set on how much could be demanded in an aid, at 20 shillings for each knight's fee or £20 worth of land held at a rent.

Distraint of Knighthood

Civil duties for knights increased during the century. In the courts of the lord's honour they received experience of law and business. In shire and hundred courts they had the opportunity to become involved with local government. They also oversaw the venison in royal forests and forest pasture-rights. Knights of the shire were expected to sit in judgement, at least in the juries of Grand Assize (for land settlements, including on-site inspections), and often in others. Suspected felons might be placed under the custody of a group of knights until called to trial. There always seem to have been enough knights to fulfil these duties, even when after the revolt against John and the accession of Henry III, rebels returned to their allegiances. Common writs were produced to allow such men, for a price, to buy back lands they had previously held. All this required juries of knights, and the pressure of work grew appreciably. Men eligible for knighthood began to avoid it.

What worried the king, however, was not the loss of jury members but the loss of men in armour. In 1224 everyone in possession of a knight's fee was ordered to become a knight by Easter of the following year. This process was distraint of knighthood, an attempt to increase the number of knights by force. In 1234 the king ordered that all those holding one or more knights' fees directly (in chief) from the king should get some armour and be knighted, but he rather undermined this by granting exemptions to certain people in return for cash. In 1241 another order was sent out, this time to anyone holding land worth £20 per year. Further demands were made in the 1250s, including one in 1254 in which the king's son figured. In 1282 all those with £30 of land were instructed to equip themselves with a horse and armour (though they did not actually have to be knights), and in 1285 all freeholders worth more than £100 per year were required to be knighted. This qualification fell in 1292 to all those with £40. From 1294 wealth alone became the qualification for service, not knighthood.

Whether or not there was a so-called 'crisis of the gentry' in the 13th century is heavily debated by historians; certainly a number of men of knightly rank found life

hard, and distraint a nuisance, when there were plenty of mounted troops available who were not technically knights. Pay had now risen from 8d a day for a knight to 2 shillings, and 4 shillings for a banneret, but thereafter stayed the same until the 15th century. The monarch also tried to attract new knights by making the ceremony of knighthood more special and by knighting groups of candidates together. Edward I also used Round Tables and tournaments as a lure to knighthood, harking back to Arthurian and other romances as a stimulant.

A rare early picture of war-horses fighting, from an English bestiary of about 1255. It is sometimes thought that stallions were trained to use their natural aggression but actual evidence is difficult to find, especially from this period. Their riders meanwhile battle it out on foot. (By permission of the British Library, MS Royal 12 F XIII, f.42v)

Tournaments and Round Tables

Many knights enjoyed tournaments, but the idea had been looked on in England with suspicion. In 1204, however, King John provided money for two of his foreign mercenaries to buy linen armour, presumably for tournament use. In 1215 tournaments were used as the occasions for meetings of the barons, such as that at Staines staged while the barons held London and waited for French assistance. The Church had always been against tournaments because of their violence and threatened excommunication on participants, but in 1219 even the presence of the Archbishop of Canterbury failed to stop the proceedings at Staines. Henry III also relaxed the ban until the rebellion of Richard Marshal. Illicit tournaments continued to be held in addition. One at Blyth in 1237 between northerners and southerners ended in an all-out battle and the papal legate was needed to quell the ill feeling. Even so the violent contests continued, with trouble fuelled by the enmity between the discontented barons under Henry III and his French favourites. In 1248 William de Valence was soundly beaten with clubs but wreaked his revenge at Brackley a year later. The French knights were beaten in 1251 at Rochester and fled, only to find their way barred by the barons' squires who took clubs to them.

Gradually permission was granted to hold events in England rather than cross the sea to France. At first the contests were still largely mock battles between two teams of mounted knights, sometimes assisted by footsoldiers. The area chosen was often a stretch of countryside between two towns or villages and casualties could be heavy. Gradually the arena grew smaller and, by Edward's reign, individual combats between two mounted knights with lances, called jousts, were growing in popularity. At the same time lances were increasingly rebated (blunted) or fitted with a coronel head with prongs instead of a single point, to dissipate the force of a blow in what were known as

The late 13th-century wooden effigy of Robert of Gloucester in Gloucester Cathedral. His knees are protected additionally by poleyns. (TopFoto/Woodmansterne)

Medical Services

The chances of receiving decent attention when wounded depended very much on status and luck. The great magnates might have a surgeon, or could hope the king would lend his own man when on campaign together. The first accounts of an organized medical service come from 1298–1300, during the wars with Scotland. The king had his physician with two servants; his surgeon; and another man. Their services were limited and most ordinary soldiers were simply released from service to find help nearby. Families could also help: knights' wives were often proficient in using salves and in stitching up cuts. The royal surgeon wears a long, formal garde-corps, denoting his status. Though herbs and poultices, egg yolks and boiled nettles might be used to soothe wounds, elder oil was for centuries a recognized treatment for open wounds such as this sword cut to the shoulder. The assistant has misguidedly prepared a red-hot iron, the standard remedy for sealing bleeding vessels after amputation. (Graham Turner © Osprey Publishing)

jousts of peace. However, even these remained dangerous contests: in 1268 the heir to the Earl of Warenne died in a tournament at Croydon.

As well as attracting magnates with little to do, tournaments were frequented by younger sons with little prospect of landed wealth, who could use the tournament to win renown and take knights prisoner, when horse and armour or a ransom was paid as forfeit; William Marshal made his fortune by doing the circuit in this way. Moreover the tournament was a useful area for richer men to recruit landless younger sons to their followings. Profit was bound up with honour, and in 1252 both were seen when the Earl of Gloucester had to travel abroad to win these back, since his brother William had lost horses and armour. Notions of chivalry also attached themselves to the tournament, with re-enactments of Arthurian scenes or other stories.

Less formal meetings were called behourds and seem to have been staged with the participants wearing linen armour, as happened at Blyth in 1258, the first contest attended by Prince Edward. Even so, deaths occurred at this event and Roger Bigod was brain damaged. There were also still problems with unrest. In 1288 squires dressed as friars and canons pretended to hold a behourd at Boston in Lincolnshire and ended up burning half the town down.

Side-view effigy of a knight forester in Pershore Abbey, Worcestershire, c.1270–80, showing the strapped cuirass worn under the surcoat but over the mail. (Author's collection)

Another social gathering was the Round Table, first mentioned in 1228 as a prohibited event and based on the stories of King Arthur. Jousting with blunted weapons and feasting were features of these occasions. At a contest at Walden in 1252 a death was considered an accident until the lance head used was found to be sharp instead of rebated; the knight responsible had had his leg broken by the dead man at a previous tournament. The first English king to hold a Round Table was Edward I in 1284, though this took place at Nefyn in Wales, to celebrate his victories there. Unlike his father, Edward enjoyed participating in tournaments and a number were held until the costs of real wars in Gascony, Wales and Scotland curtailed them. However, the kings now realised their popularity could be boosted by patronizing such events. In 1260 Edward took a large company of knights overseas to tournaments, only to be beaten, as he was again two years later.

Crusade

Throughout the 13th century some knights chose to venture on crusade to the Holy Land. The impetus for English knights to take part had come with Richard I as one of the leaders of the Third Crusade in 1190. After his death the monarchy remained influential as to who should be allowed to go, though the nobles now were effectively in control of the crusading forces who left the country. For the Fifth Crusade (1218–21) a number of English magnates and barons went overseas, including Ranulf Earl of Chester, Saher de Quincy Earl of Winchester, and Robert FitzWalter. Some, under the leadership of Simon de Montfort, father of that Simon who would make his name in England, joined the crusades against the Albigensian heretics. After the Holy Land was lost in 1291, campaigns against the Moors in Spain or the Teutonic Knights' crusades in Eastern Europe were alternatives.

A crusading background was good for family values. It was a surer way to heaven, since a crusader dying in battle did not have to wait in purgatory, and his lands were expected to be safe while he was away.

Both crusades and tournaments probably assisted in making the knightly class increasingly exclusive.

Campaigning

Preparations

Mustered troops could be ordered and drilled up to a point, a fact not lost on Simon de Montfort who noted how well the enemy advanced at Evesham in 1265. However, many magnates had little experience of real hostilities and when the Welsh wars broke out it was men such as Otto de Grandison and Hugh de Turberville with fighting experience in France who found themselves favoured by the king. Like Turberville, Luke de Tany had been Seneschal of Gascony and, despite a poor record, was given his own command in 1282 because of his previous position.

The dismembered body of Simon de Montfort is graphically portrayed in this manuscript illustration. Following the battle of Evesham in 1265, his corpse was treated ignominiously by the royalists. (Topham Picturepoint/TopFoto)

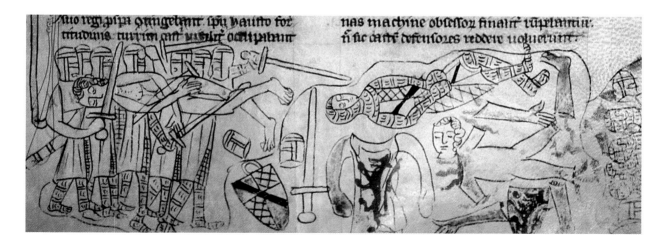

The late 13th-century effigy of William de Valence (died 1296), in Westminster Abbey, carved in wood covered in copper-alloy. His surcoat bears his shield of arms. He has laces at wrist and elbow. (TopFoto/Woodmansterne)

Edward needed to co-ordinate the army, since there were many inexperienced commanders, but he never brigaded horse and foot together. Transportation, training for foot and combining arms, the use of the fleet of the Cinque Ports, were all areas of concern for him. Sheriffs collected food and war material from the counties and from Scotland, Ireland and Gascony. The crown bought at cost price. Some was presumably deducted from the cavalryman's 1 shilling or the footman's 2d for food. Mobilization could be swift. When the Welsh revolt broke out on 22 March 1282, Edward had the first troops on the payroll by 7 April 1282 and the feudal muster ordered for 2 August.

Strategy and Tactics

Campaigning could be difficult. John made an abortive attempt to invade Wales in 1211 that failed because of a lack of supplies; Llywelyn and the Welsh collected their belongings and cattle and withdrew into the mountains. In 1265 Simon de Montfort's troops were unable to get their normal food and suffered from having to live off the land in Wales. Edward I fought no major battles in Wales – the ground was wrong for cavalry and the Welsh fought more as guerrillas. Knights were often hampered by the mountainous terrain but the English were nevertheless victorious in two engagements. Edward instead used attrition. He launched his first campaign against Wales both by land and sea, using labourers and woodcutters to make a road through the forests, building castles and cutting off the grain supply from Anglesey. In 1282 a bridge of boats was built to cross to Anglesey.

The king used similar tactics against the Scots. The first campaign in 1296 was completed in just over five months, with Scotland annexed to England. After his victory at Falkirk in 1298 he was able to provision his garrisons. He was in Scotland again in 1300, besieging Caerlaverock castle and leading his armies across the country, but the Scots withdrew and refused battle. English armies would always be hampered by problems of supply in Scotland: the further they ventured, the longer the lifeline to England became. Moreover, many English-held castles were scattered and remote, making it difficult to march swiftly from one to another, or to relieve a fortress if besieged.

The late 13th-century effigy of a knight in the Temple Church, London, sometimes attributed to Gilbert Marshal. A strapped cuirass is just visible in the gap in the surcoat under the armpit. Note the shields and bars decorating the guige. (Author's collection)

Scouts were used to locate enemy forces, after which, the commanders tried to work out the best way to proceed. Armies made use of terrain where possible, and were careful to protect a flank if feasible. William Marshal, in a speech to his troops before the second battle of Lincoln in 1217, pointed out how the enemy's division of his force meant that Marshal could lead all his men against one part alone. Other commanders were less prudent or simply hotheaded. The decision by the Earl of Surrey in 1287 to cross Stirling Bridge with the Scots in near proximity was foolhardy, since there was a wide ford two miles upstream that would have allowed a flank attack, and indeed Sir Richard Lundy had suggested this move. As it turned out, William Wallace and Andrew Murray attacked before even half the English force was across the bridge and the majority of those caught on the wrong bank were crushed.

When Edward was in direct control he proved a good tactician, as he showed at Evesham in 1265. He advanced to stop Simon reaching Kenilworth, and divided his army into three battles to block his escape. Caught in a loop of the River Avon, Simon's vain hope of killing Edward was dashed when the second battle swung into his flank while the third blocked any escape back south.

In his Scottish campaign of 1298, Edward brought 2,500 heavy cavalry and probably about 15,000 infantry. At Falkirk he faced the Scots arrayed in their *schiltrons*, tightly packed formations presenting a hedge of spears towards any attacker. They may have additionally fortified the position with wooden stakes. Again, disagreement was found among the division leaders: having skirted to the right of wet ground, the Bishop of Durham sensibly wanted to wait for the earls of the left-hand division to come level, and for the king who was bringing up the centre. But the impetuous young Ralph Bassett urged the cavalry on. Swinging out round the flanks, the two English divisions rode

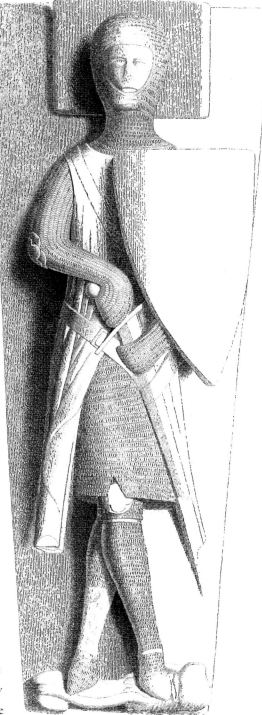

down the Scottish archers stationed between the schiltrons, and the Scottish cavalry broke and fled. However, the horsemen could not break the determined Scottish ranks of spears and it was the move by the king to bring up his archers and crossbowmen that helped prevent his knights dashing themselves to pieces. English cavalry deterred the Scots from breaking their ranks, and they were then forced to stand their ground until the archers withdrew, allowing the cavalry finally to break through. Even so, over 100 horses were killed. It should be noted that there appear to have been more cavalrymen in the battle than archers, and that crossbowmen were also used. Edward does not seem as yet to have developed his tactic of using massed longbows to decimate enemy ranks.

Knights at this time still often fought from horseback, changing to their destriers or coursers from the palfreys they used for riding. There is no evidence that cavalry routinely dismounted during the Welsh wars. The charge began as a walk, increasing speed when within suitable range so that the horses would not be blown or the formation disorganized when the final push came. The mounted charge could still be highly effective, the knights riding almost knee to knee with lowered lances in the hope of steam-rolling over the opposition. The lance usually shattered during the first charge, the stump being dropped and, if need be, the sword was drawn, or perhaps a mace or horseman's axe. Inventories show that horses killed in battle largely belong to knights and those with mounts of quality; in other words, the knights formed the front line.

As is obvious from manuscript illustrations, armour was not proof against all weapons: great sheering blows, especially those delivered with a weapon using both hands, could cut through mail and cause horrific injuries. The helms worn, though not particularly heavy, soon grew hot, muffled hearing and limited vision. Men looked to their lord's banner, which was usually carried furled and only broken out when fighting was expected. Its symbolism was of high import: if it fell or was captured there was a risk of panic, and it would be protected by several tough men. Signals were given by trumpet or by hand, especially if the noise made shouting ineffective. Trumpets were also used to call the troops to arms before battle. War cries were used to frighten the enemy and bolster courage.

Another problem with a mounted charge was discipline. As happened at Lewes, the charge by Prince Edward's cavalry was successful but the elated horsemen kept going, pursuing their opponents so far as to put themselves out of the battle as well. The threat of the front line being completely penetrated was one reason commanders sometimes used a reserve, as did Simon de Montfort at Lewes. The knights who burst through might turn and strike the rear of the enemy line. The reserve was also quite often the position of the commander, with subordinates controlling the forward battles.

Knight c.1290

By the late 13th century many knights were wearing a coat of plates, or occasionally even a cuirie, beneath their surcoat but over their mail coat. This figure of a knight of the Hastings family has substantial poleyns protecting the front and sides of the knee. The coif is now separate, and hidden under it he has a whalebone collar. From about 1275 ailettes were sometimes worn by knights, being small rectangular or, rarely, diamond-shaped or circular, boards attached to the shoulders and painted with the knight's arms. It used to be thought that ailettes provided protection for the neck but, since some parchment examples are described, it seems they were wholly for display. The helm is more pointed, with a chain and toggle to the belt to sling it and help prevent loss in battle. Crests were secured by laces through a ring of holes on the helm, and this join could be disguised by wrapping a cloth around it and allowing it to hang down the back of the helm, where it may have helped give protection from heat. This would become known as the wreath and lambrequin in later heraldic display; at this date it was less fussy. Sometimes the ends of the cloth hang down like a scarf, at other times it appears to be like a single broad rectangle of cloth.

1 Helm, Italian, c.1300.

2 Kettle hat.

3 Separate coif, with rear slit tightened by a lace, obviating the need for a ventail.

4 Couter, from effigy of William Longespée the Younger, Salisbury Cathedral.

5 Suggested appearance of a reinforced surcoat.

6 Coat of plates, showing vertical plates riveted inside.

7 Reconstruction of a gauntlet covered in whalebone plates.

8 Reconstruction of a rowel spur, from fragments, c.1300,

Museum of London. The ornamental swan may allude to the Swan Knight legend with which some families associated. The decorated spur arm was worn on the outside of the foot.

9 Sword belt secured to scabbard by two laces, from late 13th-century effigy of Gilbert Marshal, Temple Church, London.

10 Great sword, Burrell Collection, Glasgow, c.1270–1330.

11 Sword, c.1250–1350.

12 Sword, Royal Armouries, c.1250–80.

13 Garnache with hood.

(Graham Turner © Osprey Publishing)

Sieges were more prevalent than set-piece battles. There was less worry of losing all in a single engagement, though a protracted siege was expensive and it became increasingly difficult to hold troops together. Great keeps, or donjons, were, by their size, difficult to take, as King John found at Rochester in 1215 when he arrived to confront the rebel barons. Having undermined a corner of the donjon, his men found the defenders still resisted for a time from behind the cross-wall inside. The siege lasted almost two months.

By the end of the century castles had perhaps reached their peak of development, as witness the imposing constructions of Edward I in Wales. Several of these, such as Harlech and Beaumaris, were of concentric form, with an inner and outer wall supporting one another all round, and with every defensive trick, such as arrow loops, overhanging wooden hoardings to command the base of the wall, and projecting mural towers to enfilade the wall and effectively cut it into separate sections that could be closed off if gained by an enemy.

But castles were not just for defence, they were bases for mounted knights who could ride out perhaps ten miles and back in a day, or as temporary bases for royal troops to operate against rebels, or vice versa. Edward's Welsh strongholds were as much instruments of conquest as defended bases. Similarly castles provided fortified resting places for field forces, and their garrisons could be used to enlarge such a force. Harrying the lands of one's enemy was sometimes a prelude to a siege, and was a way to deny food, kill peasants and so his economy, and insult his lordship.

Sieges could be costly and involve much organization, sometimes drawing craftsmen from all over England, as that of Bedford by Henry III in 1224 shows. The king summoned much of the kingdom's resources, with carpenters, miners, stone-cutters and quarriers brought to the scene together with all sorts of equipment, such as timber, ropes and tallow for siege engines. We also glimpse the necessary luxuries of the lords: as well as his armour, King Henry's tents were sent by cart from London, together with comforts such as wine, pepper, almonds, cinnamon, saffron and ginger.

Yet the real business was dangerous. Lord Richard de Argentan was hit in the stomach by a crossbow bolt that went through his armour, and six other knights were killed. It took four assaults, each time advancing further into the castle, before the defenders yielded. Quarter was usually given if a place surrendered but was in the gift of the besiegers if a castle were taken by force. At Bedford the garrison had already been excommunicated by the Archbishop of Canterbury and King Henry, angry at the resistance he had met in a siege lasting eight weeks, hung William de Bréauté outside the gates with his knights. As a note of leniency he did, however, allow them to be absolved of their excommunication. At Rochester, too, John seems to have wanted to hang the garrison, until it was pointed out that this might prompt other rebels to do the same to royal garrisons.

Perhaps the most celebrated siege in 13th-century England was that of Kenilworth in 1266, when supporters of Simon de Montfort took refuge there after their leader's death at Evesham. The siege by Henry III and the Lord Edward lasted six months and only ended on terms of surrender. Mining was impossible because of the wide water defences. As well as using siege towers and catapults, several attacks were launched by knights on the siege lines causing much damage and loss of life. This was one reason knights were important to the defence of a castle. Yet food was equally important, and lack of provisions was a major reason the defenders asked for a truce, saying that if no help came in 40 days, they would surrender. They were then allowed to march out with full military honours.

Siege warfare also demonstrated, as at Bedford, that knights could fight effectively on foot, since a mounted man was not much use against a wall unless a gate was forced. Conversely he was needed in siege towers or on scaling ladders, or as a strong pair of hands, as at Dover in 1216 when the French Prince Louis mined a gate tower, only to find the breach blocked by timbers hastily inserted by Hubert de Burgh and his men.

Knights could have long military careers. William Marshal was 70 at the battle of Lincoln in 1217. Some, however, did not like the idea of campaigning. Knights knew the fear of death in combat but they were trained to fight and knew it was their duty to do so. They might hope that their enemies would wish to capture rather than kill them, since their ransom was a tempting tool of moderation. Certainly in some battles few knights were killed and this can only partly be ascribed to better armour. There was also the desire to capture knights for themselves (in war or tournament), or for plunder. Valour and loyalty might be rewarded by the lord or by the king, in the form of wealth or forfeited lands.

Opposite:
Stothard's drawing of the effigy of a de Vere in the Church of St Mary, Hatfield Broad Oak, Essex. The figure has a separate coif and gamboised cuisses with small poleyns attached. Its date is debatable but may be c.1300. (Author's collection)

fent

PART II

English Medieval Knight 1300–1400

Introduction

The 14th century was a time of great changes for the English knight, not only in terms of his armour and costume, but also in the method of his recruitment. In 1300, armies were composed largely of men summoned to perform their feudal duties; by 1400, the king could command a professional army raised largely by contract and paid in cash.

This was just as well. When the century opened, Edward I was still embroiled in his struggle to force the Scots to recognize his authority. On his death in 1307 his son, Edward II, continued the war with an army strong in mounted knights, but lost decisively in 1314 to Robert the Bruce at Bannockburn. Unfortunately, Edward had a knack of raising up unpopular favourites to help him govern, firstly Piers Gaveston, then the Despensers, men who were hated by some of the most powerful barons. The Earl of Lancaster led an opposition to Edward's rule but was beaten at Boroughbridge in 1322. However, Edward's favourites perished and his queen and her lover, Roger Mortimer, plotted his downfall, Edward reportedly suffering a gruesome death in Berkeley Castle in 1327. His young son came to the throne as Edward III and soon took control, incarcerating his mother and executing Mortimer. A king interested in spectacle and war, Edward gradually won over his lords; knights found themselves fighting for him in Scotland where, after several victories, a treaty was agreed in 1357 and David was recognized as king in Scotland.

Meanwhile, following clashes in the Channel, England had drifted into war with France in 1337, after which Edward laid claim to the French crown itself. The conflict carried on intermittently for so long (116 years) that it became known as the Hundred Years War. At first things went well for Edward, with a naval victory at Sluys in 1340

Sir Geoffrey Luttrell, from the *Luttrell Psalter* of c.1335–45. He receives his lance and helm from his wife, while his daughter-in-law holds his shield. He wears some plate armour on his limbs. Large ailettes, a triangular lance pennon and the ladies' robes all display his arms. His basinet will be worn under the helm, which bears a fan crest, as does his horse's shaffron. The front arçon of his saddle encloses the knight's torso rather than curving in the opposite direction. (akg-images/British Library)

and English armies triumphing at Crécy in 1346 and Poitiers ten years later, when King John of France was captured. In 1348, however, the Black Death, having ravaged France, reached England and within two years wiped out perhaps one-third of the population.

The siege of Jerusalem, from the early 14th-century *St Mary's Psalter*. The mailed figures wear great helms or basinets, with poleyns at the knee. Separate gauntlets, ailettes and falchions can be seen. (By permission of the British Library, MS Royal II B VII, f.56)

The king's eldest son, Edward, the Black Prince, victor of Poitiers, joined Peter the Cruel in a bid to secure the latter on the throne of Castile, but his brutality alienated Edward and he returned from Spain in poor health. He never fully recovered, dying in 1376. The French now usually refused to meet their enemy in the open, while the English were too weak to besiege towns and strongholds effectively.

The once martial King Edward sank into his dotage and died in 1377, leaving his young grandson to inherit the throne as Richard II. Though still a boy, he faced hostile crowds at the outbreak of the Peasants' Revolt in 1381 with praiseworthy calm, but he was no military general. The powerful John of Gaunt, Duke of Lancaster and third son of Edward III, invaded Spain in 1386 in a bid to secure Castile for himself through the claim of his Spanish wife, but, as in France, he was denied battle and forced to make a truce. The war policy in England, as happened before and would again, always created problems at home when victories dried up, and Richard could not effectively curb his barons who protested about the cost of war (among other things). He grew more tyrannical, and banished Gaunt's son, Henry Bolingbroke, in 1395. When Gaunt died in 1399 Richard made the banishment permanent, but then Henry landed with a small force at Ravenspur. Tricked into giving himself up, Richard was forced to abdicate. An uprising in Richard's favour sealed his fate, and the unhappy prisoner died in Pontefract castle that same year. As Henry IV of the house of Lancaster, the new king would reign until 1413.

Practice at the pell in mail armour with shield and sword, from an early 14th-century French version of Vegetius, *De Re Militari*. (By permission of the British Library, MS Royal 20 B XI, f.3)

Organization

At the beginning of the 14th century knights and squires might serve in several different contexts. They might be employed as household knights, as feudal troops, as volunteers, or as paid fighting men. Many knights were quite prepared to fight when the call came for troops, but their wish was for relatively short campaigns. Some found that running their estates was their main interest. Others became county members of parliament – knights of the shire – though from the middle of the 14th century not all of them were actually knights. The more intuitive of them might rise to the rank of sheriff, might become part of judicial commissions of 'oyer and terminer', or commissioners of array to select men for war service. By the 14th century knighthood formed a bridge between county knights and the landed aristocracy, whose great estates and judicial rights had been slowly eroded by the increase in royal power and government involvement in local areas. This stability and order was reinforced by the continuation of service, now increasingly laid down by indenture.

Some knights originated as members of the free peasantry, whose family rose in government or religious lay office until their status (particularly in the legal profession) deemed them worthy of knighthood. Marriage was still a lucrative way to acquire wealth, but for landless younger sons there was not much to offer a girl's family in return. Not many of the English gentry made a career of war. The landless knights had less call on their time at home, and were often willing to stay in the field. Others pursued military careers after the Treaty of Bretigny in 1360 had removed English troops and garrisons in France, and instead joined the free companies. There were a few knightly bandits in England, gangs led by gentry such as the Folevilles and Coterels in the 1320s and 1330s, who settled matters of land ownership by summary justice.

In the 13th century the cost of the knighting ceremony and the additional duties that the rank required had led many men to avoid becoming knights. To combat this, Henry III and Edward I began to force those men with defined amounts of land or property to become knights. This was known as distraint and was still employed to a lesser extent in the 14th century. Fielding a full complement of knights was often a problem and deficiencies were made up with squires, a group who were considered worthy of coats-of-arms in the first half of the 14th century, and increasingly formed a social level below the knights. Many now found themselves disinclined to take up knightly status, however. Apart from the expense that it entailed, they enjoyed being landowners and managers, and many were busy in local government. Some would never become knights, but together with burgesses would form the new class of gentry who absorbed knightly ideals.

Household Troops

Household knights lived with their lord at whichever castle or manor he happened to be residing in. Their upkeep was paid for by him, and in return the knights were employed on various duties, such as forming a bodyguard wherever he went, escort duty, carrying messages and, most importantly, forming the nucleus of his troops in battle. This group was called the familia and their relationship with their lord was often close. Equally, the king also had his familia regis, made up of bannerets, knights bachelor and troopers. It formed the main body of men in an English army, men who could be detailed for special duties such as escorting workmen or provisions. Some became constables of Welsh or Scottish castles, or led *chevauchées* (mounted raids) into Scotland, or even held posts in the navy. Even under Edward II, a king not noted for his military interests, 32 bannerets and 89 household knights were in service in 1314–15. Under Edward III, 14 bannerets and 66 knights were with him in 1347, although the records for this French expedition do not distinguish between wages for household knights and other knights. In mid-century the name 'household knight' began to change to 'knight of the chamber'. After 1360 chamber knights are mentioned to the exclusion of 'household knight', perhaps because of more domestic duties. It should be remembered that Edward III took a less active military role in his later years and his own household was being run more along the lines of those of the great magnates. Under Richard II a new term appears: 'king's knights' were men who drew annuities from the exchequer instead of royal household

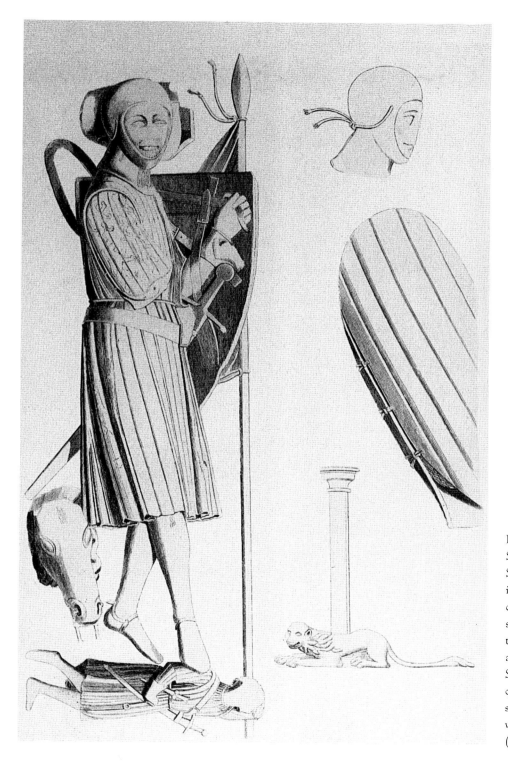

Effigy of Sir Robert Shurland, a drawing by Stothard from his tomb in Minster, Isle of Sheppey, c.1320–35. This effigy shows the inner side of the shield, with brases adjustable by a buckle. Sir Robert wears a quilted jupon with inset sleeves and his squire wears a quilted aketon. (Author's collection)

Coment le cōmoune gent: checon leua a cōtre autre z uou dra autre octre p le auer pur me ṁēt aproche.
trise. E ceo est dunt nous esperoms bien q̇ le iour de droit iugemēt tor

fees. King's knights formed the nucleus of the later 14th-century armies, but were not as close to the king himself as the earlier household knights. In 1394 Richard II had 48 king's knights for his Irish expedition, over half the total number of knights and bannerets in charge of retinues.

The Feudal Summons

The feudal summons was already becoming outmoded by the early 14th century but had been maintained by the barons themselves. In the 13th century the number of men a baron agreed to send had been drastically reduced, although feudal agreements meant both king and baron knew the numbers expected. On the Caerlaverock Roll in 1300, 40 knights and 366 sergeants appeared, but only three years later numbers had declined to 15 knights and 267 sergeants. In 1310 the Earl of Pembroke provided one knight and eight sergeants but ten barded horses, the latter now a more important requisite; the earl's obligation was actually five knights, but one knight was worth two sergeants. Generally speaking, the proportions of knights to sergeants had altered greatly by the first quarter of the 14th century, contrasting to those a century earlier in which perhaps over half the mounted troops were knights.

The old, the sick, and female or religious landowners could send money in lieu of service, with which the king could hire troops. This scutage (literally 'shield money') had been increasingly popular since the 12th century. Equally, some knights were simply too busy or too disinterested in military matters to attend in person, and scutage allowed them to pay the king instead of performing their military service. Ecclesiastics sometimes contracted military men to provide soldiers for the feudal summons.

For the campaigns in Scotland of 1300, 1303 and 1306, Edward was granted a levy of scutage raised. All who served, who paid their fines pro servitio (for service) in full, or who were doing duty elsewhere, were allowed to take a levy from their sub-tenants at 40 shillings per fee. Despite low quotas, the tenants-in-chief were able to take scutage from their own tenants at the old 12th-century rates. As in 1292, in 1305 there was a complaint that tenants were being pressured to pay arrears of scutage, but Edward said the rolls should be searched so that service could be proved. Prelates, earls and barons had sanctioned a levy of scutage of 40 shillings per fee for these two campaigns, to be taken within two years if Edward so wished, but the officials had apparently been pressing even those who had fought.

Opposite:
Two battle scenes from the *Holkham Picture Bible Book* of 1326–27. In the upper panel, riders wear visored helms, that of the king having a bevor at the chin as do some kettle hats. Several body-defences of coat of plate construction consist of small square plates apparently riveted at the corners to the outside of a fabric coat. The king seems to have fluted couters and spaudlers, with gutter-shaped plates on the arms and plate gauntlets; his horse has a simple shaffron, with a peytral worn over the caparison. Only one man carries a shield. The lower panel shows an infantry battle. One man has a mail coat but most wear a quilted aketon under the tunic, glimpsed at the forearms or hem. Some have mail hoods, others quilted versions, that of the left figure buttoning up at the chin. Leather gauntlets seem to be worn, only one man having plate versions. Small bucklers with metal boss and rim can be seen. (akg-images/British Library)

Obligations to Serve

Paid troops had many advantages: they did not go home after the usual 40-day feudal service was over (when the king in any case had to pay his feudal troops if he wanted them to remain), and they could be selected for the quality of their military skills. As Edward I became involved in wars with Scotland and France, he found the restrictions of feudal service were becoming a burden. Full coffers would allow him to take armies of professional fighting men out of England for long periods of time if necessary. Thus by 1300 his armies also enlisted members of the baronage for periods of service by contract, whereby they were paid to follow the army for a designated campaign or time. Perhaps lack of interest in Scottish campaigns that promised little reward had something to do with it, as well as hard economics. Most had already served in this way when the 14th century opened, but feudal service remained, largely because aristocrats did not want to be seen serving for pay like common mercenaries. Some served for nothing, especially if it entailed a personal campaign against a hated enemy, for example by Marcher lords. In raising troops in 1297, 1298, 1307 and 1319, the king had ordered no feudal summons. For that of 1316 Edward II asked for as many additional troops as the tenants could bring, but now homage was demanded as well, with a threat of confiscating lands if not

Effigy of a knight, probably Sir Robert Hilton (died 1372) in Swine Priory, Yorkshire. Notice the single staple at the chest from which hang two chains to sword and dagger, the latter suspended from the belt by a looped cord. The aventail has a decoratively wavy leather upper edge, a form seen on other effigies. (Courtauld Institute, Conway Library, copyright Maurice H. Ridgway)

obeyed. No exact obligation or pay structure was laid down, and it caused much bitterness and could not be implemented. Service from £50 landholders was also demanded with similar threats. In 1327, Edward III ordered his first and only feudal summons, the last of such demands. The summonses of 1314, 1322 and 1327 had not been stunning successes, but the usage of terms such as 'fealty' and 'homage' continued to be used when agreements were made. In the early 14th century new lands in Scotland were given under feudal obligation, to provide castle garrisons, while in Ireland it continued into the 15th century. It was revived in England in 1385 for a Scottish campaign (though no troops were really necessary), perhaps so that Richard II could confirm that such summonses could still be demanded.

The king might use a special summons that appealed to the chivalric nature of his lords. Thus in 1300 they were asked to bring as many as they could plus their formal quotas. For Scotland Edward I then tried using a structure based on wealth rather than knighthood. He had done this before in the 13th century but had come unstuck when reducing the qualification from land held worth £40 to £20. Now, again with a £40 level, men argued that either they were not tenants-in-chief and did not have to serve, or else were and so owed feudal service anyway. Backing off, Edward changed tack, and in 1301 sent 935 men summonses for wages. This too failed.

Edward II, successful after the battle of Boroughbridge but smarting from his failed 1316 summons, now expected all cavalry not retained to muster at Newcastle for the 1322 Scottish campaign. This had wildly varying results, such as 56 bannerets and knights from Essex but only two from Huntingdon. Two years later all knights were asked to meet at Westminster to discuss things, and a distraint was issued to force knighthood. Lists of knights and men-at-arms were drawn up by the sheriffs, some 1,150 knights and 950 men-at-arms from those lists surviving. For the war in Gascony commissioners were to array all knights, squires and men-at-arms, noting who formed part of a magnate's retinue and who were ready to serve. Then demands came for men-at-arms, light horse and infantry, with a total of about 650 fully armed horse. In 1325 the sheriffs demanded that all men be ready to serve, and a new distraint of knighthood went out. That the commissions of array used for infantry were now extended to cavalry was a very new departure, probably the work of Edward's unpopular favourites, the Despensers. In 1327 it was abandoned.

In the 1330s Edward III revised the 1285 Statute of Winchester, which defined the equipment of different classes of society. He demanded that a £40 landholder should have arms and horse for himself and one other. In 1344 this idea was extended, with a scale for assessing contributions to the army, embracing all those with an income of £5 or more, up to £1,000. £5 meant finding an archer, £25 a man-at-arms. Only the successful campaign with its victory at Crécy staved off a real backlash.

Sometimes barons sent men by an individual bargain struck with the king. In 1306 Thomas and Maurice Berkeley sent ten men-at-arms for as long as King Edward remained in Scotland, in return for the removal of a 1,000-mark fine imposed for lawlessness in Gloucestershire.

None of these attempts to raise men by non-feudal obligation had any great success, and some caused serious ripples in government. Walter de Milemete, a royal clerk writing in the 1320s, puts it at the bottom of the three ways to raise men, with voluntary service as the most favoured. Between these come paid troops, and it was with pay and rewards that the king would find the successful formula for raising field armies.

The interior of Longthorpe Tower in Cambridgeshire, added by Robert de Thorpe, steward of Peterborough Abbey in about 1330 to an existing manor house of c.1300–10. This rare survivor has walls covered in paintings made for him or his son. (Topham Picturepoint/TopFoto)

Knight and Equipment, c.1330

At the beginning of the century, knights differed little from those at the end of the previous century, and it was not until about 1325–30 that the use of plate armour became increasingly common. This reconstruction of Sir William FitzRalf shows armour similar in many ways to that of the latter part of the previous century, the main defence being a mail hauberk extended into mittens. However, he now has gutter-shaped plates on his arms, together with a disc at the shoulder and another attached to the couter. Gamboised cuisses protect the thighs, with decorated poleyns at the knees, schynbalds over the shins and early sabatons over the top of the foot. His squire wears a vertically quilted aketon with upstanding collar, and carries a sword and ballock dagger.

1 Kettle hat and bevor.

2 This knight has a small basinet with riveted aventail and pendant flaps covering the joints. Note the spaudlers fashioned as lion-heads.

3 Visored basinet.

4 Visored helm.

5 Late prick spur.

6 Reconstructed tinned rowel spur, Museum of London. Rowel spurs would take over completely in the 14th century. The spur strap riveted to the arm would give way almost entirely to straps hooked into loops on the arms, though at first some passed through a slot on the inner arm, as here.

7 Hand-and-a-half sword, first half of 14th century, with 39½in. (100.4cm) blade, Museum of London.

8 Sword of first half of 14th century.

9 Sword, c.1290–1330; the style of cross was uncommon after 1300.

10 Sword belt fastening, using hook and eye attachments, from the brass of Sir Robert de Septvans.

11 Axe.

(Graham Turner © Osprey Publishing)

Wages and Contracts

Pay was more attractive than feudal summons. By 1300 the crown usually paid a knight 2 shillings a day, a sergeant or man-at-arms 1 shilling, but others were forced to offer higher wages as need arose. Edward III induced service by paying twice the rate between 1338 and 1339 but had to fall back to the lower level. Even this tended to be based on the horses owned. Some men-at-arms with only two horses found their wages held at 12 pence.

Advances, called prests, might also be paid out to help a man bring together and maintain his following, an idea that had been in use since the 12th century. The sum was offset against the total wage, but Edward I paid few in his later years, because of shortage of money. Edward III paid many prests to foreign fighting men in his army but some English knights also received them. After a very generous initial advance of £200 in 1339, William Stury received £2 and 16s 6d the next year. From the 1340s wages could be increased by paying a quarterly bonus called a reward to those supplying troops, usually 100 marks for every 30 men-at-arms, a bonus that could be paid at one-and-a-half times or double this amount.

Wages were frequently in arrears, so much so that huge debts accrued. The Earl of Lancaster was owed £2,343 in 1343 following the campaign into Brittany. John of Gaunt's chevauchée of 1373 ran up debts of nearly £20,000 over seven years, a huge sum largely caused because no money was sent from England as promised. Soldiers sometimes had to wait ten years for payment, and some only received it when they gained political influence. Cavalry assessments show how members of a retinue, both knights and squires, might come and go during a campaign.

The use of contracts, or indentures, increased gradually in the late 13th and early 14th century. Two copies of the terms were set out on one piece of parchment and a wavy or zig-zag line was drawn horizontally to separate them. The parchment was cut in half along this line, one half going to the contractor and the other to the contracted knight. The unique shape of the pieces was a useful protection against forgery or deceit. It was, perhaps surprisingly, uncommon for the terms to be broken, even though one reason for such written contracts was a safeguard in the law. Contracts known as money fiefs (fief-rente), purchasing service for a fixed sum per year, had been used since the 11th century, and were used by Edward III to buy foreign allies.

Contracts were a simple way of securing castle garrisons beyond the campaigning season. Thus in 1301 John Kingston contracted to hold Edinburgh castle with

St George gives Edward III his shield and lance, from the treatise of Walter de Milemete of 1327. Reversing heraldic animals on the wearer's right ailette or right side of his horse's caparison was sometimes done to imply they were moving forwards; it was not normal to do so on the surcoat, suggesting here a mistake by the artist. (The Governing Body of Christ Church, Oxford, MS 92, f.3r)

30 men-at-arms and 54 foot and others, between the end of November and Whitsun, for £220 paid in four instalments. In 1316 Edward II made contracts for peace and war. In 1317 the Earl of Pembroke agreed to bring 200 men-at-arms for land worth 500 marks and a wartime fee of 2,000 marks paid quarterly. These terms of agreement were beneficial to the great lords and designed to attract them to a contractual agreement in the hope that it made them less dangerous to the crown.

In 1337 contracts were used for the first time to raise an army for an expedition to Scotland. The method was not a major success, and many also deserted. Despite this, contracts were still drawn for provision of garrisons. Contracts were few when the king accompanied an army in person, for example in Edward III's forays in the Low Countries in the late 1330s. Similarly, for his French expeditions of 1346–47 or 1359 no formal contracts were generally needed.

Where the king was not present, contracts recorded in indentures were more usual and a common formula soon developed. Edward III usually paid quarterly at the accepted rate, the first in advance. From the mid-1340s there is written evidence of another incentive, the regard. This was a form of financial assistance in kind, provided by the king in addition to the terms of the contract; fees might also be used. Thus in 1347 the king contracted with Thomas Ughtred for a year's service of 20 men-at-arms (six being knights, including Ughtred) and 20 mounted archers, for a fee of £200, half paid soon after the agreement was made. Once at the coast, wages would be paid in quarterly instalments, the first in advance. Ughtred also received livery of foodstuffs as other royal bannerets, a good horse, compensation for any animals lost, and provision of ships to and from France. A fairly standard form of contract developed. The amount of wages paid (usually quarterly in advance) was set out, plus the regard, the standard being 100 marks for 30 men-at-arms per quarter. In Edward III's later years a double regard was common, and occasionally, even double wages.

Captains in their turn made contracts with their followers. John of Gaunt added two-thirds of the profits of war to the standard terms mentioned above. The sub-contracts were not always as generous as those agreed between king and captain, and sub-contractors could be hired on differing scales of wages, fees and regards. Gaunt's contract with Roger Trumpington in August 1372 grants him for life, for himself and a squire, 40 marks per year in war and 20 marks in peace, taken from specific manors and paid by Gaunt's receiver at Michaelmas and Easter. The wages for himself and his squire are taken together with other wages paid to others of his rank. The year of war starts on the day he sets out from home to join Gaunt in accordance with instructions that will be sent to him, and he will be entitled to wages for reasonable travelling time there and back. He will provide adequate equipment for his men and horses himself. Gaunt would recompense him in accordance with his rank, for warhorses taken or lost in service, or prisoners or other prizes taken or won by Trumpington, his esquire or servants. In order to ensure the terms of a contract were being followed, musters were at first generally confined to garrisons, and others may well have been slipshod in fulfilling the terms that they had agreed. Lists were drawn up in order to note the names of deserters or for non-attendance. Even so, knights sometimes recruited poorer quality troops – and fewer men – than had been agreed. In mid-century the ratio of men-at-arms to archers was about 1:1; for example, in 1342 the retinue of Ralph, Lord Stafford consisted of three bannerets, 16 knights and 31 esquires, plus 50 archers. In Edward III's later years, however, the ratio had already often become as much as 2:1. In 1369 Henry, Lord Percy's retinue comprised one banneret, 12 knights and 47 esquires, plus 100 archers. Other soldiery might include armati (mailed horsemen or mounted infantry), hobilars (light horsemen) or bidowers (Gascon light infantry). However, by mid-century men-at-arms (bannerets, knights and esquires) and mounted archers were the usual forces recruited.

Opposite:
Brass of Sir William de Setvans, Chartham, Kent, c.1322. Still largely covered in mail, his mittens hang loose, revealing the cuffs of the aketon. Ailettes are shown flat. The seven fans for winnowing grain are a pun on the knight's name. (Author's collection)

Below:
Effigy of John Plantagenet, Earl of Cornwall (died 1336), from his tomb in Westminster Abbey. The layers of body armour are clearly visible, and he wears enclosing vambraces and gauntlets. The aventail seems to be attached quite high on the basinet; the leather edging appears to have a decorative pendant fabric curtain. (© Dean and Chapter of Westminster)

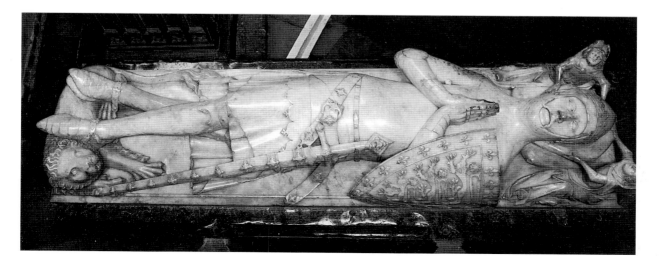

Restor, the restoration of horses lost on active service, was often part of an indenture agreement. Edward I usually replaced horses lost on service. One 1346 indenture of Edward III with three men notes that it was the English custom to do so (not exclusively, in fact). Each man was expected to have only one horse valued, but in 1357 the Earl of Salisbury was allowed his own mount as well as his horse of arms. If a horse was killed, the presentation of ears and tail to the royal clerks then resulted in action. Some were given back to the royal caravan because they were deemed no longer fit (one sorry steed ended up as a royal carthorse). The low valuations, and administrative difficulty in checking claims for a set price asked by the owners, saw a move to drop restor early in the century, but it was not until war with France erupted again in 1369 that it was largely abandoned in favour of compensation payments for costs.

Training

Training for knighthood began at an early age. Most boys came from knightly backgrounds, though some were from the ranks of prosperous merchants, lawyers or government officials. The latter might have achieved knighthood as recognition of their services, but most sons of knights began their training earlier. This was similar to that of the previous century, a mixture of manners and training in arms. Some might be taught by a clerk or chaplain to read and write in French or Latin. English was only just becoming the language of the court during the middle of the century but most people probably spoke it as their first tongue. Pages had to learn how to wait at table and how to look after horses. At the age of about 14, those who had done well became esquires and would be assigned to a knight, when their military training with armour and weapons began in earnest. They accompanied him to the hunt, in itself good physical exercise that had the bonus of bringing additional food to the table. They were taught how to break a freshly killed deer, but the use of the bow or crossbow was limited to the hunting field; it was not a knight's business to use one in battle.

Chaucer's squire gives a portrait of a young man seemingly vibrant with the joys of youth (and presumably a privileged upbringing). Unlike the rather sober picture of his father, the knight, the squire seems to have boundless energy; he is dressed in garish finery while he sings, dances and plays the flute, or courts young women all night. Interestingly, apart from jousting there is no sign of the military side of his work in Chaucer's description, and in the early 15th-century illustration in the Ellesmere Manuscript the squire is in civilian dress, unlike his father. He is clearly an accomplished young man, able to write and draw. Young men being trained for knighthood were now becoming educated as well, learning that would stand them in good stead in managing their affairs or if they pursued careers in government.

Opposite:
Brass of Sir Robert de Bures, Church of All Saints, Acton, Suffolk, c.1331. Note the decorated poleyns and gamboised cuisses. (Author's collection)

Effigy probably of Richard Stapledon, c.1332, with his fighting unit of squire and page, the latter holding his horse. The squire appears to be wearing an aketon beneath his surcoat.
(By courtesy of the Dean and Chapter of Exeter Cathedral)

At some time usually between the ages of 18 and 21, a squire who had performed well was dubbed knight. During the 14th and 15th centuries this was sometimes done before a battle, and produced new knights keen to fight bravely to uphold their honour, and who might be needed to lead troops, something squires were not supposed to do. Edward III made new knights before a raid into Scotland in 1335. For the new knights, it also meant they received a higher wage and were more likely to be captured for ransom rather than killed outright in battle. It also removed the problem of the costs involved in the lavish ceremony. Knighting was also performed after a battle, such as at Crécy in 1346, when Edward III declined to send help to his hard-pressed son, the Black Prince, telling the messenger to let the boy win his spurs, which he did.

For a full ceremony, the aspirant might be given a symbolic bath to cleanse him and be placed in a bed, from which he would arise dry, thus foreshadowing paradise. He may also have spent the night in vigil at the chapel, with his sword on the altar. The knighting ceremony now included prayers to help the knight fight for England. Distraint of knighthood was still in evidence, though it was not such a problem as it had been in the 13th century. Sometimes the knighting of the king's son was the opportunity for knighting other noble youths. A notable example occurred in 1306 when Edward I

Training

Squires and knights needed to practise constantly in order to keep muscles supple and to hone their skills. It is possible that on occasion double-weight weapons were used, so that normal weapons would feel much easier to swing. Most of these illustrations are based on those seen in the Flemish *Romance of Alexander*, of 1335–48. **1** Wrestling from pick-a-back. **2** Fighting with wooden swords. **3** Practising controlling the powerful warhorses by riding against the quintain, a post with a shield attached to it. **4** Running with a lance against a seated knight. **5** Running against a quintain on which a pivoting arm has a shield set at one end and a weight at the other; striking the target spun the weighted end and a man had to pass quickly and duck to avoid it. Other combative sports such as quarter staff were also indulged in. (Graham Turner © Osprey Publishing)

Sir Nigel Loring, who died in 1386, wearing the robes of the Order of the Garter embellished with garters. (By permission of the British Library, MS Cotton Nero D VII, f.105v)

knighted his 21-year-old son together with 276 squires, a number so large that the grounds of the Temple in London had to be taken over. For the squires, only their horses and armour had to be paid for. Apart from Prince Edward and a few companions at Westminster, the rest kept vigil at the Temple. Having been knighted at the palace by his father, Prince Edward returned to Westminster to knight the others. In the crowds two knights were killed, a number fainted, and fighting broke out; only when order was restored could the ceremony continue. There was good reason for this pageantry: the king needed men for his next adventure into Scotland.

Armour and Weapons

The 14th century saw the greatest change in the armour of the medieval knight. In 1300 the main body armour was mail; by 1400 most knights were completely protected by plates of steel. Mail would continue to be the predominant defence well into the 14th century.

In 1300 the mail coat usually reached just above the knees, and might have a small slit at the front (and presumably the rear) for ease of movement. It was long-sleeved, often terminating in mittens held in place by a thong at the wrist, usually threaded through the links. These had a glove or leather palm, furnished with a slit to allow the hand to emerge. Some knights now wore separate gauntlets, however. These gauntlets had a flared cuff, but most seem to have either been lined or externally covered with plates, often of whalebone but sometimes of iron or steel, secured by rivets through the material. These too seem to have been of mitten form.

The mail was extended up to form a coif or hood, the mail about the throat loose to facilitate putting it on. The ventail was a flap of mail pulled up and across the chin and even the mouth before action, and tied or buckled at the side of the head, sometimes laced via a thong threaded through at the temple to further secure the hood. A padded coif or arming cap, quilted front to rear, was worn underneath to provide a comfortable seat for the hood and to help absorb blows. From at least the mid-13th century a separate form of mail coif had appeared, though in 1300 many still preferred the attached form of coif. A shorter form of mail coat, the haubergeon, with sleeves to the elbow or forearm, might still be seen occasionally.

Mail stockings or chausses were worn over cloth hose, and had leather soles to prevent slipping. The upper end was secured by a lace to a belt at the waist. A very few might still wear simple strips of mail over the front of the leg and foot, laced behind and also supported at the waist.

Being flexible, mail yields when struck, sometimes allowing a blow to bruise or break bones without tearing the links; if they were damaged they might be driven into the wound. A padded coat or aketon (also sometimes confusingly called a wambais, gambeson or pourpoint) was therefore worn underneath mail. The long-sleeved aketon was usually quilted vertically, consisting of two layers of cloth stuffed with wool, tow, hay or something similar. Some may have been made instead from many layers of linen, as in 15th-century descriptions. In the 1326 inventory of Edward II's possessions in Caerphilly castle, a green canvas aketon covered with red kid is recorded. Some may also have had a standing collar, perhaps even of solid material such as whalebone or iron, but some knights certainly wore what appears to be a separate collar beneath or even over the mail.

Plate armour was beginning to become popular in 1300. From about 1320 the most commonly mentioned item is the coat of plates, also called the pair of plates, hauberk of plates, côte à plates, or 'plates'. This consisted of a poncho-like garment lined with an arrangement of plates which were riveted inside the cloth over the front of the body. Vertical plates lined the side flaps, which were tied or buckled at the back, perhaps additionally laced to the back flap by a ring at each upper corner. The coat of plates was usually worn over the mail but under the surcoat, making it difficult to see at this period. Occasionally, the plates were fastened over, rather than under, the cloth. Surviving examples from battle graves at Wisby in Gotland (1361) show that some coats consisted of rows of small vertical plates at front, sides and back, with extra plates over the shoulders and scales at the armpits. One opens at the right side and right shoulder, another at the left side and both shoulders. Swiss examples open at both shoulders and were probably laced shut at the sides. The cuirie, possibly a leather body armour, is also mentioned, and 13th-century depictions suggest it was buckled at the sides, perhaps reinforced by plates. A rare example of a coat of scales over mail occurs on an effigy from the second quarter of the 14th century in the church at Moccas, Herefordshire.

Plate leg-defences were usually restricted to poleyns over the knees, either riveted over the mail or else attached to gamboised cuisses, quilted tubes worn over the thigh and attached at the waist. A few might have schynbalds, plate shin guards, or even, rarely, a completely enclosed greave on the lower leg, hinged on the outer side and buckled shut on the inner side, to protect the leather straps. Very rarely, a plate *couter* was worn at the elbow.

Making Armour

Some armour was made by groups of workmen almost as a production line, with a particular craftsman using his skills to produce a particular piece of equipment, such as buckles. This sort of industry would become more common in the following century when amounts of plate armour required greatly increased. For the making of mail, however, this form of production was probably usual from the start. This man is drawing hot iron wire through a hole in a wooden board to achieve the right thickness. On the bench lie links that have been completed, and the equipment and tools used to form them. All this work was repetitive and time-consuming, and may well have been done by a team of workmen, perhaps including apprentices. (Graham Turner © Osprey Publishing)

Brass of Sir John de
Northwode in Minster
Church, Isle of Sheppey,
Kent, c.1340. Here he has
scale forearm-defences
instead of plate. The
hemlines of his defensive
layers suggest the mail coat
is worn over the coat of
plates, yet he has chains to
sword and dagger, which
would necessitate them
passing through the mail
to a solid chest-defence
on the coat of plates.
(Author's collection)

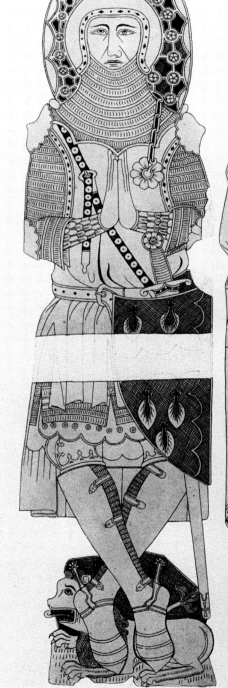

Ailettes were flat pieces of wood, leather or parchment, mainly rectangular, more rarely circular or diamond shaped, and decorated with the knight's coat-of-arms. These flimsy items were worn on the shoulder purely for identification and show, and were discarded after about 1350.

The helm, a helmet which covered the whole head, was usually, by the 14th century, conical or sugar-loaf shaped, rather than flat-topped. It was lined with leather or cloth padded with hay, wool or tow which was stitched to a leather or canvas lining band riveted around the upper part of the helmet (avoiding the breathing holes); the helm was laced or buckled under the chin. The lining was cut into scallops which could be adjusted with a draw-string, thus ensuring the helm fitted correctly whenever it was put on, and especially that the vision slots lined up with the eyes. Some were fitted with a visor and some with a pivoted bevor, a plate to give additional protection to the throat. A leather, wooden or whalebone crest was sometimes worn, laced through holes in the metal that were hidden by a cloth wrapped round like a scarf or hanging down like a curtain. However, the helm was increasingly confined to the tournament.

The cervellière was sometimes also called the basinet (although the helmet we now regard as the basinet was also developing in the early years of the century). The latter was small and globular, covered only the ears and often had a visor. Some were conical and did not cover the ears, resembling instead the old conical helmet without its nasal, or noseguard. Another conical variety was much larger, reaching almost to the shoulders, and when provided with a visor looking very much like a visored helm. A few might have a nasal, instead. The cervellière, or low or tall basinet (not the deep form) might be worn under the mail coif until the 1330s, but even before 1300 a few might have a simple mail curtain, or *tippet*, riveted inside the helmet, thus obviating the need for a coif. This was probably rare until about 1320, though it is difficult to know what was worn under many helmets shown resting on mail. The helm might be worn over either the cervellière or the smaller forms of basinet.

Kettle hats might occasionally be worn by knights wanting more ventilation at the expense of safety, while the broad brim was a good defence for siegework in deflecting missiles. At first it was made from several pieces with applied bands to cover the joints and an applied brim. After about 1320 it seems to be made from a single piece or else a few large ones riveted together, and some had high pointed skulls. It was sometimes worn with a large bevor.

Most knights wore a surcoat, a gown pulled on over the head, split up the fork before and behind for ease of movement. It was usually sleeveless, though a few had elbow- or

wrist-length sleeves, and it was often lined in a contrasting colour. Richer versions were made from silk. It varied in length from the ankles to just above the knees (rare) and might bear the coat-of-arms, though many did not. It is uncertain if it was developed to protect armour from rain or heat, or whether it simply copied Muslim fashions seen on crusade. A few may have been lined with plates over the chest. By about 1330 the surcoat became shorter at the front until it was cut off horizontally at the thighs. This has sometimes been called the cyclas. It was not long, however, before the rear of the skirt was also shortened.

A window of c.1340 in the choir of Tewkesbury Abbey depicting armoured men. All wear plate gauntlets, but only the left-hand figure has full vambraces, this figure also possessing complete greaves. Instead of mail at the throat, two have what appears to be a defence in coat of plates style. All have ailettes shown standing up at the back, presumably an artistic style to display them. (TopFoto/ Woodmansterne)

Knight and Equipment, c.1350

By the mid-14th century the surcoat tended to shorten, especially at the front, as seen on this figure based on the brass of Sir John d'Aubenon. He wears layered armour: a quilted aketon, then a mail haubergeon, then a coat of plates with floriated rivet heads. The lower cannons cover the forearm completely but the upper arm still only has gutter-shaped plates over the shortened mail sleeves. Circular besagews protect the armpit. Poleyns, schynbalds and plate sabatons are worn. The mail aventail is riveted inside the basinet, which is fluted and has a gilt finial.

1 Visored basinet and plate collar.

2 The helm of the Black Prince, with decorative breathing holes on the wearer's right side only, c.1376.

3 Decorated basinet fitted with pendant flaps.

4 Inside view of a poncho-style coat of plates with shield-shaped shoulder pieces attached, based on finds from Wisby in Gotland.

5 Evidence for a solid breast-defence seen in the guard-chains running through decorated lion-heads.

6 Arm-defence.

7 Lower arm-defence of scale.

8 Gauntlet with plates riveted to a glove.

9 Sabaton of scale, together with enclosed greave.

10 Gilt copper-alloy rowel spur, Devizes Museum.

11 Sword with relatively short blade reinforced by a flattened diamond point, c.1350.

12 Sword, 1st half of the 14th century, found in London. The fuller on this type runs just over halfway down the blade, while the tip is of diamond section. This example has the mark of a fleur-de-lys within a shield punched in the fuller and on the tang.

13 Sword belt fittings, from effigy of Maurice, Lord Berkeley (died 1326) at Bristol.

14 Garnache with tongue-shaped lapels, worn over super-tunic, and wide-brimmed hat.

15 Cote-hardie worn over jupon, and hood.

(Graham Turner © Osprey Publishing)

The Increase in Plate Armour

The armourer needed new skills to make plate armour. Plates were shaped over an armourer's anvil embedded in a tree trunk. A controllable fire, fanned by leather bellows, was necessary for heating the metal, and controllable light sources were needed to enable the armourer to check the colour of the metal to enable him to remove it at the required time for further treatment. Mushroom-headed stakes were set into a wooden bench for shaping, much of which was done when the metal was cool. Large snips were needed to cut the steel sheets for working, but all plans of the basic flat shape, if indeed they existed, have vanished. Probably much of it was carried in the armourer's head. The shaped pieces were black from the furnace and were usually burnished and polished to a bright finish. Most would need rivets of some sort: those for attaching a lining band to which a lining was stitched; those that acted as a pivot between two plates and, towards the later 14th century, those that slid in a slot in another plate, usually on the elbow and lower cannon joint. The coat of plates used many rivets in securing it to its backing.

Evidence from German effigies suggests that the breastplate began to appear in about 1340. At first it was quite short, but by the 1360s it became deeper and curved. It was fastened to the inside of the coat by two semicircles of rivets, with narrow waist lames with the wider hoops below these. Another form of breastplate appeared in the 1370s, less globular and with a notable medial ridge.

A list of armour for the Wardrobe of Edward III drawn up for the years 1337 and 1341 refers to separate breastplates, though these, and others in Dover in 1361, are specified as for the jousts. If contemporary German effigies are anything to go by, these early breastplates were perhaps flat with curved edges, or shaped rather like an inverted heart, presumably being attached to the front of the covering by straps and buckles. An effigy on a 1340 tomb at Abergavenny, Monmouthshire possibly shows a small, flat breastplate with a medial ridge worn under the surcoat. By about the third quarter of the century a larger form covering the whole chest as far as the waist also appeared on German effigies. From about 1380 the breastplate, rounded in the chest and sometimes with a medial ridge, was usually worn without the coat of plates, but often with a *fauld* of plates that might curve down to cover the abdomen. They seem to have been strapped and perhaps laced in place over a cloth or leather jupon, and some may have been held by a *saltire* of straps across the back, as on a figure in Basle Cathedral. The back-defence was presumably of the coat of plates form until about 1400, for at about this date the effigy of John, Earl of Salisbury, displays hinges down the wearer's left side under a heraldic jupon, suggesting the fabric has a lining consisting of a large ridged breastplate with a (presumably) one-piece backplate. The hinges continue down the side, suggesting that the waist lames connected the breast and back to a shirt of hoops.

By mid-century, plate armour for the limbs had also become more popular. Until about 1320 many knights seem to have worn no more than mail chausses and gamboised cuisses, quilted tubes covering the thighs and knees and presumably suspended from the waist belt. By this date the knees were often additionally protected by plate or cuir-bouilli poleyns, either laced or riveted to the mail or the cuisses. However, solid plate schynbalds were increasingly worn over the shins, and, more rarely, greaves that enclosed the lower leg entirely, being usually hinged on the outer side to protect the leather straps on the inner side. Greaves became increasingly common by mid-century, and were sometimes worn with sabatons over the top and sides of the foot, leaving the sole of the shoe in contact with the ground. The strips were connected by internal leather straps and by pivoting rivets. They were probably strapped under the foot or pointed to the shoe, that is, a pair of points (twine or leather laces terminating in a metal aiglet) stitched to the top of the shoe, or threaded through holes in it, passed through a pair of holes in the sabaton

Opposite:
Brass of Sir John de Creke, Westley Waterless, Cambs, c.1340–45. His aketon, mail coat and coat of plates with floriated rivet heads are all visible. Hinged tubular plate defences are visible on the lower arm, emerging from the shortened mail sleeve, with gutter-shaped upper arm-defences. Note the lion's-head design of the couter disc and spaudler. The lower end of the cuisse emerges decoratively from below the poleyn. Plate sabatons additionally cover the mail of the foot. (Author's collection)

A basinet, probably of the 14th century, found at Pevensey, Sussex. It is of unusual form and is decorated with a line of shields. (By permission of the Trustees of the Armouries, IV.444)

and tied in a single bow. The upper end was probably attached to the front of the greave by points. Some sabatons appear to have been made from overlapping scales, either of iron, copper-alloy or leather, attached by a rivet at the top of each scale to a fabric or leather backing. Others may have been made from plates riveted under a cloth covering.

By about 1350 the all-enclosing poleyn was gradually superseded by a smaller form that had appeared some ten years earlier. This covered the front and outer side, the latter usually extended to form a circular, fan-shaped wing to deflect cuts, and occasionally another on the inside. Later wings were often oval in shape. The cuisse was also changing in about 1340, to a form made from small plates riveted to a covering so the heads were visible, rather like the later *brigandine* worn on the body. The poleyn was secured to the lower part of the cuisse, and the cloth edge of the latter was often visible below it, cut in a fringe that overhung the armoured lower leg. From about 1370 a new form of cuisse appeared, made from a single plate shaped to the leg and protecting the front and outer side, though as early as c.1324, a figure on the canopy of Aymer de Valance's tomb in Westminster Abbey appears to have both plate cuisses and a fan-shaped side-wing on his poleyn. Later cuisses are shaped slightly over the top of the knee, and were attached to the poleyn by a pivoting rivet at each side. The cuisse of the boy prince in Chartres Cathedral suggests that the top edge was rolled out to stop weapon points snaking up past it; a stop-rib was sometimes added to the upper surface from about 1375. At about the same time, an additional outer plate was sometimes hinged to the cuisse. The cuisse was strapped round the leg and was probably also suspended like later examples by a leather tab riveted to the upper edge and pierced for points.

From the beginning of the period a small, circular, slightly shaped plate was occasionally attached to the point of the shoulder. This *spaudler* is sometimes seen without any other plate arm-defences. For the first quarter of the century a small elbow cop or couter was occasionally riveted over the point of the elbow. However, though some references suggest that a form of arm-defence (perhaps of leather or even coat of plates construction) was worn occasionally, it is not until about 1320 that gutter-shaped plates, strapped over the outside of the arm with the couter, appear in artistic representations. A circular plate, the besagew, was sometimes attached in front to guard the armpit and a disc at the front of the elbow. Besagews at the armpit tend to disappear after about 1350, and only reappear in the 15th century.

By about 1335 tubular arm-defences were already known, the upper and lower cannons together with the couter being called the *vambrace*.

An ornate copper-alloy rowel spur (the rowel missing) of c.1300–40, for the left foot decorated with gilding and enamel and with an unusual bent neck. It has three shields (perhaps of the Noon family) on each arm, plus one curving out at the rear, one at each ring terminal and others at the buckle and terminal for the leather. (Courtesy of King's Lynn Museums)

The Mine at Cormicy, 1359

During the siege of Rheims several English nobles were ranged about the French countryside to block ingress. Lord Bartholomew Burghersh (on right) was lodged in the town of Cormicy, where the enemy-held castle had a strong tower and looked safe from attack. He ordered a mine dug and, when all was ready, invited the castellan, Sir Henry de Vaulx, to come out under safe conduct and see the danger he was in. When Henry de Vaulx arrived and saw that the tower's foundations were only held up by props he accepted honourable surrender for all his men. Sir Henry acknowledged that if the French Jacquerie ('Jack Goodmans') had got the better of a garrison in this way they would never had been treated so generously. (Graham Turner © Osprey Publishing)

Occasionally forearm-defences of scale are shown. The cannon might be closed entirely and slid up the arm, or, as with an upper cannon from an effigy from Lesney Abbey, open slightly on the inner side and closed by straps and buckles. However, at this date the upper cannon was sometimes still of gutter-shaped design. The tubular lower cannon was usually worn under the loose three-quarter sleeve of the mail coat, from which it protruded. Cannons hinged on the outer side and buckled on the inner, became more usual. Some couters were now of laminated construction. By 1360 a heart-shaped wing

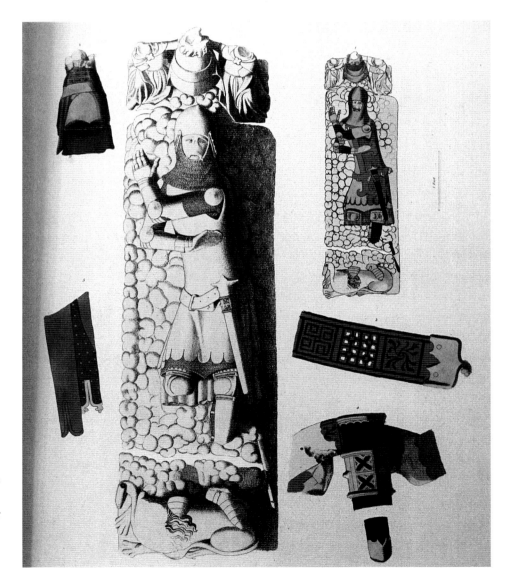

Effigy of Sir Oliver d'Ingham, died 1344, a drawing by Stothard from his tomb in Ingham, Suffolk. The black colouration of the limb pieces noted by Stothard may represent cuir bouilli, or armour left black from the hammer, or painted perhaps in an effort to prevent rusting. The short sleeve of the mail coat covers the top of the upper cannon. He wears a great sword of some length. (Author's collection)

Brass of Sir Hugh Hastings, St Mary's Church, Elsing, Norfolk, c.1347. Sir Hugh's basinet has a bevor and visor. His thigh is protected by a cuisse made in the manner of a coat of plates, presumably with small plates under the fabric. The poleyn at the knee seems to be strapped over a layer of fabric. He wears no plate armour on the lower legs. The right-hand figure wears what appears to be a basinet with wide brim. (Author's collection)

had replaced the disc-shaped wing of the couter, which itself now consisted of a single shaped plate with one or two lames to connect to the upper and lower cannon. In some late examples the rivet attaching the lame to the lower cannon may have run in a slot in the latter, forming a sliding rivet to allow the forearm to twist. Laminated spaudlers had appeared by 1335 and were soon being riveted permanently to the upper cannon of the vambrace. In the last years of the century a larger shoulder-defence, the *pauldron*, emerged, in which the plates extended over the chest and back.

Extensions of the mail sleeve into mittens remained popular as the century opened, and might still be found 50 years later. Mail gauntlets with flaring cuffs were rarely seen, but gauntlets of metal plates riveted over or between a fabric glove (presumably tinned or coppered to prevent rusting under the covering) were in use. They might have a large plate over the cuff or several strips. By 1350 the so-called 'hour-glass gauntlet' had appeared, and within about 20 years became the dominant form for the rest of the century. Many such gauntlets also had *gadlings* over the finger-joints and knuckles, low spikes for use as a kind of knuckleduster.

By about 1330 the tall conical basinet had begun to extend down to cover the ears and neck, and within 20 years, together with the globular form (some of which were now pointed), it had extended further down to the base of the neck and the cheeks. The very deep basinet went out of use by about 1350. From 1375 the point of the skull of all basinets tended to be set further back.

In the 1320s the riveted mail *aventail* began to be replaced by a detachable version secured over staples, and this would become almost universal after 1350. Some aventails were covered by a decorative cloth, while a few were tied down to the jupon at intervals by laces. A plate bevor was occasionally fixed to the basinet from about 1330, and by the end of the century a few were extended to overlap the edges of the basinet and to cover the whole aventail. By 1400 large bevors riveted to the basinet formed the first great basinets.

From about 1330 the basinet was often worn with a visor. This was at first often formed with a swelling over the face. The vision-slits were usually flanged to deflect a weapon point, and some seem to have been pointed at the bottom or extended horizontally to form a throat guard. After about 1380 the visor became drawn out in front, sometimes in a rounded form but more usually into a snout, and now had a flanged slit over the mouth. Each arm usually had a removable pin to allow the visor to be detached. The snouted form of helmet was dubbed a 'pig-faced basinet' in the 19th century and it is sometimes claimed that the term Hounskull, which appears to come from a contemporary German term: *Hundsgugel* ('hound's hood'), was also used in England. One unusual hybrid is to be found on the Hastings brass, where a figure wears what appears to be a basinet, but in this case fitted with a broad brim.

The basinet might be decorated by a plume of feathers, perhaps one or two pheasant feathers, set in a hole at the apex of the skull. Very rarely it might carry a crest. From about 1375, however, a number were decorated around the skull with an *orle*, a roll of cloth, or sometimes leather, which may be jewelled or embroidered. Others bore a simple circlet or crown. An ornamental pendant sometimes hung from the centre rear of the helmet.

The shield was soon to lose its place on the battlefield. In the second half of the century a rectangular form of shield had appeared, usually concave, the upper and lower surfaces curving or bent outwards to the field. A cut-out was sometimes added to the top corner to accommodate the couched lance, it being mainly used on horseback. The shield was increasingly relegated to the tournament, where safety made its use desirable.

𝖂𝖊𝖆𝖕𝖔𝖓𝖘

The sword was the revered weapon of a knight, girt about him when he was knighted and usually blessed at the altar before the ceremony; the cross-guard made a crucifix when needs were pressing. Some knightly weapons were richly decorated, and a glimpse at representations in detailed effigies hint at the richness also of the scabbards and sword belts.

One type that had been extremely popular in the 13th century had a fairly broad, slightly tapering blade with a fuller running as much as three-quarters of the length. Others were broad bladed, but the blade does not noticeably taper, while most widen just before the hilt. These swords have a long grip, some 6 inches (16.25cm) on average, though some lack this and are sometimes narrower in the blade. Some swords of this type are large, 37–40 in. (94–101.5cm) long, with the grip as much as 9 in, (23cm) long. Known as 'great swords' or 'swords of war', they were designed to be swung in two hands.

By contrast, another form of sword was quite short, with a grip less than 16cm (4 in.) long and a wide, strongly tapered blade with a fuller running about halfway and a 'wheel' pommel. This type was used for 'armour piercing', as the blade was acutely pointed, with a flattened diamond section and no fuller, to impart rigid strength for a thrust. A narrower-bladed form with long grip (between 7 and 10 in., 17.75 and 25.5cm) appeared at some time around mid-century. Some of these thrusting swords were made with a short section of the blade in front of the guard left blunt (later called the *ricasso*), enabling the user to hook his finger over it and hold the sword further forward, the better to deliver a thrust.

Dual-purpose weapons for cutting and thrusting were made from the beginning of the century, with a tapered blade which was fullered for just over half its length, but with the lower part of the blade made in flattened diamond section. Another type of weapon has a long tapered blade, fullered for about one-third of the length, with a long grip. One group dating from about 1355 to 1425 has a long tapering blade usually of hexagonal section, and a long grip. The pommel is a flattened oval or else a late 14th-century 'scent-stopper' variety. Some carried a falchion, a single-edged, cleaver-like weapon whose blade expanded toward the point to add weight to a cut.

The sword hilt was covered by a grip of wood, bone or horn. On swords with a flat form of tang, the grip consisted of two pieces cut out to accommodate the tang, then glued together over it. As thinner tangs became popular in the second half of the century, a one-piece grip was bored longitudinally before the heated tang was forced up through the hole, widening it as it burned through it. The core was usually covered additionally by winding cord or wire round it, but might also be bound in diaper fashion by cord or leather strips, all designed to prevent the weapon slipping in a sweating hand. The cross-guard was often straight or gently curved down towards the blade. Some swords had a small flap of leather folded over the cross-guard and down

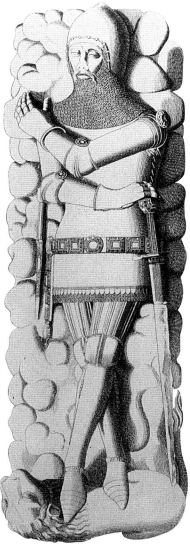

Effigy of Sir William de Kerdiston, a drawing by Stothard from his tomb in Reepham Church, Norfolk, c.1361. The thighs are protected by what appears to be stud and splint armour, which disappeared in about 1380. (Author's collection)

over the blade. Called the *chappe* (literally 'cape'), this flap overlapped the mouth of the scabbard when the weapon was sheathed, and helped prevent water running down inside and rusting the sword.

Pommels came in many shapes. The most common was the disc pommel or a variant, the wheel pommel, but many other styles were seen with varying frequency, including a faceted version and a flat form of chamfered disc pommel (both types from about 1350). One form of pommel seen up to about 1325 has the form of a petalled flower. A spherical pommel survives on a sword of about 1300 from London, and a bevelled cube on an effigy at Halton Holgate (Lincolnshire). A 'tear-drop' style flourished until about mid-century. A lobated pommel was used in northern England and southern Scotland until about mid-century. A type rarely seen before about 1360 was the 'scent-stopper' pommel, so named from its likeness to the stopper of a scent bottle. Some examples were faceted.

Scabbards were fashioned from two wooden slats bound with a leather covering. The lower end was often protected by the addition of a metal chape. The mouth of the scabbard might have a metal locket to prevent damage, and both were sometimes

Probably one of a number owned by the Black Prince, this jupon fastens down the front, and has lost some of its shape from earlier mounting. Four squares of silk velvet form the quarterings on front and back, laid on a linen foundation with a layer of wool between, quilted vertically. The heraldic charges were embroidered in gold thread on separate pieces of applied velvet, the seams covered with gold cord. The inserts of the sleeves are longer at the back than the front, and the sleeves each bear two quarters. (By courtesy of the Dean and Chapter of Canterbury and the Trustees of the Armouries)

ornamented with engraved or openwork designs. Sword belts would change dramatically in design, from a two-point attachment of leather, or increasingly, metal mounts, to the hip belt that appeared in about 1340 and would become standard for the rest of the century. Usually decorated with gold, gilt or silvered plaques often set with jewels or enamel, the belt was normally clasped or sometimes buckled at the front. In some instances the sword was still hung from a diagonal strap, while the horizontal hip belt was used only for the dagger on the other side. The dagger carried in the last quarter of the century was often a form of *rondel* dagger, with a disc or rondel at the base of the grip, but a pommel instead of the more usual second rondel at this end. These daggers were usually of triangular section, single edged and tapering to a point, being sturdy but very sharp weapons. *Quillon* daggers were also worn, or occasionally *ballock* daggers, although they were more usual with civilian dress. Like scabbard leather, sheaths were often highly decorated with punched or engraved designs, and civilian daggers might be fastened behind the pouch, slung from the belt, or hung from a cord on the belt.

An extremely rare cuir bouilli tubular upper right arm-defence of the first half of the 14th century. Now flattened, it is provided at the top with a pair of holes for lacing to the undergarment, and decorated with moulded leaves and flowers. (The British Museum, 56, 7–1, 1665)

The lance was carried on horseback, with a shaft of Cypress wood according to Chaucer, although ash was just as likely. At first it was a simple staff tipped with a steel head, but in the early years of the century a steel disc, the vamplate, was sometimes nailed on in front of the hand. By the end of the century, the hand grip was usually waisted somewhat and the vamplate more conical in shape. A leather strip was often nailed around the shaft behind the hand. This, a simple form of *graper*, was designed to ram against the armpit to prevent the lance sliding back on impact. By the end of the century early lance-rests had probably appeared, riveted to the solid breast-defence to take the impact. The lance might be used to carry a small pennon, nailed on the shaft behind the head, on which were painted or embroidered the arms of the owner. When fighting on foot the lance was sometimes cut down to a more manageable 5 feet (1.5m) in length, but it was not as effective as the long-handled axe.

The long axe, sometimes provided with a rear spike and later a top spike, was primarily for use on foot. Smaller axes for horsemen might have a rear spike. Later manuscripts sometimes show a very large bladed weapon with no spikes, the lower end curled round the haft. Maces and hammers were also becoming more popular as plate armour increased. The mace usually had a flanged steel or iron head nailed to a wooden haft. Short or long hammers were usually furnished with a rear spike and sometimes the corners of the hammer face were slightly elongated. By the end of the century the pollaxe was also coming into use, a staff weapon with an axe blade and top spike, backed by a hammer or spike, or else having a hammer with top and rear spike.

Sir Robert Knollys with Sir Thomas Grandison, from a French manuscript of c.1392. Under the red cross of St George English troops wear quilted jupons over their armour; some laced or buttoned up the front. The commanders have exchanged their helmets for a top hat and hood-turban. One carries a baton. (The British Library/HIP/TopFoto)

Horses

The horse was, of course, vital to a knight. The destrier was the best warhorse and also the most expensive, sometimes confined to use in the tournament. So-called from the Latin word for 'right' ('dexter'), it is believed it was led on the right hand or was trained to lead with the right foot. About the size of a modern hunter, it was its build and breeding rather than great height that gave it value. Deep-chested for good windage and muscular for carrying an armoured rider, it nevertheless could run and turn nimbly in response to the spur, knee or rein. Warhorses were always stallions, partly because their natural aggression could be channelled into kicking and biting at enemy horses, but probably also because of their macho image. Some lords bought destriers valued at £100, a fortune by standards of the day. A less expensive but nonetheless valuable warhorse was the courser. Though the now out of date prick spur was designed not to penetrate too deeply, some manuscripts do show horses with bloodied flanks, also seen from the use of rowel spurs.

1 Warhorse of about 1325 with primitive plate shaffron and early peytral over a cloth caparison. The manuscript does not indicate how the shaffron was fastened; it may have been laced to the head-piece.

2 Warhorse of the second half of the 14th century. The mail trapper, presumably with linen beneath for comfort and to absorb sweat, has a cloth caparison over it. The arms are those of Sir Walter Paveley.

3 Cut leather decorated trappings of c.1380, for use on a war-horse or a good palfrey, the better sort of riding horse. Note the tied tail. Also necessary were rounceys or roncins, horses of poorer quality for a knight's retinue, and perhaps a hackney for his squire or squires. The knight's lady might ride a quiet jennet. Sumpter horses or mules were used for baggage, or else it was carried on wagons.

4–5 14th-century bridles, fitted with curb bits. These bits rarely survive but are seen everywhere in art. The curb acted like a pivoting lever, pressing the bridge inside up against the roof of the mouth while pulling the bridle against the horse's poll. Some may also have had a curb chain under the jaw, which would squeeze it, though representations are difficult to find at this period.

6 Typical 14th-century style of snaffle bit with connecting ring and side bars.

7 Stirrups.

(Graham Turner © Osprey Publishing)

Horse-Armour

The war horse often had no protection, only a decorative leather harness. However, a cloth caparison was sometimes worn, which might have been padded and could catch weapons in the folds. The caparison was usually made in two halves, divided at the saddle and often enclosed the tail, head and neck, usually including the ears. Sometimes a testier might be worn on the head, a form of padded and quilted defence. Some cloth caparisons may have concealed a trapper of mail, which was quite heavy and expensive and would be worn over a linen lining cloth to absorb sweat and provide some comfort for the horse. Some mail trappers even covered the head (though not the ears) as well.

Early forms of shaffron were occasionally worn, which may have been attached to the mail trappers. The shaffron could be of metal or cuir bouilli, and was probably used as a point of attachment for the fan or moulded crests sometimes shown on top of horses' heads. By the late 14th century shaffrons that enclosed almost the whole head might be worn, perhaps with a poll plate or short laminated crinet (neck-defence). By this date a mail crinet was sometimes worn with a plate shaffron, together with perhaps a mail curtain around the chest and rump. A plate chest-defence, the peytral, was occasionally used by the 1330s, sometimes worn over the caparison.

Civilian Dress

The basic undergarments of the knight were a long-sleeved linen shirt and drawers, or braies, which reached down to the knees or even slightly below; by 1400 they had shrunk almost to the size of modern boxer shorts. A draw-string kept them in place, and presumably they had some form of frontal slit, though this is not very clear. The shirt was roughly knee-length, with wrist-length sleeves.

From about 1335 the tunic was superseded by the jupon, also known as the pourpoint or doublet (the latter term rare until after about 1370). The jupon was of similar length, but was rather tight-fitting, with no folds, and was usually padded all over. It was closed right down the front (or to the waist for those out of fashion) by laces, or ball or flat buttons, with perhaps a row of buttons from wrist to elbow. In the second half of the century the area over the chest was further padded, while the skirt gradually grew shorter until it barely covered the hips, usually being joined to the body of the garment by a seam. By this time some had short side slits that could be buttoned. Some sleeves now stretched over the hands to the knuckles, and some were inset well over the front and back of the body. Belts tended not to be worn until the second half of the century, since before this the jupon was usually covered by the cote-hardie, a tight, belted garment, which replaced the super-tunic by 1330. It was laced or buttoned to the waist, from where it became a full open skirt to the knees. In the second half of the century the fastening continued down to the hem, which might be dagged, and which in turn began to shrink upwards like that of the jupon, until for the last ten years of the century, it was high fashion to wear the cote-hardie daringly short. Sleeves terminated at the elbows, but the back edge extended to a flap, which became longer from about mid-century. Called a tippet, this flap was often coloured white, with a white band at the elbow forming a cuff. At the end of the century a long-sleeved version appeared, buttoned down the forearm and extending over the hands. From about mid-century the belt moved to the hips and was often similar to that worn with armour. Decorated with plaques and jewels, it was probably fastened in place with stitches or hooks. From about 1375 some cote-hardies were made with a collar. The poorer classes wore a different cut of cote-hardie.

Opposite:
Brass of Sir Ralph de Kneyvnton, Aveley, Essex, c.1370. His upper torso has two semicircles of rivets that secure a solid breastplate beneath the cloth, from which guard chains attach to his sword and dagger. (Author's collection)

Left:
Early frog-mouthed forms of jousting helm of late 14th- or early 15th-century date, that once hung over the tombs of Sir Reginald Braybrook (left) and Sir Nicolas Hawberk, from Cobham Church, Kent. The lower band and rear bar on the Braybrook helm are funerary additions. (By courtesy of the Trustees of the Armouries and the Rector of Cobham, Al.30)

A falling knight, struck by a crossbow bolt, carved on a misericord in the choir of Lincoln Cathedral, dating from the second half of the 14th century. It affords a rare back view of a coat of plates, the sides held by two buckled straps and a third lower down. The sides seem to be composed of horizontal hoops, the back of small overlapping rectangular plates. The hinged outer plate of the cuisse is clearly visible. Note also the bells adorning the horse's harness. (akg-images/ A. F. Kersting)

At the beginning of the century the garde-corps, a long super-tunic with wide sleeves and a slit for the arm to pass through, dropped out of fashion, as did the tabard, which was pulled on over the head and clasped or stitched at the sides. The super-tunic with loose and short sleeves, or no sleeves, continued until the cote-hardie became popular. The garnache, a wide garment pulled over the head and falling sometimes as far as the ankles, and stitched all the way up the sides or just under the arm, or not at all, but now with tongue-shaped lapels, also continued.

The *houppelande* appeared in about 1380, a closed gown worn over the jupon and reaching anywhere from the knee to the floor. Cut from four panels with front, rear and side seams, it widened as it fell into folds, held in place by a waist belt. The seams might be left open at the bottom to varying degrees, to form vents. The houppelande had a very high upstanding collar and was usually closed in front by hooks or buttons. By the end of the century some houppelandes were buttoned right down the front. The sleeves were generous, reaching the wrist but with an enormous opening so that the lower edge trailed sometimes to the ground. The edges of the sleeves, hem, vents and collar were often dagged (cut in fanciful shapes), especially after 1380, a decorative effect also seen, but with less frequency, on other forms of clothing. Some dagging was added in overlapping layers as appliqué work. At the end of the century a new version of the cote-hardie came into use, with similar sleeves and collar to those of the houppelande, from which it was difficult to distinguish it except for its hip belt, unlike the waist belt of the houppelande.

Hose, usually of wool or linen and often parti-coloured, reached the thigh for the rich, or knee for the less well-off. In the first half of the century the tops of the hose were pulled over the braies and tied to the draw-string or buttoned, perhaps to a string from the braies' girdle. Garters of wool or linen (often embroidered) might be worn tied below the knee. During the second half of the century *estaches*, or strings, were sewn inside the jupon for the suspension of the hose, which were now furnished with pairs of eyelet holes along the upper edge. At the end of the century the two legs reached the fork and became joined. The feet of some hose were stuffed with hay, moss or tow to produce exaggerated points called 'pikes', and some were soled with leather and worn without shoes.

Shoes were laced on the inner or outer side or with a flap folding over a long tongue; some were cut away over the instep and fastened at the ankle with strap and buckle. Leather might be punched with patterns or cloth embroidered, and by 1360 the shoes became sharply pointed and often had openwork designs. Edward III's Sumptuary Law forbade knights under the estate of a lord, esquire or gentleman (and anyone else, for that matter!) to have pikes over 2 inches (5cm) long; transgressors were to be fined 40 pence.

The effigy of Edward, the Black Prince (died 1376) in Canterbury Cathedral. Depicted on the tomb chest is also a black shield with white ostrich feathers, his 'shield of peace' for jousts, which probably gave rise to the name 'Black Prince'. (TopFoto/Woodmansterne)

The helm and crest of the Black Prince, from his funeral achievements in Canterbury Cathedral. The helm consists of front and rear plates plus one forming a dome. The sights are flanged outwards, and the rivets holding the dome have brass washers inside that originally held the lining strap. Pairs of holes below these were for tying the lining laces. Two sets of four holes on top were for attaching the crest or coronet. Two cruciform holes in front were for the toggle of a guard chain, while at the back two holes were for the strap to attach it to the body armour. The leather cap of maintenance had canvas glued over the joints and was originally plastered and painted red, powdered with gold roses; the brim was painted as heraldic ermine. The lion is of moulded leather and canvas, the tail and legs of canvas held by wooden dowels. The hair was simulated by gluing on lozenges of leather that had been stamped with a fur pattern. The surface of the lion was gilded and the eyeballs and lashes shaded black. (By courtesy of the Dean and Chapter of Canterbury and the Trustees of the Armouries)

In 1395, however, poulaines, very long, pointed shoes, became fashionable for men of rank and their attendants. Boots, or buskins, tended on occasion to follow the style of toe seen on shoes. Short boots were closed by buttons or laces at the side, or, from about 1395, by being hooked on the outer side. Long riding boots were sometimes shaped to the thighs and secured by buttons, laces or buckles below the calf; open varieties could be closed by a flap across the outside of the calf, fastened by hooks or buttons. Some

boots were additionally decorated with tassels or silver-gilt. Galoches (clogs) and patterns were sometimes worn from about 1350, the latter with wooden soles and a leather strap to keep feet out of mud in bad weather.

Gloves were common, sometimes simply carried in the hand. They had long, wide cuffs and might be decorated with embroidery. Mantles were sometimes worn for ceremonial occasions. Cloaks were usually of circular cut, richly lined and fastened with a brooch in front or a button on the right shoulder. From about 1330, shoulder capes appeared, some being long, cut on the circle, to reach the thighs, and buttoning down the front. Some had hoods, and from mid-century many were dagged.

From about 1330 the hood was extended to include a tail, the *liripipe*. It hung down the back unless cut vertically, when it would hang to the side. Long versions were often twisted round the head. The hood might also be made into a turban by wearing it with the face-opening on the head, turned up to a rolled brim, and the liripipe and gorget (the part around the neck, if the hood was worn properly) hanging on opposite sides. However, from about 1380 a new form, the hood-turban, appeared. The face-opening fitted the head and the edges rolled back, while those with a long liripipe had it wound round the crown with an end hanging on one side. The gorget either fell on the other side or stood up if the material was stiff enough, and since most were dagged, gave the appearance of a cock's comb. Knights might wear a hat with a wide, turned-up brim to form a sharp point in front. From 1325 a high or round crowned hat with a rolled or turned-up brim was also seen. From 1392 some hats had a floppy bag-shaped crown that drooped over a rolled brim, while two years later a hat with a tall but often flattened crown, widening at the top, was worn over a rolled or turned-up brim. In the second half of the century some headgear sported a plume, usually of one or two dyed ostrich or peacock feathers fixed at front or rear of the bottom of the crown by a brooch. Decorative hat bands also began to appear at this time. The coif was still worn.

Men were either clean-shaven or else had a beard sometimes without moustaches and with no sideburns. Hair styles were relatively simple: in the first part of the century a roll curl across the forehead and nape was common, but after mid-century the hair was either parted in the centre and hung down, or else was cut more closely all over.

The pouch had two straps for suspending it from the belt. The ballock dagger, so called from the two swellings at the base of the grip, was sometimes worn in civilian life at the front of the belt, so mimicking male genitalia. Richard II is said to have introduced the 'hand-cloth' or 'hand-coverchief' or mokador, for wiping his nose.

Ideals and Customs

Chivalry

Chivalry was an ideal of knightly behaviour that bound knights across Europe together. The old tales of chivalrous heroes, notably King Arthur, were still read and narrated, and real heroes appear in the pages of great storytellers such as Froissart, one English notable being Sir Walter Manny. Besieged in Guingamp by the French after dinner, Manny suggested he and his friends go to attack the siege engine outside as a fitting end to the entertainment, which they duly did. Attacked as they retreated back to the fortress, Manny swore never to be embraced by mistress or friend if he did not unhorse one of the riders, and a skirmish followed. He later led a sortie from Hennebont castle to rescue two companions who were about to be beheaded by the French and was clearly a brave and skilful fighter, well versed in the ways of war.

Another work with a sense of immediacy was the *Scalacronica* of Sir Thomas Gray of Heaton in Northumberland, himself a knight who spent much of his career on the Scottish borders. He relates the story of how, when his father held Norham castle, Sir William Marmion joined the garrison. A Lincolnshire knight, Marmion had been given a gold helmet by his mistress, who told him to make it known wherever glory was most difficult to obtain. When a small Scottish force appeared, having received permission of the commander, this 'knight-errant' rode out wearing the helmet and confronted the enemy. Only when Marmion had been unhorsed and badly wounded did the garrison sally forth to save him, an excellent example of a brave, but essentially useless act. Such courage was held up as an ideal of behaviour and was frequently emulated, such as the death ride of Sir William Felton in Castile in 1367 who charged into a group of Spaniards with levelled lance.

The idealistic vision of knighthood persisted, however. *Piers Plowman*, written by John Langland in the 1380s, repeats the notion of the 'pure order' of knighthood, and incorporates ideas such as fighting to defend the truth. Most people in England spoke English (rather than French) as a first language by the early 14th century, and contemporary romances embrace the idea of a national hero fighting for his country. In two poems knights are satirized as 'lions in hall, hares in the field'. Chaucer's high-minded chivalrous knight fights in Prussia, Lithuania and Russia, Spain, North Africa, Anatolia and Armenia, and has jousted in the lists in Algeria – all very well except that it was not much practical help to his own country. Terry Jones has argued that the lack of heraldic display and the stained fustian jupon of Chaucer's Knight are signs of the professional fighting man, perhaps even modelled on Sir John Hawkwood of the White Company. Others

The tower house of the castle of Warkworth in Northumberland. Built by the Percy family in about 1390 on the remains of the old Norman castle, such buildings are descendants of the keep. Tower houses, however, were fitted out as private dwellings, the large windows and internal stairs, cupboards and closets making the wall relatively thin. (TopFoto/Imageworks)

The Black Prince's shield with the leopards of England and fleurs-de-lys of France quartered. Made from poplar wood, it is covered in layers of white canvas, plaster, paper and leather. The heraldic charges are made from moulded leather and attached by small brads. Originally there was also another shield of pointed oval form hanging over the tomb, decorated with an arabesque pattern with the royal arms in the centre. (By courtesy of the Dean and chapter of Canterbury and the Trustees of Armouries)

disagree; but even if not technically a mercenary, Chaucer's dowdy knight is a far tougher character than a first reading would imply, and almost certainly a contracted fighter.

With the upset in the Church caused by the collapse of the Templars and loss of the Holy Land, and the internal problems of the Hospitallers, knights began to lose interest in the ideals set by the religious orders and looked elsewhere for inspiration. They turned increasingly to the romances, in particular those about King Arthur and Camelot. Edward I's conquest of Wales and early successes in Scotland strengthened the chivalric ideal and ensured it did not wither despite the setbacks of the early 14th century, until Edward III was able to utilize the enthusiasm for his own war aims in France.

In 1344 at Windsor, Edward III proposed to found an Order of the Round Table, and during a 'Round Table' tournament he swore to found a chivalric order, a fellowship of knights bound together by oaths of mutual support. King John the Good of France founded a chivalric order, that of the Star, in 1351–52, but it was Edward's Order of the Garter (which was largely based on initial ideas for the French Order of the Star) that became the first in 1348. It soon had 24 member knights and before long 25 knights as well as the sovereign, which has remained the membership to this day. It may have had political overtones, but the connection with tournaments made it attractive to knights. There were also 26 priests and the same number of poor knights (religion and charity looked after by the order).

Tournaments

At the beginning of the century, tournaments were still subject to a ban, largely because they were seen as a threat to the recruitment of knights for real war. Edward I was quite keen on tournaments, however, and relaxed the bans during or after a campaign, as after Falkirk in 1302, apparently as a sort of reward for those who had supported him. Later in the century, most of the tournaments were held to celebrate a knighting or marriage, or very occasionally a triumphant return from battle. Many English knights still crossed the sea to joust, especially in the lavish tournaments held between about 1370 and 1385 at Bruges or Ghent by the dukes of Burgundy. The political use of such events was not lost on kings either. In a bid to separate William of Hainault from the French king (which nearly succeeded) Richard II organized a great tournament in London in 1390 when 60 knights held the lists against all comers.

In 1309 Sir Thomas de Maundeville was contracted to serve Humphrey de Bohun, Earl of Hereford, for 20 marks per annum for a fixed period. In peace he received hay and oats for four horses plus wages for three grooms, but in war and during tournaments the allowance rose to eight horses and seven grooms, with horses for himself from Humphrey. Some knights served by a contract solely for the tournament. This was becoming more exclusive. The rolls for the Dunstable tournaments of 1309 and 1334 show that only knights (135 of them) were expected to participate in a full capacity. Knights who arrived without their lord tended to join another retinue.

The Combat of the Thirty in 1351 was a formal foot combat between Sir Richard Bamborough, captain of Plöermel, with 30 companions (including ten German and Breton mercenaries), and the marshal, Richard de Beaumanoir, with 30 Frenchmen. Four Frenchmen and two Englishmen were dead when the two sides paused for refreshments. During the second half, however, Guillaume de Montauban mounted his horse and charged into the English ranks, knocking over seven of them. Following up, his friends killed nine Englishmen and captured the rest.

By the 14th century jousts had superseded the tourney, or team event, in popularity. There was as yet no barrier, and a man riding a powerful horse might deliberately set it against his opponent, in the hope of riding him down. Quite apart from this there was always the danger of accidental collisions, or knees being damaged from riding past too closely. The lance could be held at less of an angle than it would be when across a barrier, making it less likely to shatter. The development of chivalric ideals was increasingly being demonstrated in the lists, where a queen of love and beauty might be chosen, and ladies' favours were sometimes worn by knights. Stands were often built for spectators, especially ladies and those of rank.

The standard of Earl Douglas carried at the battle of Otterburn, 1388. A rare early survivor, it bears the blue saltire of St Andrew next to the fly instead of the red cross of St George. The motto: 'Jamais areyre' comes from the Douglas's claim to lead the Scots into battle. (© The Trustees of the National Museums of Scotland)

131

Campaigning

During the 14th century war was conducted in a number of ways. The chevauchée was a mounted raid (literally 'ride') far into enemy territory. Like the well-tried feudal tactics that preceded it, the aim was to disrupt the economy of the area by swift movement, seizing food for the soldiers and destroying crops, villages and peasants (thereby insulting the lord of the place into the bargain) while evading danger to oneself by avoiding castles unless they were easy to capture.

Successful battles required the use of cavalry and the matchless skills of the English archers. When delivered correctly the charge of the heavy horse was a formidable weapon that could smash a hole in enemy ranks. Starting from a walk, riding sometimes knee to

Sir John Dalyngrigge built Bodiam castle in Sussex in 1385 against the threat of French attacks, which never materialized. It is of square plan, with domestic buildings along the inner walls. Sir John had a private first-floor suite connecting to his pew in the chapel. There was a presence chamber and inner chamber with two bedrooms off it. The lower parts of the walls are served by early gun loops. (akg-images/A. F. Kersting)

Jousts of Peace, late 14th century

The main figure is Brian Stapleton, a squire who took part in the celebrated jousts at St Inglevert in France in 1389. By this date the first specialized equipment for jousts of peace had appeared. Saddle extensions negate the need for leg armour. He wears an early form of external independent breastplate, and a protective gauntlet for the left hand and arm, the manifer. The great helm has begun to be adapted for jousting, with the lower edge of the vision-slit projecting slightly forward, forerunner of the 'frog-mouthed' helm. The helm is strapped down at the back. For additional protection a plate wrapper, or 'barber', is strapped round the lower half of the front of the helm. The lance is fitted with a coronel head to dissipate the force of a blow. The hand is protected by a large vamplate, while behind the hand a spiked 'graper' is nailed on. His horse wears a shaffron and crinet, and peytral to help protect the chest. (Graham Turner © Osprey Publishing)

Opposite, left:
A rare mail hood, probably dating from the 14th century. It has no ventail, instead being slit up the back to allow it to be put on, after which the slit would presumably be laced shut. (The Trustees of the National Museums of Scotland)

Opposite, right:
A coat of mail, possibly English and probably dating from the 14th century. It is made from alternate rows of riveted and welded rings, the rings approximately ½in. (1.3cm) in external diameter. There is a short vertical slit in the front hem but it opens up full length at the back. (Courtesy of the Museum of London)

knee, the horsemen increased their speed, breaking into a gallop only when within striking range of the enemy, so as not to blow their mounts or lose formation. It was then that the lances were levelled for the shock. There were times when such a manoeuvre could not be used effectively, for example in the bogs and mountains of Wales. In addition, the Scots used the schiltron, a circle of dense spears, to frustrate cavalry. Bowmen could break up these masses when used together with cavalry who either broke into the gaps or forced the enemy to hold ranks under a withering fire. However, in 1307 a large force of perhaps 3,000 men under Aymer de Valence, Earl of Pembroke, was repulsed at Loudon Hill by the 600 spearmen of Robert the Bruce who made a stand with protected flanks. Pembroke withdrew after sending in only two futile cavalry attacks. The Scots were victorious again in 1314, when Edward II spectacularly lost the battle of Bannockburn; the English archers were caught by cavalry and the English heavy horse thrown back by the schiltrons.

Archers was employed effectively at Boroughbridge, Yorkshire, in 1322, this time against Edward's enemy, the Earl of Lancaster. The Earl of Hereford led some 300 men in an abortive charge on foot across the bridge over the Ure against the royalist blockade, but was killed by a spear thrust from under the bridge, and when horsemen made for the ford, the Welsh longbowmen on the opposite bank foiled every attempt to cross.

The young Edward III composed his forces so that the bulk of infantry were bowmen, and were mostly mounted to assist swift movement on the march. His men-at-arms were much more likely now to dismount on the battlefield to form the front divisions (called 'battles'). Where possible, they stood in a naturally defended position with their archers, thus forcing the enemy to wear themselves out attacking them. This style of warfare was first used in battle against the Scots. Froissart describes how, in 1327, when Edward's troops encountered the Scots, they were ordered to dismount and take off their spurs before forming themselves into three battles. In 1332 a force of the 'disinherited Scots' under the pretender Balliol (in fact pretty much an English force) invaded Scotland and after an abortive attack on the Scottish camp on the River Earn, formed a single block of dismounted men-at-arms at Dupplin Muir, with wings of archers and a small mounted reserve. The Scots, under the Regent, Donald, Earl of Mar, withered under the archery, and many of Balliol's men-at-arms remounted to chase the routed enemy. The following year at Halidon Hill near Berwick three divisions with flanking archers annihilated the Scots, the knights remounting to chase the routed Scots back to Duns.

When Edward launched his main campaign against France, the English took their new double-pronged strategy with them. The first encounter in France was in 1342 when the English, driven back from the siege of Morlaix, formed up with a wood at their backs, a stream on one flank and dug a ditch to protect the front. Despite being pushed back to the woods, the English held their enemies off. At Crécy in 1346, dismounted men-at-arms and archers beat off repeated attacks by French cavalry, whose horses were a prime target for arrows. That same year this combination defeated a Scottish invasion at Neville's Cross near the city of Durham, but there was heavy pressure on the English centre and right until a mounted English reserve was brought up and caught the Scots by surprise, the victory made complete by the arrival of reinforcements. At Poitiers in 1356 a mounted reserve swung the battle for the English, who were hard pressed in their defensive array by dismounted Frenchmen. The reserves turned the battle round and King John himself was captured. At Auray in 1364 a similar use of reserves under Sir Hugh Calveley meant that potential gaps, caused by French pressure on the low numbers of English archers, could be successfully plugged, thus eventually leading to an English victory. The great French captain Bernard du Guesclin advanced his men with *pavises* (shields) to reduce casualties from arrows, but still lost the battle and was himself captured.

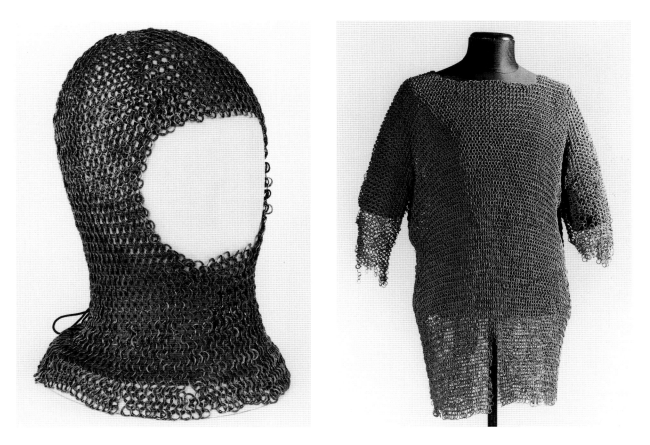

In 1351 at Saintes the French retained mounted wings of horse to try to break up the archers on the flanks, and retained this formation for the rest of the century. At Nogent-sur-Seine in 1359 they succeeded in breaking into the English formation of archers in this way, whereas the men-at-arms kept tightly packed. The significance of English archers in the French theatre is shown by the defeat at Ardres in 1351, where Sir John Beauchamp, caught by a dismounted French force as he returned from a raid, lined a ditch and held them off until they came to close quarters and another force broke up the archers. At Mauron the following year, the English partly used a bramble hedge for an obstacle. Despite losing the right flank of archers to a mounted attack, the dismounted attacks were beaten off.

In 1345 an English relieving force under the Earl of Derby charged into a French siege camp before Auberoche, the archers and men-at-arms doing much damage, while a sortie from the garrison finally broke the French forces. This form of surprise attack would occur again at La Roche Derien in 1347 during the Breton War of Succession, when an English relieving force fell on the French siege camp at night, although this time they encountered large numbers of troops and were probably saved by a sudden sortie from the garrison at dawn.

In 1388, having failed to assault Otterburn Castle, the Earl of Douglas set up camp instead. When his bitter enemy, Sir Henry Percy, arrived, he held off, perhaps fearing an

Knight and Equipment, c.1390

Sir Hugh Calveley, based on his effigy at Bunbury, Cheshire, wears a tight padded jupon over his armour. Beneath it, the coat of plates was giving way to separate breast- and backplates, the former with a skirt hanging from internal leather straps. A full mail coat and padded aketon were usually still worn underneath. The sabaton is tied to the shoe, and also laced to the hinged greave. The poleyn is attached to a plate cuisse by pivoting rivets, and the cuisse has a tab to tie it to points from the undergarment. Plate vambraces are laced at the shoulder by two points threaded through holes in a leather tab riveted to the top of the enclosing upper cannon. The helmet visor can be removed by pulling out the pin on each arm near the pivot. From about 1370 some aventails had the vervelles (staples) and cord hidden behind a decorative applied strip. The jewelled sword belt probably hung from hidden hooks at the hips, balanced by a rondel dagger.

1 A loose form of jupon. The aventail is covered by a decorative cloth covering.

2 German basinet showing the form of the Klappvisier.

3 Basinet with aventail. The top of the mail was stitched to a leather band. Slits in the band were forced over vervelles along the edge of the helmet, and secured by a cord through the vervelles.

4 Late 14th-century great basinet with plate collar.

5 Breastplate riveted to a covering, with attached fauld and holes for a lance-rest, based on a German example.

6 Independent breastplate, late 14th century.

7 Cuisse, poleyn, greave and sabaton for right leg, from the boy's armour in Chartres Cathedral. The deep lower plate of the poleyn now articulates with the greave, probably by a turning pin.

8 Hour-glass latten gauntlets of the Black Prince. A plate was shaped to cover the back and sides of the hand. Overlapping plates (scales) were riveted to leather strips that were stitched to the glove and riveted to the main plate.

9 Reconstructed tinned rowel spur, late 14th century.

10 Sword from the Great Ouse at Ely, c.1370–1400.

11 Sword belt, from effigy of Sir Humphrey Littlebury, (1360) at Holbeach, Lincs.

12 Sword belt with smaller belt now twisted round scabbard, from effigy of Lord Montacute (1389), Salisbury Cathedral.

13 Hammer and mace.

14 Long houppelande with side vents, piked soled hose and hood-turban.

15 Short houppelande, piked soled parti-coloured hose, and hood-turban.

(Graham Turner © Osprey Publishing)

ambush. Splitting his force, he sent the Umfravilles round to attack the Douglas camp from the rear. Unfortunately, Douglas had moved a large force out of the camp and Percy attacked a baggage park which he mistook for the camp. Douglas had avoided the Umfravilles and caught Percy in the flank. The Umfravilles, meanwhile, seem to have made too large a detour, and when they came upon the Scottish camp it was deserted. In the confusion of darkness, they then appeared on Percy's flank instead of the Scottish rear. The battle was lost to the English, despite the death of Douglas, who had hacked his way towards Percy. Indeed, this was a hard contest, both sides stubbornly refusing to give ground, and both Percy and his brother wounded and taken prisoner. Froissart said that of all the conflicts he wrote about, this was the most bravely fought.

After Poitiers there were no further major battles between England and France until Agincourt in 1415. It was not battles that won a country as much as hard sieges. After Poitiers the French generally refused to fight in the open, instead shutting themselves up in castles and fortified towns, and forcing the English to besiege them, or else wander the countryside.

With the Treaty of Bretigny in 1360 garrisons emptied, and groups of soldiers formed free companies under captains such as Sir Robert Knollys (perhaps the earliest) and Sir John Hawkwood. These 'rutters' as the English called them, or routiers, actually consisted of men from many nationalities, though the French often referred to them all as 'English'. Each company often consisted of only a few hundred men, archers, infantry and men-at-arms. A typical ploy was to seize one or two strong castles and use them as bases from which to terrorize an area. Froissart describes them approaching a town by stealth and entering it at sunrise, burning a house to dupe the inhabitants into thinking an army had entered instead of perhaps 60 men. In the ensuing panic they then looted the place. They hired their services out to rulers, and according to Froissart, the Black Prince used 12,000 of them in Castile. At the end of the 14th century they tended to disappear until their rebirth on a smaller scale after the renewal of war by Henry V. According to the French chronicler Monstrolet they were called 'Écorcheurs' ('skinners') after 1437 because they even took the shirts off men's backs.

English forces were also involved in Spain. At Najera in 1367 the army of the Black Prince formed three entirely dismounted lines, the main battle in the centre, to face a Castilian force including many French soldiers, also in three lines but with many cavalry. The men-at-arms again fought well, ably supported by archers who out-ranged the Spanish javelin-wielding mounted *jinetes*. They also out-shot crossbowmen and slingers, who drew back, allowing the English men-at-arms to overlap the enemy division. When the English rearguard swung in on the flank, the Spanish and French lines shattered.

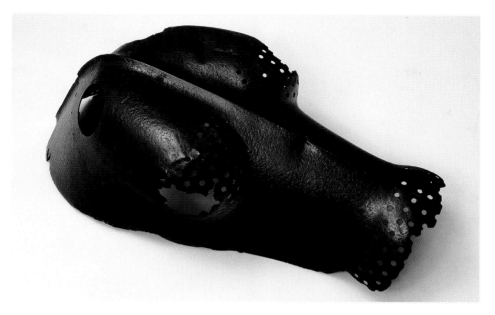

A shaffron, probably of the late 14th or early 15th century, from Warwick Castle. It has a main plate that joins a subsidiary plate behind the ears; this second plate then continues down either side of the head, being overlapped by and riveted to the main plate. (The Board of Trustees of the Armouries/HIP/TopFoto)

Siege warfare called for different measures, in which siege engineers in charge of machines, and latterly gunners with new-fangled cannon, were as important as the knight. Knights were still needed for escort duty, for forays to lay waste surrounding countryside and procure food, or for an attack should a mine or machine collapse a wall, or should ladders or siege tower be required. In captured strongholds they helped to provide the garrison.

When fighting on foot the knight relied in part on his following – his squires, household and retained men – to watch his back. He might wear a jupon with his coat-of-arms displayed on front and rear, but equally some were plain and a warrior with his visor down was then difficult to recognize. If the knight was a banneret his square or oblong banner would be held aloft unfurled when action was expected, and shadowed its owner wherever he went. For his followers, a man of rank might, by the end of the century, also have a standard, a long flag perhaps carrying the red cross of St George next to the fly, then elements of his heraldic coat, such as main charges and colours, and perhaps his motto, the war-cry shouted to rally and encourage his men. In the din of battle trumpets and hand signals were used to impart instructions.

Knights also fought from ships, notably in the famous battle off Sluys in 1340. In such battles ships came close in for archery and crossbow duels, before trying to grapple each other for an ensuing battle on the decks and rigging. Even here, Edward III arranged his ships with one of men-at-arms between two of archers.

Part III

English Medieval Knight 1400–1500

Introduction

The knight in shining full plate armour appeared in the 15th century. As such he became the stuff of medieval legend, of 19th-century romance and, more recently, of television and film. The image of the warrior clad in steel plates is always more impressive than that of his predecessor in armour of mail rings. The great boost to medieval stories given by the contemporary Thomas Malory's tales of King Arthur meant that such sub-Roman warriors were now often identified with 15th-century knights. However, behind the light of Galahad's shining goodness, the real knights of the day could present a varied tapestry of emotions. Many were loyal and true to their king and their followers, well bred and well mannered. Others were self-seekers or social climbers, ruthlessly changing sides for personal gain or preservation. Long campaigns abroad and lethal factional fighting at home could breed hard-bitten men and cultured thugs; even gentlemen could be noted for their sadistic ways. War was hard and knights fought hand to hand. Time has sometimes softened our perspective of their world and painted too rosy a picture.

The 15th-century knight no longer fought for his lord in return for land, since the feudal summons had long before given way to a system of contracts. Moreover, many now preferred the lifestyle of the landowner, man-about-town and parliamentary representative; likewise many rich burgesses were now obtaining the rank of knight. Some knights spoke English, French and Latin. At court Sir John Paston amused himself by borrowing Ovid's *De Arte Amandi* ('Art of Love') and was advised to look at the same author's *De Remedio* (Ovid's *Remedio Amoris*, 'Remedies of Love') unless he was going to spend time 'courting' a certain lady.

Previous page:
A late 15th-century depiction of a joust of war before Richard II at Smithfield in 1394. The knights wear field armour. In Richard's day the fleurs-de-lys had not yet been reduced to three in each quarter of the shield. (Art Media – Lambeth Palace Library/HIP/TopFoto)

Great lords, however, still recognized their special role in the order of things. In time of war it was their duty, the reason behind their privileges, to lead from the front. England began the century still embroiled in the Hundred Years' War with France, as she had been since 1337. Interspersed with sporadic bouts of peace, the contention for the French crown had begun under Edward III. Despite resounding victories for English armies at Crécy and Poitiers, the French had not been overcome, while the terrible ravages of the Black Death in 1348–50 had wiped out perhaps a third of the population in England alone.

As the new century opened under Henry IV, an uneasy peace still held. With the coming of his son, Henry V, in 1413, a new war loomed as the king sought foreign adventure to divert attention from problems at home. His dramatic victory at Agincourt in 1415 solved little, and it was the hard sieges of the following years that really wore down his enemies. Just as it seemed that Henry might unite the two crowns, he died of dysentery in 1422, leaving the throne to a young child, Henry VI. Despite surviving until captured in 1460, Henry would see English pretensions crushed by French insurgence assisted by Joan of Arc, until only Calais remained by 1453.

At home, King Henry, of the house of Lancaster, faced rising opposition to his poor government from the descendants of Edmund of York, one of Edward III's sons. This heralded the civil wars known as the Wars of the Roses. These dynastic struggles, which owed nothing to the modern geographical counties of Yorkshire and Lancashire, would

The Knight, as depicted in the early 15th-century *Ellesmere Chaucer*. He wears a vertically quilted jupon with unusual bagpipe sleeves, which Terry Jones has suggested may have been widened latterly. The four straps at neck and shoulders may have been for securing an external breastplate, or perhaps for tying down the edges of a mail aventail. Note the brand on the horse's rump. His fashionably dressed son, to his right, wears no armour. (akg-images)

bear witness to some of the bloodiest fighting ever seen in England. The Yorkist Edward IV would seize the crown, lose it and retake it; his son, Edward V, would disappear in the Tower of London; and his brother, Richard III, would die at Bosworth striving to destroy the invading Lancastrian, Henry Tudor. From 1485 the wars were effectively over and England was ruled by a new dynasty.

Training

The long road to becoming a knight involved the learning of similar skills to those in the previous centuries. The aspirant was taught manners and courtesy, how to sing and dance, to serve ladies and make pleasant company. He would learn to groom horses and begin the arduous tasks of becoming familiar with, and looking after, weapons and armour. His master's harness might be stored in cupboards; it had to be kept clean and free of rust (olive oil was best for this), the sliding and pivoting rivets had to be serviceable, leather straps must not be frayed. This training went on for several years until he was 14 or thereabouts. He now became an esquire to a knight, unless proven unsuitable, when he might be packed off to the Church. As an esquire, he was increasingly ordered to train with weapons, sometimes of double weight to develop his muscles. Caxton's translation of Christine de Pisan in 1489 says:

> The knyght or men of armes is to be chosen that from the tyme of his youthe hath lerned the trauayllis of armes and the maners of bataille.

Though many read these military treatises, experience in war was the best way to learn. The esquire rode with the knights in the hunt, and was taught to recognize the different hunting calls and how to correctly dismember a kill. He might learn to use a longbow or crossbow but only for the hunting field; it was not part of his duty to employ such weapons in battle. Hunting also increased riding skills, though horses were not expected to jump fences, and much land was open country or open fields. The youth was also required to follow his master into battle to pull him out of the press if wounded, or

Opposite:
The battle of Poitiers (1356) illuminated in the early 15th century. The basinets are now fitted with rounded visors. Few shields are carried and these are convex. Note the lance resting in the cutout. (akg-images/ British Library)

The early 15th-century Dunstable Swan jewel, found on the site of Dunstable Priory in Bedfordshire. This is the only surviving example of a white enamelled badge in the form of a chained animal. The emblem came into the House of Lancaster after the marriage of Henry of Lancaster to Mary de Bohun, whose family was one of those claiming descent from the legendary Swan Knight. (By courtesy of the Trustees of the British Museum, M&LA, 1966, 7–3, 1)

remount him if unhorsed. Standards of education were higher than in previous centuries, and the esquire might be taught by a priest or chaplain to read and write Latin or French.

The ceremony of knighting traditionally took place when the young man was somewhere between about 18 and 21 years old. This was often an excuse for elaborate displays of feasting and tournaments, and the richer the candidate's circle, the more imposing the ceremony. A well-bred youth might be knighted by the king himself, and on occasion squires were knighted before a battle, or sometimes after it for conspicuous service. Some squires were knighted much later in life, or remained squires until they died. A new knight still had to continue his exercises. He would cut at the wooden post or pell, test himself against opponents in the courtyard, or ride against the quintain. Some might try to catch a suspended ring with the point of the lance, a feat requiring good co-ordination and a steady arm.

By mid-century many nobles were increasingly looking to law or some other peaceful occupation, something railed against by William Worcester in his *Boke of Noblesse*, written at this time. With fewer knights to call upon, advice on warfare had to be sought from veteran captains of the French wars. Training of ordinary soldiers soon came to reflect the different ideas of individual captains in particular areas.

Arms, Armour and Horses

Armour

By the opening years of the 15th century steel plates covered the knight's entire body. The main body protection the previous century had been the coat of plates, or 'plates', in which plates were riveted inside (or occasionally outside) a canvas covering. This was then faced with a richer material such as velvet or even leather, with the rivet heads visible on the outside. The heads were often tinned or gilded and might be of floriated form to enhance the effect.

Plates were usually arranged as horizontal hoops but many had a breast-defence of two plates or even a single breastplate. The coat was put on like a poncho and fastened at the back, though a number were side fastening and closed additionally at one or both shoulders.

Many knights now wore 'plates' with an external breastplate and a fauld of steel hoops below. Beneath the 'plates' was a long-sleeved mail coat, consisting of thousands of interlinked and individually riveted iron rings. Such coats were usually slightly longer than the 'plates' and might now be provided with an upstanding collar made from thicker rings to provide stiffness. A padded aketon was worn beneath to help absorb the shock of a blow; this was necessary because mail was flexible and would yield when struck, even if the links were not torn.

By about 1425, knights increasingly replaced the coat of plates with armour which was attached by points (laces, often red) directly to an arming doublet, a padded coat provided with gussets of mail covering the armpit and inner arm. The Hastings manuscript of about 1485 (How a man schall be armyd at his ese when he schal fighte on foote) said that points were to be of fine waxed twine such as that used to make crossbow strings, and each would be fitted over the end with a brass 'aiglet' or metal point. Some might be made from buckskin, which is tough and stretchy. A few knights still wore the full mail coat underneath, with elbow-length sleeves over the plates of the upper arm, well into mid-century, a practice more common in Italy.

This French illustration of the poems of Christine de Pisan (c.1410) explodes the myth that knights could not mount their horses unaided and without a crane. It shows a knight in full plate armour, with probably a complete mail coat beneath, about to climb into his saddle. (akg-images/British Library)

Agincourt, 25 October 1415

This plate shows the struggle following the defeated French cavalry charges when both sides fought on foot. A French warhorse has been killed by an arrow. A steel-tipped arrow has bored into the breastplate of a French knight; even steel armour was not always effective against them. Some knights still wear a jupon over their armour but many have discarded it. The knight on the left wears a breastplate and fauld attached to a red velvet covering. The older, pointed visor can be seen alongside the newer, more rounded variety. Similarly, many still use a basinet with attached mail aventail, but others have a great basinet with plate neck-defences. The shield is disappearing though some horsemen still carry them. Swords are used to hack at lightly armoured archers but only the points are useful against fully armoured knights, when an armpit is exposed or a visor lifted. Increasingly in evidence were percussion weapons: maces, hammers and staff weapons such as long axes, that could be swung in two hands to deliver a powerful blow. (Graham Turner © Osprey Publishing)

Arming a Knight in Alwite Armour

A knight was always armed from the feet upwards. Before putting on his armour he donned his leggings, often of woven wool. The Hastings manuscript of about 1485 mentions hose of 'stamyn sengill' (worsted cloth apparently made in Norfolk). On his feet he wore shoes designed to prevent skidding, described in detail:

An early 15th-century helm designed for jousts of peace, which hung above the tomb of Henry V in Westminster Abbey. The metal beneath the vision sight is ¼ inch (6mm) thick. The front ring is a replacement, and the rear hook a funerary addition. (© Dean and Chapter of Westminster)

Also a payre of shone [shoes] of thikke Cord-wene and they muste be frette [fretted] with smal whipcorde thre knottis up on a corde and thre cordis muste be faste swoid [sewn] on to the hele of the shoo and fyne cordis in the mydill of the soole of the same shoo and that ther be betwene the frettis of the hele and the frettis of the mydill of the shoo the space of three fvngris.

According to the Hastings manuscript no shirt was worn under the fustian arming doublet, which was lined with satin. The question arises as to how the hose were secured, since in mid-century they reached only to the hips, and even later, when they were higher, they were still anchored with points through the civilian doublet. Since it is unlikely that a civilian doublet was worn beneath (also contradicting the Hastings description) it must be supposed that the arming doublet was at this time provided with pairs of eyelet holes near the lower edge. It was practical to leave undone the back pairs, since even in civilian life bending forward violently could cause them to break. The arming doublet would be laced down the front with similar pairs of points passing through pairs of holes cut in the doublet. The Hastings manuscript mentions the doublet as cut full of holes, which may refer to the holes pierced through it for the points; it might also mean it was full of small bound holes, to aid ventilation, though surviving jackets of this form are not arming doublets.

Mail gussets were sewn to the doublet, as described in the Hastings manuscript, though 16th-century illustrations also depict use of points. From the Hastings manuscript we learn that a thin blanket ('shorte bulwerkis') was wrapped around the knees to prevent chafing from the plates. Around the neck a mail upstanding collar was added. This is sometimes thought to have been attached to the collar of the arming doublet, but most detailed effigies show no front fastening, suggesting that the mail collar is a separate item fastened at the back, a more secure method despite the necessity for some assistance when putting it on.

A knight arming for foot combat in the lists, from *How a Man Schall be Armyd*, a manuscript of the later 15th century and the only known medieval portrayal of an arming doublet with mail gussets. The valet is tying on a mail skirt. The knight's great basinet lies on the table and a pollaxe and an ahlespiess is propped up at the side. (Pierpont Morgan Library, M.775, f.122v)

Except for the sole, the foot was covered by a sabaton, made from a number of overlapping lames connected each side by rivets on which they pivoted. The sabaton was hinged on the outer side of the foot under the ankle and closed on the inner side with a strap and buckle. The foot could be slipped through a leather stirrup running under the sole, and might be further secured by points at the top of the shoe, which were laced through holes in the top of the sabaton. If mail *sabatons* in the Italian style were worn (rare in England) then the edges would be held by straps and the top tied through the shoe; the mail was secured to the greave through numerous holes in the lower edge. Greaves were hinged on the outer side but closed by straps and buckles on the inner side, where they were less likely to be cut. They were usually attached to the sabaton by pairs of points.

The poleyn and cuisse (knee and thigh armour) were added as one item. The upper end of the greave had a turning pin which fitted through a hole in the lower plate of the poleyn, while the latter's main plate and the cuisse were held by straps behind the knee and thigh respectively. In order to hold the cuisse against the leg and help support it, a leather tab, riveted to its top edge and pierced with holes, was secured to the lower part of the arming doublet by a pair of points hanging from a similar pair of holes in the doublet. Both legs were armoured in the same fashion.

A mail skirt, to protect the genitals and allow a man to sit down easily, was tied round the waist, perhaps supported by further points along the top edge. For foot combat in war

151

Knight, c.1425

The evidence for armour at this period comes largely from brasses, effigies and manuscript illuminations, since very little survives. Besagews at the armpits were very popular. The basinet with mail aventail would remain a common sight until about 1430, but this knight has a great basinet, used from about 1420 until mid-century. It is quite large and less closely shaped to the head than German versions, here decorated with a jewelled scarf or orle. He wears an arming sword.

1 Great basinet, with bevor and gorget plate.

2 Detached visor, secured by a pin each side.

3 Lancastrian SS collar.

4 Jewelled hip belt with rondel dagger; arming sword with fish-tail pommel on a diagonal belt.

5 Arming sword associated with the tomb of Henry V.

6 Gauntlet.

7 Rowel spur found at the battlefield of Towton but of a form common at least 25 years earlier.

8 The cote-hardie, belted at the hips, was often worn over the doublet and until 1410 it barely reached the fork but then lengthened to the knees. It eventually blended with the short houppelande. It consisted of four pieces seamed at front, rear and sides, which until 1440 might be left open a short distance from the hem to form vents. It was closed by buttons or hooks and eyes. It was frequently lined with satin, silk, taffeta, linen or cloth, with fur or cloth for winter versions. The neck, hem, vents and wrists might be furred. This knee-length houppelande has hanging sleeves. The bowl crop appeared in 1410 as an extremely popular hair style. Pointed or forked beards were occasionally seen until about 1415.

9 Very short houppelande with high collar and baggy closed sleeves of 'bagpipe' form (with large pouch), popular until the 1430s. The chaperon was a ready-made hood-turban, from 1420.

10 Houppelande with huge open funnel-shaped sleeves of the type only worn for ceremonial use after about 1420. A padded doublet was worn over the shirt. Often called a 'paltock', it was made in eight pieces with a central seam down the back and round the waist. The quilting was usually horizontal or confined to the lining for civil use, but vertical for military use. Broadcloth, linen, fustian or sometimes leather was used, with damask, silk or velvet for the rich or for ceremonial use. The doublet was rarely uncovered after 1412.

(Graham Turner © Osprey Publishing)

or tournament, a pair of mail pants might be substituted, in which the gusset between the legs was tied in front; however this would be too uncomfortable for use in riding.

The breastplate had the fauld attached by internal leathers and, from about 1430, the lower plate was divided in two and hung from straps, becoming known as tassets, which gradually lengthened. The backplate had a culet (skirt) from which usually hung a single plate, the rump-guard. The whole was closed on the wearer's left side by hinges with pins and on his right side by straps and buckles, and by straps over the shoulders. The tassets would probably be already suspended. After about 1450 German cuirasses tended to use a waist belt instead of pins and buckles.

The vambrace consisted of a gutter-shaped upper arm-defence (the 'upper cannon'), a cup-shaped couter at the elbow, and a two-part tube (the 'lower cannon') enclosing the forearm. It was simply slid up the arm in one piece, the top edge of the upper cannon being provided with a leather tab for a pair of points at the shoulder of the doublet. The lower cannon was hinged for access and shut with a strap. By about 1430 the upper cannons almost enclosed the upper arm. West European vambraces often had separate couters in the German fashion, which necessitated points at the elbows also, for attaching them. In England the lower cannon probably attached to the lower end of the upper cannon by laces, though the exact method of this fixture is not known for certain.

The construction of Raglan castle in Gwent was begun by Sir William ap Thomas in about 1430 and carried on by his son, Sir William Herbert, later Earl of Pembroke, until executed in 1469. (akg-images/Archie Miles)

The shoulder was protected in the first half of the century by a laminated spaudler secured by points through holes at the top of one of the plates, and a strap and buckle under the arm. Often a pair of 'besagews' guarded the armpits, being hung from the spaudler or laced on. Besagews were usually circular and sometimes drawn out at the centre to a short spike. By 1440 *pauldrons*, shoulder-defences that overlapped the chest and back, were common, being attached like spaudlers. On Italian armours at this time, asymmetrical reinforcing plates were attached to couter wings and pauldrons. Gauntlets had flared cuffs, and the knuckles might be furnished with 'gadlings', raised pyramids or spikes of steel. By about 1440 mitten gauntlets were replacing those with fingers. The sword was then belted on the left side, and possibly a dagger on the right. The gauntlets might be buttoned over the sword hilt. If the knight was to ride, his spurs were buckled on.

Right:
A knight, depicted in
the northern English
Desert of Religion of the
second quarter of the 15th
century. His sleeves hang
outside the vambraces.
The strange staff weapon
has a long axe-head with
three flukes and a spike,
but a cross-bar to stop
enemy weapons sliding
down the shaft. (By
permission of the British
Library, MS Cotton
Faustina B VI, f.1)

Helmets

The helmet was the last item to be put on. In 1400 most knights
wore the basinet, an open-faced conical helmet to which was attached
a removable mail neck-defence called an aventail. The visor could
usually be detached by withdrawing a pin each side, a pointed form being
common until about 1410. By about 1420 the great basinet was increasingly
seen, with its attached plate neck-guard called a gorget. The front plate
often pivoted for access, and had a chin-defence (bevor) pivoted inside or
sometimes attached to it. A more rounded visor was now usual. The whole
was usually strapped down to the breast- and backplates.

By the 1440s the sallet and occasionally the armet had begun to
replace the basinet. The armet opened out at the sides to facilitate placing
it over the head, the cheek-pieces being fastened together at the chin by
a turning pin. The visor then closed over their upper edges. Further
protection might be afforded by a wrapper, a frontal plate shaped like a
ship's prow and with gorget plates below, which fitted the lower
part of the helmet and was secured at the rear by a strap and buckle.
The far more popular sallet was sometimes accompanied by a bevor with
gorget plates, strapped around the neck and laced through holes in the gorget
plate to the breastplate, though rich examples might use a staple instead. The
sallet was then secured with a leather chin strap. Most helmets had a leather or
canvas lining-band riveted inside, to which was stitched a cloth lining stuffed
with hay, horsehair, wool or tow, and often cut into scallops at the top, which
could be adjusted by a draw-string. Otherwise a lining was glued inside. Other
pieces of armour were often also lined. Occasionally a padded arming cap was
still worn, tied under the chin.

Shields

Shields were rarely used, except perhaps by cavalry, largely being
relegated to the tournament. Typical examples were made from
wood, which was faced with leather and sometimes lined with
parchment or cloth.

Wearing Armour

All this equipment could be put on very quickly if necessary. Once the undergarments were in place, two attendants could arm a knight from head to toe (cap-à-pied) if necessary in about five to ten minutes, and remove it in less time still. A complete war harness weighed only about 45–55 pounds (25–35kg), the weight spread all over the body, and less than a modern infantryman carries in his backpack. A fit man could run, lie down or mount his horse with ease. There was no need for mechanical aids such as cranes, a later myth which has clung tenaciously largely thanks to misguided films.

It was easy enough to move in full armour; some could (and still do) turn cartwheels, or vault into the saddle. The greatest drawback was the lack of ventilation. The body's heat could not escape easily and the wearer soon got hot, especially when the helmet was in place, since much heat is lost from the head. Some died in the press of battle from suffocation, as did Henry V's cousin, the Duke of York, pulled from the crush of bodies at Agincourt (in October) without a scratch. In summer sunshine the metal became hot to touch, in winter it was cold to the touch but hot inside.

The metals used to make armour ranged from iron to impure mild steel containing slag, which could not be removed by the processes available. However, it could turn a sword and was designed to make a weapon point skid off. A v-shaped stop-rib below the neck was welded on to guide a point to right or left of the throat and so away. Ribs were also added at certain other points, such as the pauldron.

Wealthy men might purchase harness from the top armourers of northern Italy or south Germany (Augsburg, Nuremberg or Landshut). A knight of average means might buy a workaday Milanese armour, brought back by merchant ships on return journeys. Sir John Cressy bought such a harness in 1441, costing £8 6s 8d, while armour for a squire cost from £5 to £6 16s 8d. Wills and inventories show that armours from Lombardy were popular. Pictorial evidence suggests that much English armour was of the style worn in England, France and the Low Countries. Some of this may have been Italian export armour, designed in the style of the area where the armourers wished to make a sale. However, much was probably often purchased from merchant armourers, who offered the relevant parts to make up an armour, which they were sufficiently skilled to adjust to fit the individual purchaser. Armour that does not fit properly is very uncomfortable, especially over the ankle bones. In 1473 Sir John Paston, then with the Calais garrison, negotiated with an armourer in Bruges for a harness, and in January 1475 mentions riding into Flanders to get horses and armour.

Confrontation on the Road, 22 May 1448

Sir Humphrey Stafford, his eldest son, Richard, and their retinue were riding towards their inn at Coventry when they saw Sir Robert Harcourt and his men coming towards them. Harcourt passed Sir Humphrey but when he met Richard the two started arguing. Harcourt then drew his sword and caught the other a glancing blow to the head, but Richard managed to draw his dagger. As he lunged at Harcourt he stumbled and was fatally stabbed in the back by one of Harcourt's men. Sir Humphrey rode back but he too was wounded from behind and fell. His men now attacked and managed to kill two of Harcourt's followers. Next day Harcourt was indicted as principal in the murder of Richard Stafford by the city coroners and arrested. Partly by his own efforts he evaded trial, so on 1 May 1450 Sir Humphrey gathered about 200 men and approached Stanton Harcourt in Oxfordshire by night. He probably knew that the Duke of Suffolk had been murdered, who well might have supported Harcourt in law and in strength. Now Harcourt locked himself in the church tower and staved off all attacks, even the burning of the room under the tower. Harcourt was pardoned, while Sir Humphrey was killed in a fight with Kentish rebels in June. However, Sir Humphrey's bastard son killed Harcourt in 1469. (Graham Turner © Osprey Publishing)

Weapons

The main knightly weapon was the sword, with those from Cologne, Milan and Savoy being popular. At the beginning of the century some swords tapered to an acute point, with a blade of flattened diamond-section for stiffness; others had a broader blade that tapered more acutely nearer the point but with edges sharp enough to cut. During the second quarter of the century, a form of blade appeared that was flat in section but which had an upstanding mid-rib. A few broad-bladed weapons had two short fullers (channels) near the cross-guard, with a short single one below, and were probably Italian imports. Some swords were heavy, perhaps 5 pounds (2.2kg) or more, and some over 50 inches (1.2m) long, designed as thrusting weapons to combat plate armour. Long, narrow blades tended to have a long grip, to help balance them, and an elongated pommel like a 'scent-bottle'. Larger hand-and-a-half swords were also known as bastard swords or 'swords of war'. Many swords had a metal flap on the cross-guard over the blade, which fitted over the scabbard to stop water penetration.

The front section of the blade was sometimes left blunt, since men tended to hook their finger over it; this section was called the ricasso. Some Continental sword hilts developed a loop to guard the forefinger and a second loop then appeared to the rear cross-guard. Swords also, on occasion, had a ring on the side of the guard. The design of such guards continued to develop throughout the 15th century, and some incorporated a knuckle-guard, although such models were rare in England until the 1500s.

Scabbards were of wood covered in leather, often dyed and sometimes decorated with metal mounts down their length. Locket and chape (mouth and tip of the scabbard) might be gilded, pierced or set with precious stones. Slits near the top of the scabbard were sometimes made to accommodate a small eating knife and steel for sharpening or a *bodkin*. Jewelled sword belts, often of metal plaques, were worn on the hip (sometimes secured to the armour) until mid-century, but by 1415 diagonal belts had become popular. In mid-century the rear of such belts were forked, the lower part being attached to the scabbard about 12 inches (30cm) from the mouth, moving it back from the wearer's feet and putting the hilt at a better angle. Occasionally a metal or leather loop was riveted to the fauld to support the scabbard instead of a belt; a dagger might be similarly worn on the right side.

Daggers usually had triangular-sectioned blades. The rondel dagger had a disc of metal or sometimes wood set at either end of the handle, or else a disc and conical pommel. Ballock daggers had two swellings (of wood, bone or brass) at the base of a handle of wood, bone or ivory.

The lance, often of ash, had swellings either side of the hand, and a large circular steel vamplate nailed on to guard it. A circular fixture (called a graper) nailed on behind the hand was used to ram against the lance-rest on the breastplate to prevent the weapon running back when a strike was made. The war-hammer sometimes had a rear spike and eventually a top spike. Maces had flanged steel heads and usually iron or steel hafts; they could be hung from the saddle by a thong. In the early years of the century the long-hafted axe was occasionally used. The pollaxe ('poll' meaning head) or *ravensbill* had a combination of axehead, hammer or beak; the top and bottom of the haft were fitted with a spike. A rondel protected the hand, while long steel or latten strips (langets) were

Sir John Fastolf began the construction of the brick castle at Caister in Norfolk in 1432. The very tall tower set in one corner is the donjon, with fireplaces on each floor except the topmost for the use of Sir John, and with a machicolated parapet and gunports. Caister appears to have repelled a French raid in 1458, when 'many gonnes [sic]' were fired. (Author's collection)

nailed to the haft below the head to prevent it being cut. The halberd had a long blade backed by a fluke, with langets and top spike. The less common ahlespiess had a four-sided spike with a disc at the base. Bills, glaives and guisarmes were more common in the hands of ordinary footsoldiers.

Horses

A knight needed horses: without them he was not a knight, even though many fought on foot more than on horseback. The most prized possession was the warhorse, which might be one of two types. The largest and heaviest horse was the destrier, a word derived from the French for 'right' which probably meant that it was led on the right side by a valet. It has also been suggested that such horses were trained to lead with the right leg. Destriers were extremely valuable; some, indeed, were used only in tournaments. Their cost indicates that they were specially bred for stamina, with deep bodies for good lungs, and thick, powerful necks. However, they were not slow and could turn nimbly enough; nor were they the size of a carthorse, as is popularly imagined. Surviving 15th-century armour would never fit a carthorse, and shows that such animals were about the size of a heavy hunter. They were always stallions, and there is some evidence that their natural aggression was utilized by training them to bite and kick opponents.

In battle many rode a courser, an expensive warhorse but of slightly poorer quality than a destrier. In addition a good palfrey with a comfortable gait was required as a travelling mount. A knight might afford several riding and warhorses. As well as these there were serviceable horses for his valets, probably rounceys or 'ronsons'. The hackney, or 'hack', was a cheaper mount for other servants or soldiers. The knight also had to provide pack animals, either sumpters, mules or draught animals for supply wagons.

Organization

By the 15th century feudalism had given way to a new form of raising troops. Instead of lords granting fiefs (parcels of land) in return for supplying troops, they now contracted men to fight for them. This has been called 'bastard feudalism'. A captain would agree to provide the king with a set number of men and the agreement was written twice on a contract, which was perforated and cut into two parts, one copy for the exchequer and one for the captain. The cut was deliberately wavy or zig-zag, so that the two halves could be matched exactly if there was any dispute over the arrangements. The irregular line gave such a document its name: an indenture.

At the time of English expeditions to France, the exchequer usually released half the agreed cash, and the rest on embarkation, following a muster to check the actual numbers had been found. Contracts contained such details as troop numbers and type (usually men-at-arms, called 'lances' or 'spears', and archers); they set out the muster points and times, pay, discipline, plunder (usually a third), and length of service. The latter varied from a few months to two years, though six months was common. Much of the information became standardized but was amended to suit the campaign. Sometimes the king made a single great indenture to a noble who would in any case then sub-indent other captains to make up the numbers.

Not all the soldiers knew the captains they came to fight for. In a similar way, a captain contracted troops for a fixed wage over a fixed period, a retainer's contract being validated by the lord's wax seal instead of that of the king. The second copy was retained by the man, who was known as a retainer. In March 1402 John Norbury covenanted to retain in his pay Bonifacius de Provana and a retinue of 60 lances and 60 crossbowmen for one year. Indentures also included obligations to the lord, not all of them military. Often indentures to a nobleman were made for life.

The governing of indentured companies was covered during the Hundred Years' War by the issuing of ordinances of war. These were instructions to ensure such bodies of troops were properly controlled, that men did not leave or come to the army unless so ordered, and to make sure that captains themselves did not employ underhand means to fill their ranks by luring men from other companies.

The expeditionary armies in Henry VI's reign rarely exceeded about 2,000 men, except for aggressive campaigns or when the English presence was threatened. The agreed contract did not always bring in the correct ratio of troops, and sometimes larger numbers of archers were employed and fewer men-at-arms, archers presumably being easier to recruit than mounted men-at-arms, and cheaper – 6d a day as against 12d. It is possible also that the long periods expected in overseas service did not appeal to a number of English knights as much as to professional soldiers.

By the 15th century only about five to ten per cent of men-at-arms in English armies were knights, the rest being esquires and 'gentlemen'. By mid-century some men-at-arms were not even of this rank. At the beginning of the century the ratio of archers to every man-at-arms had risen to 3:1, so that, on average, each man-at-arms was served by a page or valet plus three archers, the latter usually mounted for mobility, though they fought on foot. This composition was essentially the same as the European 'lance', though this unit appellation and form of recruitment was not customary in England during the Wars of the Roses. Contingents could vary wildly, from a mere handful of men to a sizeable force. The selection from the retinue of Henry V in 1415 in British Library MS Sloane 6400 gives some indication:

The Coventry sallet of about 1460 may be on of the few survivng English-made pieces of armour. The high skull is different from the forms seen in Italy and especially Germany. (Herbert Art Gallery and Museum, Coventry)

John Irby, Esq – single man-at-arms and two foot archers

Sir John Greseley – two men-at-arms and six foot archers

Sir Thomas Tunstall – six men-at-arms and 18 mounted archers

Thomas, Earl of Salisbury – 40 men-at-arms (three knights, 36 esquires) and 80 mounted archers

Thomas, Earl of Dorset – 100 men-at-arms (one banneret, six knights, 92 esquires) and 300 mounted archers

Humphrey, Duke of Gloucester – 200 men-at-arms (six knights, 193 esquires) and 600 mounted archers

The variation in army size can be seen from the fact that, in 1415, Henry V fielded perhaps 900 men-at-arms and 5,000 archers, whereas at Verneuil in 1424 there were about 1,800 men-at-arms and between 8,000 and 9,000 archers.

Normandy

By the 15th century, a shift in strategy meant that the mobile expeditionary forces in France were being replaced in Normandy by more expensive garrisons. Annual indentures were drawn up between the king, or his regent, and garrison captains, followed by quarterly commissions of array for musters. Pay was given each quarter after approval of the muster rolls. Initially men from the conquering army made up garrisons, later supplemented by volunteers from England or from troops still in France, some of whom settled there. It has been estimated that in 1420 there were 1,028 men-at-arms and 2,926 archers in various garrisons in Normandy. Such forces ranged in size from the two men-at-arms and six archers at Pont d'Ouve to 60 men-at-arms and 180 archers at Rouen. Outside Normandy a similar situation existed, though Calais and its March had 1,120 men under Henry V.

A grisaille of about 1460 by Guillaume Vreland shows an armourer cold-hammering a plate while another burnishes a breastplate. (Friedrich-Alexander-Universität Erlangen-Nürnberg)

In 1433 the English government claimed to have 7,000–8,000 men in France; this would not have included the garrison of Guyenne and feudal troops from Normandy. John, Duke of Bedford, regent for the young Henry VI, had 100 household men and 300 archers. Some Frenchmen also served Henry V after lands north of the Loire were ceded to him in 1420, while Norman forces often fought alongside Englishmen. Between 1422 and 1450 about 45 castles and towns were regularly garrisoned. A ratio of three archers to one man-at-arms was usual, with more footsoldiers in coastal areas. Garrisons increased and decreased in line with the French threat.

For field service in Normandy, swift mobilization was needed; requirements such as escorting supply trains or siege work could last from a few days to several months, and involve a few hundred or several thousand men. Some men were recruited from retinues such as Bedford's (less after about 1430) or from the many ex-soldiers living on the land some were drawn from garrisons, and some from those given land. in return for a feudal obligation to serve.

Effigies of Lady Margaret Holland and her two husbands, Thomas, Duke of Clarence (left, died 1421), and Sir John Beaufort, Earl of Somerset (died 1410), in Canterbury Cathedral. Both knights wear tabards over their armour, and great basinets. (Topham/Woodmansterne)

Italian Armour, c.1450

The main picture is based on the Milanese harness in the Scott Collection in Glasgow, with its missing pieces restored and the barbut replaced by an armet. The breast hinges to the back on the wearer's left and is strapped on the right; this keeps vulnerable straps away from the side which was most commonly presented to an opponent. The fauld is held on internal leathers, straps which act to join plates together while allowing them some movement. Beneath, a mail skirt is tied around the waist to allow movement while protecting the genitals. For combat on foot this might be replaced by mail pants. A lance-rest on the breastplate would be held by a staple and pin. Mail sabatons were common in Italy, being attached to the greave.

1 The armet opened; it is fitted with a padded lining of hay, wool or tow, stitched to a lining-band riveted inside. A mail aventail would be attached to a leather strip pierced with holes that fit over staples along the lower edge of the armet, and secured by a cord.

2 The visor is removed by withdrawing the side pins.

3 A wrapper can be strapped over the visor and cheek-pieces.

4 A stop-rib is riveted to the main plate of the pauldron; the plates above articulate on pivoting rivets.

5 A gardbrace attaches to each pauldron by a staple and pin, the left being much larger.

6 The lames of the counter attach on pivoting rivets, to prevent gaps appearing when the arm is bent. The lower cannon is attached to the lower couter plate by a sliding rivet (moving in a slot), allowing the forearm to twist slightly.

7 The large guard of the vambrace – characteristically Italian in its size – fits over the left couter wing via a staple and pin.

8 The gauntlet has a leather glove stitched to a canvas or leather lining-band riveted inside the cuff and secured at the hand by rivets and straps. Each exposed finger end additionally has a leather strip stitched to it, on to which are riveted overlapping steel scales. The left gauntlet has one plate over

the fingers, the right, which requires more flexibility for gripping weapons, has two.

9 The cuisse has a leather tongue pierced with holes to attach to the doublet. The poleyn, with large Italian side wing, has lames above and below that allow the leg to bend without exposing the limb itself. The greave is strapped on the inner side of the leg.

10 An Italian sallet, c.1450.

11 Italian sallet covered in velvet and decorated with gilt copper mounts, c.1480.

(Graham Turner © Osprey Publishing)

Livery and Maintenance

Great lords employed knights and men-at-arms in private retinues, indeed sometimes so many that they formed private armies. Under this system of 'livery and maintenance', the retainers wore their lord's coat with his livery colours, usually the two principal colours from his coat-of-arms, and they were maintained at his expense. It was a practice that meant nobles could field large bodies of troops and were a permanent threat to stability. Violence on occasions spilled out into open warfare with heavy casualties, and it was the duty of the king or noble to intervene to stop quarrels getting out of hand. A strong king was necessary in such circumstances and a weak or unlucky monarch could find himself facing a revolt.

It was the king's lot to pass titles and land rights to his nobles, and for them to pass them through their own heirs and retainers as best they could. However, the nobles and gentry had the wherewithal in men and money to resort to violence if necessary when involved in disputes. These were sometimes valid questions of land ownership or rights, but could also concern cases of simple avarice:

> ... the squire is not satisfied unless he lives like a knight; the knight wants to be a baron; the baron an earl; the earl a king.

If they could not be controlled by the upper strata of society through the crown's active intervention, then unrest would break out as private quarrels were pursued by force of arms. Always a threat, this problem increased during the Wars of the Roses, when families joined opposite sides in order to carry on private vendettas.

Retainers could be called out at any time, and acted as bodyguards for their lord, accompanying him around the countryside, to his manors, to the court or tournament, or to war. They learned their trade as squires, yeomen or grooms, and wore their lord's livery. *The Black Book of Edward IV* gives the following guide to the maximum number of retainers allowed by various ranks of noblemen:

King: 600	Viscount: 80
Duke: 240	Baron: 40
Marquis: 200	Knight: 16
Earl: 140	

Opposite:
A sallet/close-helmet of about 1485, from Pluckley Church, Kent and now in the Royal Armouries. This very rare form of helmet is known from two other English examples and the Beauchamp Pageant, all with English connections. It may be English, Italian or Flemish made for the English market, and has a pivoting bevor. It originally had a riveted reinforcing bevor covering the lower edge of the missing visor. The apex has been pierced to fit a funerary crest spike. (Author's collection)

For the duration of the Wars of the Roses, some 35 years, a maximum of about 50,000 men were ever in arms at one time, usually in short campaigns.

It was, however, difficult to maintain a force of ideal size, especially with an itinerant aristocracy, when for example a retainer might arrive at his lord's house or castle with his own followers.

Some lived so far away that they were known as 'extraordinary retainers'. As with the old feudal practice of being enfeoffed to more than one lord, so retainers might hold contracts of several masters, which gave them more money, more chance of receiving favours and better protection. These men were known as 'well willers'. The problems caused by the common practice of being retained to more than one lord meant that a retainer was careful to insert clauses in his contract which excused him from having to face one of his other employers on the battlefield.

By contrast, those closest to their lord had no contract but lived by the older bond of loyalty. This practice means that there might have been many more men retained than is evident from records. The bond between retainers and their lord could be strong, a trait that compared to an aristocrat's bond with his king, such as the example of William, Lord Hastings, and Edward IV. When speed of action was necessary it was the household retainers, or 'feed men', close at hand who were called upon. The same men were also convenient to form a guard and escort for their lord on visits to estates or other lords or the king's court. At times of war, however, enough men had to remain to look after a lord's estates and to see that crop production was carried on as usual.

A knightly retainer would have to supply a number of men to his lord, who often had many retainers. An indenture dated 20 September 1468 between Anthony, Lord Scales, and John Norbury Esquire was for one man-at-arms and 118 archers for 91 days. Indentures like this enabled the lord to supply the king with an agreed number of men while still keeping plenty for his own use. The most powerful nobles could call upon many thousands of men. In 1484 the Duke of Norfolk could raise 1,000 retainers and levies from his East Anglian estates alone.

Archers would usually make up the largest proportion of the men a retainer could call up from his own estates. Billmen or soldiers carrying other staff weapons usually made up the remainder. Men-at-arms, who might fight mounted or on foot, were more likely to come from a retainer's own family or men in his household, again a small number compared to the archers. Unlike in the early part of the century, the ratio of archers to men-at-arms had changed noticeably, and could be as high as 8:1. For Edward IV's expedition to France a knight was paid two shillings a day, an esquire one shilling.

During the Wars of the Roses there was a revival in the use of 'Commissions of Array', the summoning of town and county militias, particularly by the Lancastrians. Such men had to be 'well and defencibly arrayed' according to the proclamation of 1463, which demanded that every man between the ages of 16 and 60 in 16 counties be ready to serve Edward IV at a day's notice. The ordering and enforcement of the Commissions usually fell to the sheriff of each county concerned. Nobles too might summon militias. In 1471 the Earl of Warwick decreed death for anyone shirking his call to the militia, and the demands increasingly became less choosy about exactly who was called up. Large numbers of militia were, according to a commission of 1468, divided into companies of 1,000 men, subdivided into groups of 20 and 100. However, because of the fickle nature of loyalties, and the bitterness inherent in civil wars, troops might join whichever faction they preferred, regardless of the original summons. On occasion both sides called up the same militia force.

An inventory of Sir John Fastolf's possessions taken in 1448 mentions silk surcoats embroidered with his armourial bearings. Another in 1461 reveals that his castle at Caister was well defended by four breech-loading guns with eight chambers, two firing 7in. (15cm) stone balls, two firing 5in. (12cm) stones. A serpentine with three chambers fired a 10in. (25cm) stone, another a 7in. (15cm) stone. Three fowlers fired 12in. (30cm) stones, while he also had two short guns for ships (he owned several for trade) with six chambers. Two small serpentines and four guns lying in stocks fired lead pellets. There were also seven handguns and equipment for the guns. Together with this firepower were 24 shields of elm, two of whalebone; eight old-fashioned suits of white armour; ten pairs of body armour, worn out; 14 horn jackets, worn out; ten basinets; 24 sallets; six gorgets; 16 lead hammers; nine bills; other pieces of armour and weapons; zinc caps; wire of little value; four great crossbows of steel, two of whalebone, four of yew; two habergeons and a barrel to store them in.

The Battle of Wakefield, 30 December 1460

Richard, Duke of York, having brought an army north against the newly raised forces of Henry VI's queen, Margaret of Anjou, spent Christmas at Sandal Castle. Five days later the larger Lancastrian army appeared. Reluctant to risk desertions during a siege, and wary of relief forces, they held part of their army in a wood while the rest lured York's men out. Archers opened the fighting, and when the Yorkists were far enough out, the Lancastrians stood and clashed with their enemies. The second division then appeared and the Yorkists were doomed. The duke, shown in an Italian armour with tabard over it, was killed. His young son, the Earl of Rutland, caught fleeing by Lord Clifford, was personally stabbed by him with the words (according to the 16th-century chronicler, Hall): 'Thy father slew mine and so will I do thee and all thy kin'.

The old Earl of Salisbury was caught and executed next day. Some knights wear heraldic tabards; one has his armour painted black, thought to protect it from rust. The knight on the far right wears a brigandine and a form of sallet, whose lower edge reached further down than the visor. By about 1450 these had become level, and the tail had slightly lengthened. Lying in the foreground a retainer in his lord's livery wears a jack, a padded coat usually made from numerous layers of linen, or else of two layers stuffed with tow, and quilted. Sir John Fastolf's inventory of 1459 shows that he owned one of black linen stuffed with mail and six others stuffed with horn, as well as 24 caps stuffed with horn and mail, and six pairs of sheepskin gloves with mail. (Graham Turner © Osprey Publishing)

Campaign Life

Life for the knight on campaign could be miserable or comfortable, depending on several factors. The actual rank of a knight would play a large part. A duke took several tents, campaign furniture, even hangings for the interior of his tent, and copious supplies of food and wine. A poor knight took what he could afford: a tent for himself, and supplies for his few followers.

The setting for the campaign also affected the way a knight lived. English armies in France could, when necessary, take food from the surrounding countryside or from captured towns, in which case a knight with a keen eye could see himself and his men well stocked. The chevauchée was also a good way to deny the enemy his own provisions, and it was a slap in the face to the lord supposedly protecting the area. Similarly, booty was forthcoming, either from battlefield plunder, items from towns or else from ransoming important prisoners, who were far more willing to give themselves up to another knight than to a ruffian archer or billman. The benefits of plunder, however, might be offset by the knowledge that the army could be on campaign for weeks or months, that sieges were liable to drag on, and that, especially in the latter case, disease was very likely to strike. The campaigning season for medieval armies was traditionally the months from spring until autumn, but in reality knights found themselves on campaign in less than ideal conditions. The battle at Towton in Yorkshire, fought in a bitter blizzard in March 1461, is well known, the battle of Wakefield fought the December before is less so.

It was a captain's duty to ensure that his men were kept under control where possible. Henry V forbade plundering in France and hanged an archer who stole a pyx from a church. However, Henry did endeavour to ensure that his men were paid and adequately fed, though even he could not always prevent the slaughter and looting that followed the fall of a town, as happened at Caen in 1417. Since this was accepted practice in cases where surrender had initially been refused, there was little even the king could do.

When a town was taken, a garrison was installed, including knights, all commanded by a captain. Some knights might remain in the town for years, or at least until their contract expired. If single they might even marry French womenfolk. During Henry V's reign some knights would have settled in Normandy, being granted estates in return for military duties. Nobles would also have received large parcels of land in return for duties such as the upkeep of the local castle and its garrison.

Much of a campaign was taken up in marching, in hot sun and soaking rain, over unmade roads sometimes turned to bogs. Often knights sat in front of a castle for weeks with little to do unless an assault was planned, but the chance to win renown via a scaling ladder was also highly dangerous. Sometimes knights would ride off with their escorts to visit a tournament, where rules of chivalry would prevent them being arrested.

A typical knight had several followers, at least one of whom would have been a valet, whose duty it was to look after his master. Damaged armour would need repairing by the armourers who moved with the army; swords had to be honed. The knight's followers would find him lodgings or tents that could be paid for with coin, or else would erect his own tent.

A knight's status meant that he also had money enough to pay for food or other items. However, a noble had to rely on his retainers, his household and feed men, to supply the hardcore of his forces. These were the only reliable followers he had; some of them were knights like himself, who went with him in peace or war. The retainers themselves also brought tenants, but if these tenants refused to come, or deserted, if the arrayed troops supplied to the lord did not materialize, then he could not deliver an effective force for a campaign. Mercenaries included Welsh lords who, like their English equivalent, tended to join whichever side suited their own ideas for striking at old enemies.

In England during the Wars of the Roses, the campaigns tended to be much shorter. For one thing England is much smaller than France, but there were significantly few sieges of towns or cities during this period, most of the conflict taking the form of violent battles or skirmishes. Despite this, Andrew Boardman, using figures by A. Goodman, has calculated that an average campaign lasted only 23 days. However, it was not foreign soil over which the armies marched, and therefore any pillaging would cause widespread distrust and unrest among the king's subjects; the only exception was campaigns into Scotland during this period.

Commanders were aware that if money ran short then pay and food supply suffered and men would desert. It meant that the troops were best recruited and moved swiftly while they were relatively happy. The author of the *Boke of Noblesse*, which was addressed to Edward IV before his French expedition in 1475, suggests that unpleasant excesses by troops in earlier campaigns were caused by a lack of proper and regular pay. One factor made these campaigns different from those in the earlier part of the century. Lords and arrayed troops often chose the opposite side to that of a rival so they could resolve differences by force. Thus a number of titled men perished, being killed on the field or executed afterwards instead of being taken prisoner for ransom, such was the sense of revenge felt by families for one another. The chivalric code between knights was passed over in the pursuit of bloody retribution, and the chance of dying a violent death during a campaign was perhaps greater than had previously been the case.

The Necessities of War

In order to carry enough provisions for a large force, many wagons were needed, sometimes more than could reasonably be procured. The armour of the captains, armoured knights and other retainers would be carried in carts, the pieces perhaps wrapped in hay in locked barrels, but other soldiers, both mounted and foot, carried their own, together with any spares, a blanket and a day's food ration. Food was an obvious essential, together with ale and wine casks. However, room also had to be made for the large number of arrow sheaves carried for the use of the archers, each bound sheaf consisting of about 24 shafts. Spare heads and shafts were also necessary.

A well-armed force might also have cannon in its train, for which specially cut stone balls or, towards the end of the century, cast iron balls, had to be carried, as well as gunpowder and all the paraphernalia necessary to lay and fire the guns: rammers, powder ladles, sponges, scourers, linstocks, etc. Occasionally older forms of siege engines, such as catapults (some built on site or from transported sections) and sheds were called upon, requiring ropes, grease and nails. Mobile forges were a necessity both for armourers and farriers. Bedding and tents for the wealthier men, together with creature comforts – folding chairs, beds, sideboards, chests of various sizes – added to the bulk of material carried. As well as food for the troops, fodder was sometimes also carried for the horses used by mounted contingents, and for pack animals and draught horses or oxen.

Despite all these preparations, food and drink sometimes ran short, especially where a large force was concerned, and had to be either taken by force or bought in bulk from towns or cities. For this, large amounts of money had to be carried in barrels or chests. Scourers, victuallers or harbingers rode ahead of the army to locate towns on the route

Richard Beauchamp is knighted by Henry IV, an early 15th-century scene shown in the costume worn later that century. From the late 15th-century *Beauchamp Pageant*. (By permission of the British Library, MS Cotton Julius E IV, art. 6, f.2v)

of march and agree sales of provisions, as well as billets if necessary. However, supply carts, pulled by teams of horses or oxen, were rather vulnerable targets. The Duke of York found this out when one such train, returning laden with vital provisions purchased by his scourers from Wakefield in 1460, and needed for a force of only 5,000 men, was pounced on by Lancastrians near Sandal Castle. His attempt to rescue it ended in his defeat and death at the battle of Wakefield.

As earlier in the century, some knights formed part of a castle garrison. These were retainers of great lords given control of fortifications, the most powerful being the marcher lords in the north, the families of Neville (warden of the West March) and Percy (warden of the East March). These men, who had control of the northern borders, could field powerful forces if necessary, and it was fortunate for the king during the first part of the conflict that the two families felt enough rivalry to prevent them from forming a dangerous northern coalition. The king's deliberate support for one family over the other helped keep them divided. The castles themselves only seem to have held small garrisons, of perhaps 20 or so men. A far larger garrison was posted in Calais, over 1,000 men to protect the March and the fortifications of Hammes and Guines, together with the English wool staple. Political unrest adversely affected cash flow, and this caused dangerous tension in the garrison, as in 1460 when the soldiers broke into the wool warehouses to take the payment due to them.

At the Kingmaker's Court, 1465

Richard Neville, Earl of Warwick, plots with friends while his one-time ally, Edward IV, talks with his in-laws, the Woodvilles. Courtiers wear dress that befits their rank, and is a conscious statement of their power and wealth. Civilian dress has changed in some ways from the early part of the century. The earl wears a long black gown (as the houppelande was now called), which often now had vents. It was fastened down the front with hooks and eyes or was double-breasted. He carries a fashionable three-tasselled 'gypcière' at his belt and wears a felt Turkey bonnet, popular from 1450 to 1485. Warwick's followers wear his badge of the ragged staff. The hose had reached the hips by mid-century, and the doublet was fastened by laces, buttons, ties or hooks and eyes. A petticoat or waistcoat (with or without tight sleeves) might be worn between the shirt and doublet, for warmth. The two figures in the foreground wear jackets over their doublets. Evolved from the cote-hardie, they sometimes had side vents and might have vertical folds. The right-hand figure has hanging sleeves, and both wear long pointed (piked) shoes. The bowl crop lengthened from about 1450–75, but already in 1465 a 'page-boy' style with fringe and long hair sometimes to the shoulders, was becoming popular and would remain so. Beards were rare. (Graham Turner © Osprey Publishing)

Into Battle

The knight of the 15th century often fought on foot. He had been trained to fight mounted, with a lance, but it was often more effective to dismount most of the men-at-arms and to keep only a small mounted reserve. This was partly due to the increasing threat from missiles. In France during the early 15th century, the English forces used tactics learned the previous century. If the armoured fighting men were kept near the blocks of archers and all waited for the enemy to advance, it meant the latter arrived in a more tired state, all the while harassed by the arrows from the archers and compressed by a natural tendency to shy away from them. This bunching could then work to the advantage of the English who used their archers to strike at the press of French soldiers, now aggravated by those behind pushing forward, as happened at Agincourt. The groups of mounted men-at-arms who tried to outflank the archers at the start of the battle were foiled by the woods which protected each end of the English line, and found to their cost the price of facing archers when mounted.

When archers were in a strong position, ideally defended by stakes, hedges or ditches, a cavalry charge was extremely dangerous. Even when the horses were protected by armour, there was always some exposed part that an arrow could strike, and arrows went deep. Shafts fitted with broad hunting heads made short work of flesh, and the horses became unmanageable even when not mortally wounded. The mounted knight then became useless as he fought for control or was thrown to the ground as the animal collapsed. It is worth noting that only a few hundred at each end of the French line attacked, and of these a few still reached the stakes despite the volleys of presumably thousands of arrows launched at them. Yet it was the dismounted men-at-arms who did most of the fighting in this battle, and it was they who, according to one chronicler, pushed the English line back a spear's length before everything became jammed up:

The battle of Agincourt, as imagined in the later 15th century. Note how the horses only wear shaffrons and, in one case, a crinet. The swords are acutely pointed. (Topham Picturepoint/TopFoto)

But when the French nobility, who at first approached in full front, had nearly joined battle, either from fear of the arrows, which by their impetuosity pierced through the sides and bevors of their basinets, or that they might more speedily penetrate our ranks to the banners, they divided themselves into three troops, charging our line in three places where the banners were: and intermingling their spears closely, they assaulted our men with so ferocious an impetuosity, that they compelled them to retreat almost at spear's length.

English Armour, 1450–1500

Examples of the west European armour worn in England are rare and we are thrown back on visual evidence to reconstruct it. This example may have been made in England, probably London, or imported from Flanders. Some armour might be of Italian export type, made in the style required in England. The knight carrying the pollaxe is based on the FitzHerbert effigy, of c.1475. Much of the detail is similar to that of Italian armour. English armour is also much like Italian armour in style but with a number of variations. Sabatons of overlapping lames, each joined by a pivoting rivet, were commonly used rather than mail over the foot. A strap under the foot acts as a stirrup, and some were tied through the toe-piece with points. The wing on the poleyn was not as large as on Italian examples, and was heart-shaped. The plackart was often attached to the breastplate by a rivet rather than a strap. Besagews were still sometimes worn, though not here. The wings of the couters were more likely to be symmetrical. The vambrace was often made in three parts in the fashion popular in Germany. Gauntlets were laminated at the wrist, and some had several lames over part of the fingers on both hands. A reinforcing plate might be strapped to the left hand. The armour is often fluted and cusped to some extent. After about 1470 the tassets are strapped on halfway up the fauld, instead of hanging from the edge. By about 1440 the English knight's helmet was likely to have been a sallet, of a more upright form than in Germany.

1 Sallet, c.1460, showing lining of canvas stuffed with hay. Stitched to a canvas or leather band held by rivets, the lining was cut into sections connected at the top by a draw-string.

2 A lined bevor, laced or stapled to the breastplate, was not always worn with the sallet.

3 Yorkist collar with lion pendant.

4 Boar pendant of Richard of Gloucester.

5 War-hammer c.1450.

6 Flanged mace c.1470.

7 Hand-and-a-half sword with scent-bottle pommel, c.1450. A membrane of leather is fitted over the cord binding.

8 Arming sword with fish-tail pommel, second half of the century.

9 Exploded view of the hilt. The wood was usually covered in leather and perhaps overlaid with cloth or leather strips, or wire.

10 Hand-and-a-half sword with scent-bottle pommel, c.1450. The lower half of the grip is covered with leather.

11 Hilt with scent-bottle pommel, late-15th century.

12 Short, broad-bladed arming sword and scabbard, from the effigy of Sir Robert Harcourt (died 1471). It is supported by a typical strap arrangement.

(Graham Turner © Osprey Publishing)

Arrows versus Armour

Archers carried specialist arrows, bodkins with needle-pointed heads to punch through mail links, or armour-piercing heads perhaps tipped with steel to penetrate steel plates. Tests have shown that the spin of the arrow in flight enables the head, striking at right angles, to drill a hole into armour plate. The range at which an arrow was shot, as well as whether iron or steel-tipped heads were used, would determine its potency. Most surviving oxidized red bodkins seem to be of iron, which tests suggest curl up when they strike plate. If they struck mail they would burst the rings apart as they

The Dauphin defeated by Sir Richard Beauchamp, who wears an armet with plume and heraldic tabard over his armour. Others wear open or visored sallets, with kettle hats also seen on the right of the picture. Some wear brigandines. English longbowmen oppose French crossbowmen. (By permission of the British Library, MS Cotton Julius E IV, art. 6, f.20v)

went through, a serious threat to anyone in plate armour exposing a mail gusset, for example at the armpit. Crossbows were equally powerful although they did not employ bodkins. Handguns were also now appearing in armies, though not in any great number at this period.

Since plate armour obviated the need for a shield, and fighting dismounted meant the rein hand was free, it became common for knights on foot to carry a two-handed staff weapon in addition to the sword hanging at their side. At first this was often a lance cut down to a length of around 6–7 feet (1.8–2.1m). Increasingly, other staff weapons were carried, which could deal more effectively with plate armour. One of the most popular was the pollaxe, designed to dent or crush the plates, either to wound the wearer or so damage the plates that they ceased to function properly.

Mounted men were very useful in a rout, for they could catch up a fleeing enemy and cut him down with minimum risk to themselves, especially if he was lightly armoured. Indeed, catching archers out of position was the best way for cavalry to scatter them before they got a chance to deploy. In the Hundred Years' War this was not too much of a problem for English knights, since the French did not use archers on a large scale. During the Wars of the Roses, archers fought on both sides in Yorkist and Lancastrian armies and, for the most part, the men-at-arms found it best to stick with the tried-and-trusted methods and fight on foot.

Organization and Identification

Armies still tended to organize themselves into three divisions or 'battles', as they had in previous centuries: the vanguard or 'van', the main battle and the rearguard. Each division included soldiers of all types who served the various lords or the king. A man of rank, be he banneret, lord or king, was recognized by his banner, a large square or rectangular flag bearing his coat-of-arms. The lord might also wear a surcoat with his arms, at first a tight or loose jupon with or without sleeves, latterly a loose tabard with loose elbow-length sleeves rather like that worn by heralds. However, surcoats were increasingly discarded and, with a lack of shields, it was essential that the banner-bearer remain close to his master, following his horse's tail, as it was said. The rallying flag was the standard, a long flag ending in a point or swallow tail. It was usually divided horizontally into the two principal colours from the lord's coat-of-arms, which also formed the livery colours worn on the jackets of his retainers. The end nearest the fly

Equipment, 1450–1500

This knight wears a brigandine over mail skirt and sleeves, together with plate armour on the limbs. He carries a glaive.

1 The brigandine was made from a canvas jacket, which was lined with small plates secured by rivets through the front. Sometimes two large addorsed 'L'-shaped internal plates (less commonly, one) covered the chest. A smaller version, sometimes with backplate, was popular from mid-century. The brigandine was usually faced with leather, fustian, velvet, silk, satin or cloth of gold. Rivets might also be set in horizontal lines, the heads tinned or of gilt latten. Laces sometimes replaced straps, and late examples sometimes fastened at the sides instead.

2 Upstanding mail collar, made from thicker rings for stiffness.

3 Linen drawers possibly with cod; some may have had a slit instead.

4 Doublet and hose, 1450. The hose had reached the hips and were pointed to the doublet. Stirrups are worn, though footed hose were more usual.

5 Doublet and hose, late 15th century. The hose now reached the waist, still pointed to the doublet. The puffed shoulders (mahoitres) were a Burgundian fashion.

6 Rondel daggers.

7 Ballock dagger or knife, with two swellings at the base of the hilt, often worn with civilian dress.

8 Dagger.

9 Ahlespiess.

10 War saddles consisted of a wooden tree, the arçons sometimes reinforced by 'steels' screwed to the front and rear faces. Long trappers appear to have become less common as the century progressed, but they remained popular for use in the tournament.

11 Stirrup of later 15th-century form. Stirrups were often

asymmetrical, with broad sides and foot-rest, the suspension-loop sometimes masked by a plate. At the beginning of the century a small triangular tongue was often added in the centre of the foot-plate. As the century progresses stirrups become increasingly solid in form.

12 Rowel spurs increased in length as the century went on, only shortening again suddenly in about 1500. One form developed a deeper body during the first half of the century. In the second half a less angular body was used, typically with the longer shank.

(Graham Turner © Osprey Publishing)

was probably furnished with a red cross of St George on a white ground. Along the rest of the flag were symbols from the coat-of-arms, together with heraldic badges, again repeated in the badges sewn on to livery jackets or worn in hats. A lord might give the order not to move more than ten feet (or a similar measurement) from the standards, but if the line slightly shifted it would not be too difficult in the confusion of battle to strike out accidentally at an ally.

Knights fighting mounted might have their coat-of-arms on a small pointed pennon nailed to their lance. In order to carry out heraldic identification and to deliver messages, important nobles employed their own heralds wearing tabards of their master's arms, and trumpeters with the arms on hangings below the instruments.

The noise of many men hammering away at each other must have been deafening. When the visor was down, it was not only the hearing but also the vision that was impaired, though lateral views were better than might be supposed. Helmets lacking ventilation holes made it difficult for the wearer to see his own feet without bending forward, and they also quickly became hot and sweaty.

Chivalry

The strange force that bound together knights from all over Europe was chivalry, a word the French roots of which show its original association with horses and horsemanship. By the 15th century it had come to include the essential qualities expected of a knight: good manners, respect for women, protection of the Church and the poor, courage in the face of the enemy. All these ideals had become increasingly fused together during the centuries and were to be heard in the romances which were told and retold in knightly halls and courts throughout Europe. Knighthood too was a bond, since knights shared a common interest and were of a certain rank in society. Knights recognized foreign names and faces from tournaments in which they had fought opposite one another (or sometimes together), or from court visits. Such intercourse often bred respect for a worthy opponent.

However, chivalry was also in some respects a game, a courtly pursuit where gentlemen could show off their breeding and knowledge of how to behave in polite society, especially in the presence of ladies. They knew full well that in war chivalry often went by the board. Knights might well spare one another out of respect or humanity, but often more from a sense of lucrative gain to be made from a fat ransom. This was seen especially in France during the first part of the century. Indeed, such profits could be ploughed back into land and castles, such as Ampthill in Bedfordshire, built from spoils taken by Lord Fanhope in France. In 1421 two English esquires, John Winter and Nicholas Molyneux, agreed to become brothers-in-arms in the wars in France, to pool their winnings and use them in England to buy lands and manors. However, a tight situation called for drastic measures. The massacre of knightly prisoners at Agincourt by order of King Henry V himself is a case in point – Henry ignoring chivalry at a moment in the battle where the captured Frenchmen might have taken up arms as soon as the English were preoccupied with fresh attacks that now threatened them.

Increasingly, bands of professional men-at-arms were seen on the battlefields of Europe, men to whom a coat-of-arms was a relatively unimportant symbol that carried with it expectations of courage in the face of extreme danger which many of them preferred not to stay and face. Such moral courage was not profitable and the absence of recognisable arms prevented a slur on the family name. In England the practice of sparing men of rank was increasingly marred during the Wars of the Roses. Now families joined opposing sides in the hope of being able to use this opportunity to

The late 15th-century *Beauchamp Pageant* depicts Sir Richard Beauchamp and Sir Hugh Lawney shattering their blunted lances in a joust of peace in 1414. Sir Hugh wears an armet, the visor of which has been flung up. The manifer on his left arm can be clearly seen, as can the polder-mitten of Sir Richard. (akg-images/British Library)

settle old grievances. Such motives did not sit well with chivalrous ideals, and those on the losing side might well find themselves at the receiving end of the coup de grace instead of a proffered hand.

Chivalry was also used in diplomacy. Occasionally an effort was made to prevent a war by the offer of single combat between champions. Though frequently no more than verbiage, in 1425 Philip the Good of France made a serious challenge to Duke Humphrey of Gloucester, and even went into training and took fencing lessons. Despite having arms and tents made ready for the expected combat, diplomacy won the day and the contest never took place.

The great English secular order of chivalry was that of the Garter, established by Edward III in 1348. Most of the Knights of the Garter were military officials of the English crown, and this military background was a necessary part of the qualification for entry for those not of royal birth, until Thomas Cromwell became the first 'secular' member in the 16th century.

A knight could be degraded and removed from the order of knighthood for three felonies: treason, fleeing during a battle, and heresy. Latterly wasteful living was added. The ceremony to remove a shamed man from the ranks of knighthood is illustrated in the case of Sir Ralph Grey in 1464, who was convicted of treason. His spurs were hacked off, his coat-of-arms torn from his body and his armour was broken up. His sentence also decreed that his coat-of-arms be replaced by another that bore his arms reversed, but Edward IV excused him this part of the punishment.

The 15th century saw a resurgence of romance literature, resulting from a borrowing of such material in the pageants of this period. The stories of Charlemagne were translated from a 13th-century version in 1454 by Lord Berners, called *The Boke of Duke Huon of Bordeux*. New versions of stories about King Arthur were now being produced, the most famous being *Le Morte d'Arthur* of Sir Thomas Malory, which was printed by Caxton in 1485 and widely distributed. Here was an author not producing work for the king but for his own peers, gentlemen and gentlewomen. The work of the 13th-century Majorcan writer, Raimon Llull, was translated by Caxton into English as *The Book of the Ordre of Chyvalry or Knyghthode*, carried out, we are told, at the request of 'a gentyl and noble esquyer'. Other authors such as Gilbert de la Haye were also producing versions of the literature of chivalry.

Malory wrote at a time when the ideals of knighthood were subsumed by ceremonial. Lancelot, despite his weaknesses, is Malory's ideal of chivalry, rather than Galahad, since the writer viewed chivalry largely as a secular entity. He makes Arthur into a great

Tournament Armour

The first reference to specialized armours for the popular jousts of peace with blunted lances comes in the reign of Edward IV. Prior to this, combatants basically wore field armour with a frog-mouthed helm and some reinforces. A 1446 French description of specialized armour for such courses, compared with later Flemish armours, allows a reconstruction of a later 15th-century harness.

1 A frog-mouthed helm; the 1446 work says it has buckles for the helm and other pieces. Later helms might have had hasps and staples, or screws. Most helms had holes and slits through which points and straps for securing a lining passed. They also usually had ventilation holes on the right side, away from any lance heads. Some, as here, even had large openings on the right. Sometimes an armet with frog-mouthed visor was used, and some late 15th-century helms may have had a removable visor, allowing the helmet to be adapted for foot combat as in 16th-century examples. A large manifer was worn over the gauntlet on the left arm; on some Flemish armours this is supported by a cord running through a staple on the breastplate or brigandine. A small gaignepain or glove was worn on the right hand. A thick shield, laced to a staple on the breastplate, was buffered at the back by a wooden or leather poire stapled to the breastplate. The 1446 work says the left shoulder has a small one-piece pauldron; on the right is a small laminated pauldron fitted with a besagew. The bend of the right arm was guarded by a polder-mitten. In England some jousts of peace were run with leg armour.

2 The helm for jousts of peace, associated with Henry V.

3 High saddle for jousts of peace. The long front extensions guard the rider's legs, and sometimes leg armour was discarded.

4 Lance with coronel head for jousts of peace. A metal graper is fitted behind the hand, whose points bit into a piece of wood sitting in a special lance-rest. A vamplate protects the hand.

5 Sharp head for jousts of war. Such jousts were usually run in field armour, often with armet and wrapper. A grandguard covering the left shoulder and chest, and pasguard for the left elbow, appeared in mid-century. For jousts 'at large' or 'at

random' (without a barrier) these pieces were removed after the lances were shattered and swords came into play. Similar armour was often worn for the tourney or mounted team event. The central figure is dressed for the club tourney, with a brigandine, (though a cuirass could be worn), plus a great basinet.

6 Great basinet from Wimborne Minster in Dorset, 1490–1500. Such helmets could also be used for foot combat. Field armour fitted with a great basinet strapped or double-stapled to the breastplate and strapped to the backplate was usually employed for such contests.

(Graham Turner © Osprey Publishing)

187

Sir Richard Beauchamp strikes Sir Colard Fynes in a joust of war with sharp lances. The large reinforce can clearly be seen on Sir Colard's shoulder and left arm. (akg-images/British Library)

knightly hero, drawing on English romances. Unlike in French romances, many familiar knightly names, such as Gawain, are Arthur's commanders as well as brave knights. Malory echoes the reality of English courtly life, when great lords were also the king's commanders in war. He also portrays the demise of courtly love, the idealism of holding a lady in high repute. As Iseult herself says to Tristram, love is an obstacle and will provoke ridicule in other knights for his taking her with him to Arthur's court, 'A! se how Sir Trystram huntyth and hawkyth and cowryth within a castell wyth hys lady, and

forsakyth us.' Personal feelings can spell doom to knighthood, as in the tragedy of Lancelot when he finally succumbs to Guinevere. It is enough that a knight perform good deeds. Caxton comments in his preface to Malory's work:

> For herein may be seen noble chyvalrye, curtosye, humanyté, frendlynesse, handynesse, love, frendshyp, cowardyse, murdre, hate, vertue, and synne, but t'exersyse and folowe vertu …

Tournaments

The tournament was still a good place for the exercise of arms, but by now it had become as much a spectacle as training for war. Jousts of peace between two mounted opponents with blunted lances required specialized equipment and high saddles, so that a shattered lance was increasingly the accepted outcome rather than unhorsing. By the 1420s the tilt had appeared in Italy, at first a cloth barrier but soon a stout wooden one, which separated the contestants to avoid collisions (deliberate or otherwise) and to help keep horses from running wide. The tilt did not help increase skill for war.

However, some still preferred jousts of war with sharp lances (à outrance), the armour being largely that worn in battle, and such contests were more dangerous, sometimes resulting in fatal injuries, though killing the opponent was never an objective. In one version, 'jousts at large' or 'at random', no tilt barrier was used; once the lances were dropped, the reinforces were removed and the two contestants could continue with swords. The tourney or team event was similar, but involved two groups. Descended from the original form of the tournament, it still provided a spectacle. The club tourney, however, differed in that only clubs or rebated swords were used. Foot combats reflected the increasing tendency to dismount in battle, though in the sport set numbers of blows were agreed and delivered, with officials intervening if this was transgressed.

As aspiring bourgeois members of society rose to knightly rank, so those who were of such rank by birth used chivalry to identify with the king to preserve their status. Hence the threat from restive lords lessened, and monarchs were less suspicious of tournaments as an umbrella for intriguing nobles. Tournaments were now seen as a reflection of a ruler's wealth and magnanimity. However, in England the expense of these festivities was becoming prohibitive, and in the 15th century they became increasingly rare. Some events were held, such as that to celebrate the coronation of Joan of Navarre, the queen of Henry IV, in February 1402, depicted in the later 15th-century *Pageant of Richard Beauchamp*. Knights wishing to participate in or view such scenes often had to travel abroad, especially to Burgundy, where the dukes put on lavish displays to emphasize their power. In the case of the *pas de la belle pèlerine*, held near Calais by the Bastard of St Pol in 1449, heralds visited England and Scotland to proclaim the event. The *pas d'armes de l'Arbre d'Or* was based on the story of Florimont, the knight of the Golden Tree who served the Lady of the Secret Isle. It was held in the market place at Bruges in July 1468, to celebrate the marriage of Charles the Bold, Duke of Burgundy, and Margaret of York. On the sixth day Anthony Woodville, Lord Scales, brother-in-law to Edward IV, challenged the Bastard of Burgundy, whom he had fought in a duel the previous year. Such was their comradeship, now sworn brothers-in-arms, that the Bastard declined the challenge and instead asked Adolf of Cleves to step into the role of defender. There followed some excellent jousts: Cleves shattered 17 lances against Scales' 11 but the main casualty was the Bastard himself, who was kicked above the knee by a

Oxburgh Hall, Suffolk, was built in brick in about 1480. The home of the Bedingfield family, it blends the idea of a castle with the fortified manor. The large windows and false machicolations on the gatehouse turrets show that this is not a serious military building. (akg-images/Robert O'Dea)

horse while he watched, and at one point was feared to be dying. After the tourney, feasting ended the whole event, with 30 centrepiece gardens each with a golden hedge and golden tree. A whale arrived accompanied by giants, and sirens appeared from the whale to sing; the giants then fought a battle with 12 sea-knights. The Duke of Burgundy was awarded the prize for the tournament but refused and gave it instead to John Woodville, the English queen's brother.

Challenges to combats à outrance were not uncommon in the 15th century, though these too usually involved meeting knights from other lands. These were much less spectacular than the types of displays just described and involved a variety of sharp weapons instead of the blunted lances that predominated in the *pas*. There was more variety in the combat too, with knights fighting on foot as well as mounted, as in real

This scene of John of Gaunt feasted by the King of Portugal gives a good idea of a rich man's life in the late 15th century. Food is placed on a table while musicians play. From Jean de Wavrin's *Chroniques d'Angleterre*, made in the 1470s for Edward IV. (akg-images/British Library)

191

Foot combat in the lists, with great basinets much in evidence though outdated on the battlefield. (By permission of the British Library, MS Harley 4375, f.171v)

war. While all tournaments were risky, these combats were more dangerous. Despite this rougher quality, they too gradually acquired a courtly element, and challenges were sent out as formal letters. The knights who took part were those who enjoyed the extra thrill of fighting with sharp weapons; they might be men out to win renown, or bands of knights grouped into a kind of order to demonstrate their skills in arms. The challenger often wore a badge or something similar, such as a garter, and this might also be the chosen prize.

In 1400 Sir John Prendergast accepted a challenge from an Aragonese esquire, Michel d'Oris, but despite letters passing via heralds, the combat came to nothing. John Astley fought a combat at Paris against Piers de Massy on 29 August 1438, watched by King Charles VII. In this episode Astley struck his opponent in the head with his lance, killing him. Astley was challenged in January 1442 by an Aragonese knight, Philip Boyle, and the contest took place at Smithfield. Boyle was slightly wounded; Astley gained the advantage and was about to thrust his dagger into Boyle's face when King Henry VI, who was watching, stopped the combat. The king knighted Astley there and then, giving him in addition 100 marks a year for life.

As has been seen, in 1465 Anthony Woodville, Lord Scales had issued a challenge to Anthony, Bastard of Burgundy. Because large-scale affairs were relatively uncommon in England, this event attracted a number of writers. Woodville was probably aping the Burgundian lifestyle. The story goes that the ladies of Edward's court surrounded

Richard Pynson's woodcut of Chaucer's Squire, c.1491. He wears fashionable civilian clothes and long 'piked' riding boots. (TopFoto/Fortean)

Opposite:
An Italian armour of about 1490 from the Sanctuario Maria delle Grazie, Mantua. The couters have now reduced in size, and in about 1500 the main plate of the cuisse would curve up to follow the plate above it. The visor pivots are now hidden behind the extended arms. (Author's collection)

Not all knights were well treated in defeat. At the Battle of Tewkesbury on 4 May 1471, Edward IV and his army faced the Lancastrian army of Edmund Beaufort, Duke of Somerset. Edward routed his enemy and the Lancastrian forces fled in all directions, some through the town and some to the abbey. Here sheltered the Duke of Somerset, Sir John Langstrother, Sir Thomas Tresham and others. One story tells how Edward raged through the abbey, killing as traitors many of those they found. Another story says he pardoned them. If the latter is true, the trials of Somerset and other nobles two days later, and their summary execution in the market place of Tewkesbury, speaks volumes for the callousness present in these wars. Condemned men were often stripped to their linen shirts. The prisoner on the left wears no shirt under his arming doublet. (Graham Turner © Osprey Publishing)

Woodville and tied a gold band round his thigh, with a 'flower of remembrance' and articles for a joust. Two years later the challenge was accepted. Despite detailed regulations that included the forbidding of spiked horse armour, the Bastard's horse was killed in a collision with his opponent. This aroused suspicion, which Scales was able to refute, though a piece from his sword was apparently found in the dead animal. The resultant foot combat was stopped by the king after a few strokes of the axe gave Scales the advantage, although further combats between English and Burgundian knights took place.

For a knight of quality, appearance at any large spectacle would necessitate a show of wealth on his part, not only in his armour and weapons but also in his horse trappings, the costumes of his attendants and, occasionally, in the largesse he might distribute.

Medical Care, Death and Burial

Knights who were injured or sick faced two obstacles on any road to recovery. Firstly, dependent on their rank, they might or might not get the chance to see a surgeon. Secondly, if they did get medical attention, a great deal depended on the quality of the physician and the nature of the wound. The king and the great nobles would have surgeons in their pay and such men would travel with their master when they were on the move. Thomas Morestede is styled as the King's Surgeon in his agreement with Henry V for the invasion of France in 1415, where he is also to provide three archers and 12 'hommes de son mestier' (men of his service). In addition, William Bradwardyn is listed as a surgeon and both he and Morestede came with nine more surgeons each, making a total of 20 for the army.

Some surgeons were retained by indenture in the same way as the soldiers. John Paston, who was hit below the right elbow by an arrow during the battle of Barnet in 1471, managed to escape with other fleeing Yorkists but lost his baggage. His brother sent a surgeon who stayed with him and used his 'leechcraft' and 'physic' until the wound was on the mend, though John complained it cost £5 in a fortnight and he was broke.

The medical care itself was a mixture of skill and luck, since astrology and the doctrine of humours played a large part in medical care. Surgeons of repute were taught at the school of Montpellier in the Languedoc-Roussillon region of southern France, but even these men would have limited skills. Many could treat broken legs or dislocations successfully, even hernias, and carried out amputations, though a lack of knowledge of bacteria made it a risky business for the patient. Some used alcohol, opium or mandragora to dull the pain. Neither instruments nor hands were necessarily washed. Open wounds could be treated by stitching, and egg yolks were recognized as a soothing balm. However, blood was staunched by the use of a hot iron.

Arrows might go deep, though by this time it was less common to be hit by one with a head bearing barbs, especially when wearing armour. Yet arrows were often stuck in the ground for swift reloading, and conveyed on their tips a lethal dose of dirt which, together with cloth fragments, would be carried into the wound. Abdominal wounds were usually fatal, and surgery in this area was fairly lethal, since any tear in the gut would allow material into the abdominal cavity (not to mention dirt from the weapon used), resulting in peritonitis and death. However, skeletons from the battle of Towton in 1461 show that men did survive quite horrendous wounds. Bones show evidence of slashing blows which bit through muscle into the bone itself, in some cases shearing off pieces. One individual in particular had been in battle before, having been struck across the jaw with such force that the blade cut across to the other side of the mouth. He also had wounds to the skull, but survived all of these, with some disfigurement, to face action once more at Towton, knowing what that might entail – in this instance his own death. Although knights might

Relatives search among the dead after a battle. This later 15th-century picture depicts the aftermath at Hastings in 1066. (By permission of the British Library, MS Yates-Thompson 33, f.167)

wear better armour, it was (theoretically) their job to lead from the front. Some unfortunate knights neither escaped nor perished, but were left for dead, robbed and left half-naked in the open unless by chance they were discovered and succoured.

Much of the Towton evidence comes from men who were infantry. Compression of the left arm bones strongly suggests that some were almost certainly longbowmen. They appear to have been killed during the rout or after capture, and some have several wounds, especially to the head, suggesting that once cut down, further blows were delivered to finish them off. Presumably they had no helmet, or had discarded or lost it while being pursued. The victims were then placed in grave pits. Knights and men of rank might escape such a fate. After Agincourt, the Duke of York's body was boiled and the bones brought back to England for burial. Similarly those of lords would be found either by their retainers or else by heralds, whose job it was to wander the field and book the dead (meaning those with coats-of-arms), which gave the victor a good indication of how he had fared. The families would then transport the body back to be buried on home ground, in the case of the nobility next to their ancestors. Otherwise they were buried locally, usually in a churchyard.

During the turmoil of the Wars of the Roses, with men supporting rivals to the throne, treason was an easy and swift charge to bring. For example, after the battle of Wakefield in 1460, Richard Neville, Earl of Salisbury, was captured and executed next day. Men of rank killed while in revolt might also undergo the degradation of public humiliation. This was not common during the first part of the century, since much of the time knights fought in France, where they were usually treated as honourable opponents. Warwick the Kingmaker, having been slain at Barnet in 1471, was brought to London and displayed for all to see, before his body was allowed to rest at Bisham Abbey with other family members. Richard III was exposed for two days in the Church of St Mary in the Newarke in Leicester, naked except for a piece of cloth, and then buried in a plain tomb in the house of the Grey Friars nearby. Salisbury's head, with those of the Duke of York and his young son, the Earl of Rutland, both killed at Wakefield, was stuck on a spike on the walls of York, the Duke's complete with a paper crown.

Being treated to the indignity of having one's head spiked on London Bridge or on other town gates served as a warning to all those passing beneath. However, a number of attainders were reversed, such as that of Sir Richard Tunstall who, despite being placed in the Tower, managed to persuade Edward IV that he was more use alive and gained his favour. Children of those who died accused of treason did not usually suffer because of it, though their father's lands might pass to the crown until they inherited them.

In contrast to this brutality, there is evidence that humanity and regret did exist. Chantry chapels were set up on various battlefields to pray for the souls of those who died, for example at Barnet, some half a mile (800m) from the town, where the corpses were buried. Richard III endowed Queen's College, Cambridge, for prayers to be said for those of his retinue who perished at Barnet and Tewkesbury. Nobles might make provision for men of their retinues to be cared for if wounded; Henry of Northumberland told his executors to carry out such wishes if he should be killed at Bosworth.

About 30 nobles were killed during the Wars of the Roses, together with numerous knights, those spared being the result of political necessity or on behalf of a family, rather than for any high-minded notions of chivalry. However, other nobles, including men who never fought, survived largely because the Yorkist monarchs, with a narrow band of noble supporters, needed to win Lancastrian support. Despite Edward IV being finally forced to destroy the Beauforts and Henry VI and his son, the Yorkists' years of rule were by no means all of blood. Henry VII and Tudor propagandists would try to maintain this argument in an effort to stabilize the crown and remove bastard feudalism.

Opposite:
A late 15th-century composite South German 'Gothic' armour, mounted on a horse armour made at Augsburg in about 1480, probably for Waldemar VI of Anhalt-Zerbst. The German armour is visually quite different, being long and fluted while the Italian is rounded and smooth. Sabatons are worn on the feet. The arm-defence shown here is joined as one, but often it comprised separate lower and upper cannons and couter. The plackart is riveted to the breast instead of being strapped on, the lance-rest riveted in place instead of having a staple. A sallet and bevor is worn. English lords might have worn armours such as this very occasionally, though there is little evidence. (The Board of Trustees of the Armouries II.3; I.379)

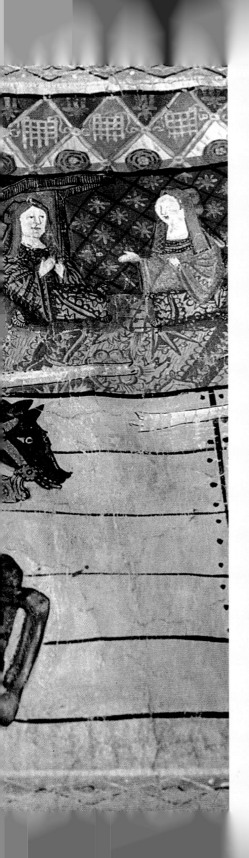

Part IV

Tudor Knight

Introduction

Knighthood in the Tudor period had come a long way since 1066. Increasingly, knights could be made from gentlemen who did not have a knightly background, while other eligible candidates were content to remain squires – men of standing, yet happy to forego the expense and the burdens of sitting in parliament or attending law courts. Those who fought often did so as officers in an increasingly professional army.

The Tudor period in England began with a new dynasty in a Catholic land after years of struggle, and would end with a Protestant country whose monarch had ruled for nearly 50 years. The battle of Bosworth in 1485 effectively ended the Wars of the Roses and ushered in the Tudor dynasty. Henry VII, whose father was the Welsh nobleman Edmund Tudor, became king of a country sick of war and uncertainty. Having removed all potential threats, his reign became one of parsimonious husbandry so that, on his death in 1509, he left a prosperous throne to his son and namesake. The earlier legacy of political unrest enabled Henry VIII to wreak his will on a country that allowed him to get away with much providing he held it securely. Despite this, Henry was always wary of potential revolt. Three times he invaded France and made various truces, including that with Francis at the spectacular Field of Cloth of Gold in 1520. However, his vain attempts to play the giant in Europe with fellow rulers Francis I of France and the Emperors Maximilian I and Charles V of Germany ultimately proved futile. Henry kept the Scots in check but his greatest legacy was breaking England away from the Catholic Church in order to divorce his first wife, Catherine of Aragon. There followed the destruction of religious houses across England, their wealth stolen and precious objects melted down. The Pilgrimage of Grace, a rising of northern folk in 1536–37

Previous page:
The Westminster Tournament Roll was made to commemorate the 1511 tournament held at Westminster. Henry VIII's trapper bears a heart with the words 'Coeur Loyall' (Loyal Heart) and he is shown breaking his lance against his opponent – although the score cheques show that in reality this did not happen. (Ancient Art and Architecture)

Opposite:
Brass of Sir Humphrey Stanley in Westminster Abbey, 1505. His tassets are still strapped on in the earlier English fashion, a little way up the fauld rather than from its lower edge. (Author's collection)

against corrupt officials, was crushed ruthlessly. By the end of Henry VIII's reign his finances were in a parlous state.

When Henry died in 1547 his sickly son, Edward VI, took the throne at nine years old, surrounded by powerful advisors. When Edward died in 1553 Lady Jane Grey, granddaughter of Henry VIII's younger sister, was put forward as Queen, but executed in 1554. Edward's sister, Mary I, took the throne and reintroduced Catholicism by fire and sword, even sending her younger sister, Princess Elizabeth, to the Tower of London. Mary married the Catholic Philip of Spain in a move guaranteed to alienate many Englishmen. When she died in 1558 Elizabeth took over the throne.

Elizabeth I brought back Protestantism and saw off the threat from Mary, Queen of Scots, granddaughter of Henry's sister, Margaret, having her beheaded in 1587. Elizabeth faced the Spanish Armada in 1588, which was chased up the Channel before dashing itself to pieces in the stormy waters around the northern and western coasts of Britain. She toyed with important suitors but never married and so left no heir when she died in 1603. Now the son of Mary, Queen of Scots, James VI of Scotland, took the throne as James I of the house of Stuart.

Organization

Henry VIII

There was no standing army in England for much of the 16th century. Whatever the advantages a standing army may have offered, the monarchs still recalled the nobility backed by their private retinues in times of war. How much more effective and dangerous could they be, then, if they commanded a standing army that was even better trained? Standing armies were, moreover, more expensive and had to be fed even when inactive during the winter. Generally speaking, the lack of troops ready for immediate action did not cause too great a problem and invasions could be planned well ahead of schedule, with enough time to raise the required forces.

The only bodies that might be regarded as a standing force were small. Two were royal guards; the 'King's Spears', active between 1510 and 1515, comprised men of noble or gentle birth formed together as a royal bodyguard. There were 50 men in all, each supported by a light cavalryman, an archer and a mounted attendant. In 1539 a similar body called the 'Gentlemen Pensioners' was set up (surviving as the Corps of Gentlemen-at-Arms). Of lesser rank were the Yeomen of the Guard created by Henry VII. Fortresses and castles maintained garrisons but although some were large, such as at the touch point of Berwick, others only held a handful of men. In all, this force of 2,000–3,000 men was widely scattered and not generally useful for repressing unrest or providing troops for foreign adventures.

During the early years of the 16th century the magnates still came to the muster with their retainers as they had in the 15th century, being contracted or indentured for a set period. Henry VIII appears to have given up the contract itself but gentlemen and nobility still brought retinues for foreign expeditions. These retinues varied in size from a few hundred to well over 800, their numbers depending upon the amount of property held – Sir Henry Willoughby was contracted to supply 830 men for the Guienne expedition in 1512. The retinue was usually made up of varying numbers of men-at-arms, archers, handgunners, billmen, halberdiers and pikemen. Tenants might perhaps send substitutes but landowners, if not ill or too young, might have to serve as captains even if already in government positions. Those tenants from royal manors or religious estates were attached to the steward, who might be an aristocrat.

By the time of the 1513 invasion of France some retinues were being divided up into companies 100 or so strong, led by a captain; this was seemingly an attempt to provide more orderly groups at least on the march, though groups of men below 100 – such as the 66 brought by Thomas Lucy – were not joined with others to make up the numbers. For the 1522 invasion far more units consisted of companies of 100 men under a captain (at 4 shillings a day) and a petty-captain. By mid-century this was the accepted format, the above officers being joined by a standard-bearer, sergeant and four vintenars (corporals) each responsible for 25 of the men (privates). Thomas Audley in his *A.B.C. for the Wars* (written for the boy Edward VI but harking back to experiences under Henry VIII) remarks that 200 is a better number for a captain, since then he would receive 8 shillings and be less likely to palm off some of the men's pay to supplement his own. Nor can captains provide such kindnesses as wagons for the sick when only in receipt of 4 shillings. Audley also suggests using only one lieutenant, standard-bearer and sergeant, and removing the vintenars so their wages could be given to a gentleman or worthy soldier of the captain's own band; this would appear as 'dead-pay' later in the century, but was then achieved by cutting the company to 90 men while giving pay for 100. Audley remarks that officers were often chosen by favouritism, not for their military experience.

In 1518 Henry wrote to several captains proposing to appoint some experienced leaders to retain companies ready for action whenever required, paid for by the king, who would decide how many men could be retained. A surviving draft document outlines the details, saying that the men would be provided with a coat of Almain armour (imported from Germany, hence the name), a jacket in the green and white royal livery, the king's badge and that of the lord retaining them. They would be mustered once or twice a year but would only receive horses when called, when they would also receive their wages. Statutes against retainers would be enforced if a captain recruited more than required – a safeguard against increasing power. In 1551 the Privy Council nominated a number of captains from their members to make up cavalry contingents from their own retainers, for which the captain received a generous imprest. Some said this was the Duke of Northumberland's way of getting extra men to increase his power, but in any case the idea was dropped less than two years later. Nervousness in the Privy Council blocked private suggestions too. In Edward's reign a number of gentlemen, including Sir Thomas Wyatt, came up with the 'King's Militia, or Ordnance of Soldiers', which set out proposals that included avoiding the recruitment into the militia of young fathers or those men worth over 20 shillings per annum, or those unwilling to serve the king. The captain would be chosen annually from a body of likely candidates. However, this proposal fared no better than the rest.

For the 1513 expedition the statute of pay drawn up for Henry VII's proposed invasion of France in 1492 was repeated almost verbatim. Captains were ordered to make sure their men received their wages within six days of the money arriving from the treasurer-at-war. They also had to ensure that the full complement of men agreed with the king were actually present, complete with their colours; prison and forfeiture of goods and chattels awaited those not complying.

In 1539, Sir Richard Morison wrote in the Preface to his translation of *The Strategemes, Sleyghtes, and Policies of Warre* (by Frontinus), one of England's first military books, that the noble captains of England often said they needed no instructions or books to teach them to rough up their enemies.

The commissioners of musters in the shires recruited the militia, which formed the second part of the army. Instructed as to what type of soldier was required and how many, they could endeavour to recruit the desired troop types, resulting in a far more ordered force than was the case for the retained men. Not until the second half of the century would this change be complete, however. When there was not time for issuing commissions the troops were mustered by the sheriffs, who were even more inefficient than the commissioners.

By the 16th century the retinues and militia, though two elements that received pay from their lords or captains respectively, were starting to blend when in battle. Retinues were fragmented as the overall commander saw fit, so that archers were formed together,

or billmen or pikemen. It is not known what flag men posted to another area of the army would follow.

Mercenaries were also hired for Continental operations. These were usually Germans ('Almains') and Burgundians. Friction occurred with such men; the Germans in particular seem to have been much less ready to obey orders.

Henry VIII meets Maximilian I during the siege of Thérouanne in 1513. The German horsemen (on the left) mainly wear sallets, while the English cavalry have armets; all wear cloth bases. Their lances are tipped with coronel points as though for jousting, possibly a symbol of peaceful negotiation. The battle of the Spurs is depicted in the background. (The Print Collector/HIP/TopFoto)

Henry VIII introduced several military reforms, including naval dockyards at Deptford and Woolwich, coastal forts to protect south and east England, an updated armoury in the Tower, an upgraded artillery train and moves to combat a shortage of heavy horses, since only the King's Spears and the nobles were able to serve with armoured mounts, many gentry serving as demi-lances or on foot.

Knight, c.1525

This knight is based on the 'Genouilhac' armour in the Metropolitan Museum of Art, New York, probably that made for Henry VIII in 1527 at Greenwich and the earliest surviving English garniture, consisting of a number of pieces that could be made up for field or tournament use.

1 The close-helmet comprises a visor, upper bevor and lower bevor, all pivoting from single points on each side. The helmet rotates on a flanged collar, secured by a sprung stud on the front edge of the skull that locates a hole in the lower bevor and is secured by a small hook. The disc at the rear may have helped keep the strap of a wrapper in place. The interior was fitted with a padded lining stitched to internal leather bands riveted in place.

2 Interior of the unique three-part breastplate.

3 Greenwich pauldrons were composed of equal-sized lames overlapping upwards. Internally these were held on five or six sets of leathers rather than with sliding rivets at the outer side. Haute-pieces (to deflect lateral blows) on the pauldrons of Greenwich armours can be seen as late as 1585 and were detachable. The vambrace was attached by a point from the arming doublet through a leather tab. The couter wing attached via a pivot hook.

4 The sabaton closed via a pierced stud and pivot hook. The rowel spur arms slid through slots and a pin secured it at the rear through a pierced stud.

5 The tilt reinforces are based on Henry VIII's 1540 garniture and comprise a grandguard over the chest, pasguard at the elbow and manifer over the forearm and hand. A hole in the manifer fits over a pierced stud on the gauntlet and is secured by a hook; the disc protects it.

6 Locking gauntlet or 'close-gauntlet' for the tourney: the fingers were secured by a pivot hook, preventing loss of a weapon.

7 A type of close-helmet (like similar armets) found in English churches c.1500–40, with 'sparrow's beak' visor. A reinforcing plate is riveted to the front or left of the bevor.

8 Sword with finger-guards, possibly North Italian, c.1520.

9 A long-sleeved shirt of linen or other fine stuff was worn next

to the skin. At the start of the century it was low-necked but slowly rose to a high neck.

10 A padded doublet was worn over the shirt, over which came the jerkin. Long hose of shaped cloth were tied to the doublet by twine or silk points tipped with metal aiglets. The upper part (upper stocks) was sometimes slashed and puffed and after 1515 was made fuller. The stockings (nether stocks) were stitched on anywhere from the knee to below the seat. Broad and square-toed shoes and boots were often slashed. Open-fronted shoes were fastened by a strap around the instep. Boots were either close-fitted and laced, or loose and knee-length.

(Graham Turner © Osprey Publishing)

Edward, Mary and Elizabeth

Commissions to raise troops, held by a chosen person, were also used by Edward VI and Mary, but increasingly rarely by Elizabeth (except in 1586 when six commissioners raised 1,500 volunteers), because of the work of the lord lieutenant (the lieutenant of Henry VIII's time). Elizabeth only issued indentures for a man to lead troops to their port of embarkation. The retinues raised by landowners were no longer used. Regular forces like Edward VI's 'gendarmery' did not reappear. The two royal guards and the militia alone survived.

In 1558 Mary abolished the Statute of Winchester. Now all those with land of £1,000 value or more per year were to keep the following, all of which was to be inventoried and inspected on occasion and none sold:

> six horses for demi-lances, three of which should have harness and armour for the
> rider; ten horses for light horsemen, together with harness and armour for
> the riders; 40 corselets (infantry cuirasses with full arms, tassets and open
> helmets); 40 lighter armours for foot ('Almain rivets'), or 40 coats of
> plates or brigandines; 40 pikes; 30 longbows, each with 24 arrows;
> 30 light steel caps; 20 bills and halberds; 20 arquebuses; 20 morions.

Those with less income had a suitably reduced burden: men with £5–£10 per year had to provide one coat of plates, one bill or halberd, one bow with arrows and one light helmet.

In 1585 the cost of a horseman was assessed at £25 and the clergy was ordered to raise £25,000 to fund the English force.

The constant need for expeditions gave little pause for any radical alteration in the army structure but, even if it had, the huge costs of maintaining English forces could barely have stood the increased expenditure. There is little evidence that the funds necessary to uphold a standing paid force could easily have been prised out of the populace either, regardless of the release from threats of conscription this would entail. Any nobleman who hinted at private forces, such as Essex, risked accusations of treason. Elizabeth could not, as her father had done, physically take part in military affairs and give opinions based on experience.

A great basinet of Henry VIII, c.1510–20. Designed for foot combat over the barriers in the tournament, it was bolted to the cuirass and has a blind (possibly later) visor – the wearer looked through the ventilation holes. (The Board of Trustees of the Armouries, IV.2)

Generals, according to Barnaby Rich and Robert Barret, had to be of noble birth in order to command the respect of their men. However, Matthew Sutcliffe pointed out that this could lead to young, inexperienced men being chosen, or worse, those with little military ability. It was a throwback to earlier centuries that the nobility earned its position in society by leading in war; moreover, lingering feudal memories would not tolerate ordinary men in high rank. This persisted until the end of the 16th century and the queen, advised by her nobles and with a similar mindset, appointed generals who, on the whole, were not of top quality. Generals also ruled in the Netherlands and as lord deputies in Ireland. Lord Mountjoy was perhaps the most able general of Elizabeth's reign – he proved his skills when sent to deal with Ireland and showed a modern efficient approach rather than the chivalry still practised elsewhere. The Earl of Essex sometimes showed great leadership and his courage in battle was not questioned, but he could also make mistakes. He, like the far less able Leicester, was quite willing to put his private affairs first, ending up on the scaffold for treason. The unwillingness of high-ranking nobles to commit themselves to their military tasks was a great drawback. It was sometimes compounded by their being restrained by the orders emanating from the queen or Privy Council, neither of which was actually in the field.

The high marshal was second-in-command, in charge of justice and camp management. Under him came the provost marshal, either the army officer or the peace officer. A general or lieutenant general of the infantry usually took part, and similarly a general of horse, both ranked just below the high marshal. The master of the ordnance was in charge of the stores. He had his own company to guard the guns, which he commanded in action, and controlled ancillary groups such as wheelwrights and pioneers. Below these ranks came numerous lesser officers, such as the forage-master. The sergeant-major (or sergeant-general or sergeant-major-major) was a rank created to connect the general to his captains of companies; to do this the sergeant-major had four corporals of the field, one for each 'battle' (van, main and rear) and one spare.

Finally, after about 1572 (when volunteers went to the Netherlands) and in imitation of Continental armies, English forces adopted the regiment, comprising groups of companies under a colonel. Some, such as Sir John Smythe, a practised soldier, disliked smaller-sized regiments because they needed more officers. However, captains returning from the Low Countries wanted small regiments, and even Continental ones were reducing from 5,000 to 3,000. English regiments reduced from 4,000 to around 1,000-strong, with up to seven companies of about 150–200 men. The sergeant-major-general now contended with colonels ranking far higher than captains. Cavalry companies settled at about 100 men. These paper estimates, however, tended not to be borne out in practice. Captains in the Low Countries dismissed eager men and pocketed their pay. In fact, captains had a reputation for feathering their nests at the expense of army efficiency, a topic that did not go unnoticed by Sir John Smythe. Some unscrupulous captains sent men on hopeless or suicidal missions so they could pocket their pay, or to remove junior officers they detested. Their men had poor uniforms and lost rations so they had to forage for themselves. They sold companies or rented them to their lieutenants. The lieutenant deputized for the captain; the ensign-bearer was of gentle birth and was expected to step in if both captain and lieutenant fell.

The lord lieutenant took over leadership of the militia from the sheriff. There were perhaps between 200,000 and 250,000 men between 16 and 60 years old eligible for the county militia, but only about 20,000 were chosen. Men for special training were now formed into the Trained Bands and where possible exempted from overseas service. This meant that instead of training gentlemen, farmers, yeomen of good stock and labourers, the bands became a hidey-hole for those avoiding foreign service. 'Untrained men' covered conscripts and volunteers. Of the latter, the gentlemen volunteers were a small group (roughly four per company), presumably with an eye to becoming captains. Conscripts, however, included labourers and criminals. Smythe asserted that time wasters made sure they were elsewhere when a levy was made. Sir John Norreys said such people impaired efficiency.

For Ireland the question arose of whether to recruit Irishmen. They received a lower wage, but might often desert, taking equipment, tactical knowledge and sometimes Englishmen with them.

Bow versus Bullets

Arguments raged as to whether or not to keep the bow. Sir Roger Williams reckoned that one musketeer was worth three bowmen, while Sir John Smythe was vehemently in favour of the latter. The Privy Council tried in 1569 to make provision for guns but made no headway against popular opinion. Finally in 1595 it took the bold step of ending the use of bows in the armed forces.

Training

From Boyhood

By 1500, men of knightly rank did not always wish to fight, and not everyone had come from a background of mounted warriors. There were plenty of other activities, such as running estates, farming, mercantile interests in towns, local government and attending parliament as knights of the shire. Some were naturally attracted to the battlefield, however. Peter Carew, born of a knightly family in 1514, kept playing truant from grammar school, even when his father coupled him to his hound as a lesson. Faring no better at St Paul's school, his father shunted him off as a page to a French friend, but he was so bad that he was made a muleteer until rescued by a relative (a Carew of Haccombe) en route to the siege of Pavia. This relative died on the way, so Peter joined the Marquess of Saluzzo, who was killed at the battle of Pavia. Peter then changed sides and was recruited by the Prince of Orange, who was soon also killed. The prince's sister, knowing Peter was homesick, sent him with letters to Henry VIII, who took him into service, impressed by his riding and fluency in French. In 1532 Carew became a gentleman of the Privy Chamber, and was knighted for services at Tre'port in 1544. Three years later he was sheriff of Devonshire and in 1549 perhaps overstepped his duties in putting down the insurrection against the Common Prayer. In 1564–65 he captained a fleet commanded to sweep the western Channel and Irish Sea of pirates. Carew sat on committees concerned with ships, munitions, customs revenues and the defences of the Tower of London. In 1572 he acted as constable of the Tower. He dabbled in architecture and claimed lands in Ireland, and served there three times.

Boys from noble houses might be sent to other households to train as squires, but some men who were knighted for bravery entered the court circle for other reasons and ended up fighting for the king. Sir Humphrey Gilbert (c.1537–83) made a telling statement in his outline for an academy in London to teach the sons of nobles and gentlemen: they should study Latin language and literature, philosophy, law, contemporary history, oratory, heraldry and courtliness. The art of war meant learning mathematics, engineering, ballistics and military theory, all equally as useful as skill with lance and sword.

A large curb bit once belonging to Henry VIII. The curb bars are decorated; the rollers encouraged the animal to play with them in his mouth and, in so doing, salivate to produce imposing froth. (The Board of Trustees of the Armouries, VI.200)

Fewer Knights and Castles

In Elizabeth's reign the bestowing of knighthoods was deliberately curtailed. Leicester ignored this and made 14 new knights in a single day. Elizabeth then set out that only those with good social standing and finances, or who had proven themselves by some outstanding act of bravery, should warrant being knighted. The Privy Council came to expect all candidates' names to be submitted for approval and by the time of the queen's death the generals hardly dubbed knights at all any more.

Castles were now becoming redundant, as much from a desire for more comfort as from the effects of gunpowder. However, men still trained in courtyards or else in the grounds of their country house. Teaching a man to wear armour differed little from how it was done in previous centuries. Any man of knightly status could ride but he must learn to ride a warhorse in armour, and to control it with his legs while using weapons. Charging a quintain helped steady the aim and prepare the body for the jarring collision that occurred when a lance struck it. Some quintains may still have consisted of a pivoting arm, one end with a target, the other a sack of sand or a weight that swung round on striking the target to clout anyone not swift enough to avoid it. Running at the ring, a metal ring suspended from a frame, needed a keen eye to pass the lance point through it.

The Tournament

Even if many rarely fought in earnest, there was still the tournament in which to impress the sovereign. In London there were lists (arenas for jousting) at Westminster until a fire occurred in 1512, after which all the tournaments in England took place at the Palace of Placentia at Greenwich. A new royal residence at Whitehall in 1533 saw a transfer to this venue and few tournaments were held at Greenwich thereafter. Occasional tournaments were held at Richmond Palace and one at the Tower of London in 1501, while a few were held at Hampton Court in Mary's reign; on 29 December 1557 half the contestants were dressed in the Almain (German) fashion and half in Spanish. Other tiltyards elsewhere in the country were occasionally used. Henry VIII was a keen jouster and those who wished to be at the centre of things did well to follow his lead. Queen Elizabeth attended tournaments, notably the Accession Day tilts each November, so those currying favour needed to hone their skills.

Horse-armour made in about 1520 at Greenwich. It comprises a three-part peytral (chest-defence), crupper and flanchards at the flanks. The pairs of holes show how it was fastened with points. The row of rivets would have held an internal lining band to which was stitched a padded lining for comfort. Saddle steels reinforce the pommel and cantle. (The Board of Trustees of the Armouries, VI.14–16)

The Accession Day tilts, c.1586

Opposite:
This tonlet armour for foot combats was put together at Greenwich for Henry VIII after the French changed the rules of the tournament planned for the Field of Cloth of Gold. The skirt (tonlet) has leathers riveted on the inner side so that the individual lames can move; the whole can be completely collapsed. It was made partly from existing pieces, the whole then etched en suite. There are signs of haste: for example, the helmet is a great basinet for the tourney that has had a pierced bar welded inside to narrow the vision sights. The gauntlets are associated. (The Board of Trustees of the Armouries II.7/HIP/TopFoto)

The Accession Day tilts took place fairly regularly on 17 November, the date that Elizabeth ascended the throne. They were usually held at Whitehall tiltyard, which ran north–south instead of east–west, with the royal gallery at one end facing north rather than in the middle where the clash would occur. Here Sir Henry Lee, Queen's Champion at the Tilt, tries to shatter his blunted and hollow lance against his opponent to score points. Lee may have entered the arena with an impresa, which would be presented by his page. By the late 1570s impresas seem to have replaced coats-of-arms in the lists. Lee wears a partially etched and gilt Greenwich garniture of the time, with narrow tilt visor and tilt reinforces in place. (Graham Turner © Osprey Publishing)

The tourney was a group combat, or one between two opponents, each with blunted swords. Foot combat was less hazardous than in earlier centuries since a barrier divided the contestants, so much so that leg-armour was not necessary; blows below the barrier were forbidden. A long spear was used, or sometimes a sword. Jousting was popular but despite special extra tilt pieces, a high barrier to prevent collisions (the tilt), and fluted, hollow lances with blunted points, accidents could still occur. On one occasion Henry VIII forgot to close his helmet and the shower of long wooden splinters that filled his headpiece when his opponent's lance broke on him could have blinded or killed him; luckily (especially for his opponent) he was unhurt and good humoured.

Martial skill was just one aspect of the tournament: poetry and allegory flattering the sovereign was all useful material for those in the court. At Sir Henry Lee's entertainment at Woodstock in 1575, Elizabeth saw two mounted knights as she arrived, battling for their ladies' honour in a staged set piece.

Appearance and Dress

Armour

Men of rank wore full harness of steel that covered them from top to toe. Initially this might not differ from that worn at the end of the 15th century, a western European style derived from Italian forms with some German influences.

Sabatons sported more rounded toes as they moved towards a broad, bear's paw style. The lower edge of the greave now extended down to cover the back of the heel, usually with a slot up the back to accommodate the spur arm. Instead of straps and buckles the two halves of the greave were now closed by studs springing into holes in the other plate and sometimes further secured by pivot hooks. The lower lame of the poleyn was now cut off straight and grew smaller. The side wing of the poleyn was at first large with a 'V'-shaped indent, but after the mid-century it grew smaller and by about 1570 had become almost insignificant. From about 1510 the hinged sideplate of the cuisse (thigh armour) was usually changed to an extension of the main plate, but after 1550 grew smaller and then vanished. On the arms, the vambrace was now attached permanently to the pauldron or else laced to the arming doublet and the pauldron connected by a strap buckled round the turner of the upper cannon. The large couter on the elbow, which had often been laced to the arming doublet separately, was now attached to the upper and lower cannons by internal leathers and sometimes to the shoulder-defence as well. Until about 1560 some arm-defences had small cup-shaped projections riveted to the upper end of the lower cannon below the couter. Gauntlets, which had commonly been of mitten form, began to be provided with complete fingers after about 1530, and at the same time longer cuffs, more pointed and bell-shaped, came into fashion. The collar had become common by 1520 and might be used to connect the pauldrons by straps.

In the 1540s the waistline of the breastplate began to dip downwards slightly. Twenty years later this had become a point that in the 1570s became the peascod (or 'long-bellied' form) in imitation of fashionable civilian doublets. The following decade saw this style become even more prominent until it nearly reached the crotch. From about 1510 the edges that had previously been turned outwards now turned inwards and were sometimes decorated with roping, though plain angled edges were still seen until about 1570, unlike in the rest of Europe. Frequently recessed borders accompanied these edges. The backplate was often of one piece and flanged at the bottom to take a culet.

The steel fauld of the breastplate was provided with hanging tassets. At first Gothic-style single-plate tassets remained in use but from 1510 laminated versions, usually rectangular with rounded corners, became increasingly popular, and had replaced the older style by about 1530.

In the last quarter of century the waistcoat cuirass appeared, often with imitation steel buttons. Two halves were hinged to a strip up the back and fastened in front, usually with studs secured by pivot hooks.

A Greenwich helmet from Southacre Church, Norfolk, with a rounded visor seen from about 1530 to 1540. (Author's collection)

Helmets

The sallet and armet helmets of the late 15th century remained in use in some instances for about 20 years. The sallet became more rounded, sometimes with a bellows visor. New forms of armet and other helmet types superseded it. All helmets tended to have a low comb from about 1510 to 1530 (roped for the last ten years); in a few instances the apex was instead drawn up to a quadrangular point that might have an acorn finial. Combs grew larger thereafter but reduced again late in the century. The visor, fitted with a removable pin in each arm, was replaced by an arm pivoted via a screw and internal nut, or sometimes pierced and held by an internal linchpin. A plume holder was now riveted to the base of the skull at the rear, thus replacing the hole in the skull for a crest holder. The plume was sometimes further secured by piercing one or two small holes through the comb to allow binding. The close-helmet developed soon after 1500 from a form of sallet with attached bevor. This was shaped to the head and made in two sections, skull and bevor, the latter pivoting either side of the brow at the same point as the visor that now only covered the opening left by the bevor. When closed the two halves were secured by pivot hooks through pierced staples or sometimes by a sprung stud (attached inside to a strip of springy metal and depressed by another stud on the strip).

Until about 1530 the 'sparrow's beak' visor was popular. Thence the visor became split horizontally into the visor and the upper-bevor (or 'ventail'), into which it fitted. From about 1520 close-helmets were usually fitted with one or more gorget plates unless they were of the type that rotated on the collar.

The burgonet, an open-faced peaked helmet derived from the sallet, was used by light cavalry and infantry, and was provided in some garnitures for wear as officers. It was also popular for parade armours. After 1510 the burgonet was often accompanied by a buffe, a kind of bevor fitted with gorget plates. Occasionally a morion was worn by infantry officers, with tall skull and pointed brim.

The arming doublet was only lightly quilted, and throughout the century come references to arming bolsters, padded rolls worn round the hips to support the cuirass, and to quilted collars called arming partlets. Pieces of armour might be lined or padded, and from mid-century might be decorated by leather or fabric tabs known as pickadils. Over the armour fabric bases were sometimes worn or, during tournaments or parades, civilian robes.

The brigandine lined with small tinned plates continued to be quite popular until the second half of the century. The inventory of Edmund Dudley in 1509 shows two rich examples for himself plus 30 fustian-covered examples for his men. Mail coats, consisting of thousands of interlinked riveted rings, might be worn under civilian clothing, either for duelling or as protection against assassination. Mail parts were also worn late in the century by officers and captains of light horse or infantry.

The Greenwich Workshop and Style

In 1511 Henry VIII set up a small workshop at Greenwich near the royal palace, staffed by a group of Italian craftsmen from Milan, followed by a group of Flemish craftsmen. In 1514 Henry was sent a present by Emperor Maximilian I of a magnificent tonlet armour made by the Innsbruck master armourer, Conrad Seusenhofer. Presenting gifts was a recognized social function for heads of state, but Henry was apparently still unable to reply in kind from English workshops. The following year he brought in the most important group of men, armourers from Germany itself, the 'Almains'. In 1516 the royal workshop moved to Southwark, but between 1521 and 1525 it was back at Greenwich, where it remained until about 1637. As a royal workshop Greenwich was technically there to provide armours for the king, and the workmanship of the craftsmen would rival the top centres in Europe. Henry had several other armours made, some now surviving only from a few pieces. Under Mary and Elizabeth it would be courtiers who would purchase armours from the royal workshop.

By the second half of the century the Greenwich style had developed. A form of armet that had first appeared in Germany was developed after about 1525, whereby the tail became wider and the cheek-pieces hinged to it at their rear edges, a style seen until about 1615, despite the close-helmet's increasing popularity elsewhere. Greenwich visors had a gracefully curved prow like that of a ship, and for ventilation there were usually vertical slits each pierced by a hole.

The Garniture

When men of rank wanted to take part in tournaments, they might require armours for several types of contest: the tourney, jousts and foot combats, not to mention harness designed for use in battle either mounted or on foot. All this could be extremely expensive, and around 1500 a new solution was beginning to appear: the garniture. This was in effect a set of interchangeable parts that allowed armours to be made up for a variety of uses. The individual pieces of the garniture were often decorated en suite.

Decoration

Varying degrees of decoration frequently enriched armour worn by men of rank. In the early 16th century this was sometimes done by engraving with a burin (a metal cutting tool with a sharp bevelled point). However, etching was already being used to decorate metal with less effort and would become the main technique, though in the last quarter some armours might be decorated by designs on shaped punches. In etching a mild acid such as vinegar ate away part of the surface to produce the required decoration, after coating the surface to be decorated with a protective 'resist' (wax or paint) and cutting the design through the resist with a needle to expose the metal. The second method, used from about 1510 in Germany and a decade later in Italy, involved coating areas to be left untouched with a resist applied by brush, and only using a needle for fine detail. A granular effect could be obtained by liberally covering a surface with small dots of wax, a typically Germanic style as opposed to the plain ground initially used by the Italians. Thus larger etched areas were more easily achieved, and this became the main way to etch armour. Greenwich armours were at first etched in Italian style but after 1570 in German style, with native English designs.

Etched decoration was frequently enhanced by mercury gilding, an amalgam of gold and mercury being painted on to the desired area and the mercury heated to chase it off, leaving the gold fused to the surface. More rarely gold might be applied as gold leaf, whereby the surface was hatched to make the leaf stick when it was laid on and burnished. Silver foil was also sometimes added this way, the most famous example being Henry VIII's armour for man and horse of about 1515. Gilding was usually applied to borders or as decorative bands. Sometimes the gilding was only applied to the ground, leaving the raised design in steel, or the ground and the design lines were blackened (more a German feature). The surface might be further enhanced by controlled heating of the steel to produce a beautiful deep blue or russet red. An easier method of colouring was to paint the surface, commonly in black, leaving areas of natural steel to produce what is called 'black-and-white' armour. This was especially popular in Germany but uncommon among men of rank in England.

A crinet or neck-defence for a horse. Made for Henry VIII by his Greenwich workshop in 1544, each lame moves on internal leathers. It is decorated with etched and gilt designs. Below is a matching mitten gauntlet, both pieces from a lost armour. (The Board of Trustees of the Armouries, VI.69)

Knight, c.1550

Garnitures varied in their composition and some were designed purely for the field. This figure is based on the Greenwich armour of Henry Herbert, Earl of Pembroke, in the Kelvingrove Museum, Glasgow. A form of cuirass that is sometimes seen from the 1530s to about 1560 is the anime. Instead of being made from a single large piece, a number of horizontal-shaped lames are riveted together; smaller individual plates made it easier to control the thickness and strength of the metal during manufacture – something more difficult to achieve with a large sheet of steel. A close-burgonet is fitted with a falling-buffe. Mail sabatons with steel toecaps remained popular until c.1570. The horse's shaffron, peytral, crupper and saddle steels are made to match.

1 Additional pieces allow other armours to be built: a reinforcing breastplate can be added to the heavy field armour to help absorb the impact of bullets from increasingly efficient gunpowder weapons. For a medium field armour the lance-rest and lower leg-defences were left off; for a light field armour an open burgonet was worn while the arm-defences were replaced by mail sleeves (or perhaps elbow-length defences and long-cuffed gauntlets) and the upper leg-defences were removed. An officer of foot was similar to the light field but might include the arm-defences, while tasset extensions were added via keyhole slots engaging with turning pins in the lower lames of the tassets.

2 Matching burgonet.

3 A close-burgonet, made at Greenwich c.1555.

4 and **5** swords, c.1540.

6 War hammer, c.1560.

7 A wheellock petronel, the butt designed to be held against the chest rather than the shoulder.

8 The doublet began to be pointed down at the front, the padded rolls on the shoulder now being common. The jerkin also had padded rolls (wings) and the short-sleeved style shown here was popular. The long gown was now relegated to ceremonial wear but simpler versions were worn in private life. Proper trunk hose now appeared (usually slashed), no longer referred to as 'upper stocks'. The shape was achieved by padding out with 'bombast', e.g. horsehair, wool or bran. Stockings might now be knitted for the first time. The feathered cap, enhanced by jewels and brooches, was very popular.

(Graham Turner © Osprey Publishing)

Another uncommon form of decoration was embossing: raising a design by hammering from the underside of the metal. This obviously dispensed with the smooth surface necessary to make weapon points glance off, and was used rather for parade items. One of the best survivals is the so-called Burgundian Bard, a horse-armour gifted to Henry VIII by the Emperor Maximilian. Embossing was also employed to produce the grotesque masks used on some tourney helmet visors, though this was much more popular in Germany. Damascening entailed cutting channels along the design lines and filling these with gold or silver strips hammered into place. Damascening was often used in conjunction with embossing, but the process was rare in England. The practice of applying precious jewels, enamels, or gold or silver plates to helmets was still very occasionally seen in the early 16th century.

St Mawes castle in Cornwall, built 1540–43. For defence of the realm, Henry constructed a series of forts such as this one, basically gun platforms with low circular towers and rounded battlements to present a small, deflective target to cannonballs. It simply housed a garrison and commander. (akg-images/ Bildarchiv Monheim)

Arms
The Sword

The sword remained the favoured arm of the gentleman. Military weapons at the beginning of the 16th century still had long thrusting blades, but were wide enough to deliver a lethal cut from the sharpened edges. The hilt was still essentially a simple cross, the wooden grip bound in cloth or leather and often overlaid by cords or wire either twined round or in a lattice, to help prevent the weapon slipping in the hand. A pommel at the end helped prevent the hand sliding off but more importantly provided a counterbalance to the blade, so that the point of balance was as near to the hand as possible; this made the sword less point-heavy and less tiring to use. Several styles of pommel had been developed, from a simple disc or flanged wheel to a scent-bottle style. This type of cross-hilt continued to be worn with armour by a few enthusiasts until after the third quarter of the 16th century. However, by the beginning of the century some infantry swords had already developed a half loop or a ring to guard the finger hooked over the blunted first section of blade to assist a swing. This form was then seen on the swords of gentlemen. By mid-century swords usually had finger-rings and side-rings, but frequently lacked the knuckle-guards and displayed none of the diagonal guards popular in Continental Europe. The *estoc* was also known in England as the tuck. The blade sometimes had three or even four unsharpened sides to produce a very stiff weapon for maximum thrust. Ordinary followers might simply have sword and buckler.

Blades usually came from Toledo in Spain, northern Italy, or Passau or Solingen in Germany. Smiths put their name or mark on the blade but some added the name of a famous smith or centre of manufacture to fool the unwary. A sword knot of cord or ribbon, forming a loop ending in a tassel, was occasionally added; it could slip over the hand to prevent loss. It was sometimes added either through a hole in the pommel or more commonly round the grip.

A tilting lance traditionally associated with Henry VIII. It is designed to shatter on impact, and to that end is partially hollow inside and fluted on the outside. The leather strip nailed round the butt behind the waisted grip was designed to ram against the lance-rest to prevent the weapon sliding through the armpit. (The Board of Trustees of the Armouries, VII.551)

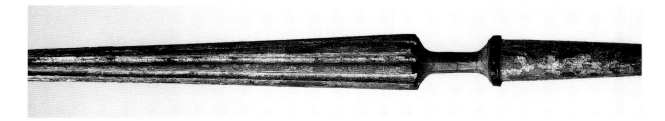

Wearing the Sword

The scabbard was made from two strips of wood covered in leather, cloth or velvet. The covering may sometimes have been made to match a man's clothing, for several are recorded for one sword. A metal chape reinforced the scabbard tip but a locket guarding the mouth was rare. On many scabbards the sides of the mouth were cut away, leaving a piece of the wood at front and back to slip up between the guards and over the ricasso (the dull part of the blade right above the hilt). Elaborate belts were developed to sling the sword from a convenient angle and to prevent the wearer from tripping over it. Early belts followed medieval practice, with three straps or slings to the waist belt, the two rearmost joining the waist belt to the rear; sometimes a single strap here bifurcated to form two connecting points to the scabbard. The front strap usually had an adjusting buckle, and a small hook connecting the strap to a ring on the waist belt became common. However, largely after 1550 the front sling (called a 'side-piece') now crossed the stomach to join the waist belt on the right. The central waist-buckle began to move round to the right hip, and a ring attached to the lower part of a slide replaced the ring on the waist belt. However, some never changed from the left-of-centre attachment. At about the same time the rear

An army in battle-order in the time of Henry VIII. Cavalry screen the main bodies. (Permission British Library)

scabbard slings were given ring attachments to the waist belt; often now these slings joined at the top and used a single hook. Increasingly, each sling was fitted with a slide and the lower end of the sling, having wrapped round the scabbard, was stitched to the central bar of the slide; the scabbard's weight ensured the loop was pulled tight. In the second half of the century the rear slings became joined into a single broad sling of leather or stuff – the hanger – its lower edge divided into as many as 12 straps with slides, wrapped round the scabbard. The side-piece was permanently attached to a leading corner. Hangers were often embroidered to match costume or sword hilt. At first heater-shaped, at the end of the century round-topped versions appeared. At the turn of the 17th century a few swords were worn with knuckle-guard upwards.

An English mounted man-at-arms, perhaps Henry VIII himself. He wears a cloth base and carries a shattered lance. (Permission British Library, Ms Augustus IIIa)

A Greenwich Garniture, c.1580

Based on the blued and gilt Greenwich garniture of the third Earl of Cumberland in the Metropolitan Museum of Art, New York, the main figure wears the armour made up for field use as a heavy cavalryman. Greenwich cuirasses tend to be flat and until about 1585 to overlap one or more waist-lames. A style of gauntlet emerged in which the metacarpal plate extends to guard the base of the thumb and the cuff similarly extends on the inner side under the thumb. The cuff is hinged until very late in the century. Greenwich pauldrons have a 'humpy look', often with a 'blister' near the collarbone covering the pierced lug and pin of the shoulder hasp that connects the breast- and backplates. By the later 16th century laminated cuisses were popular, as here. For heavy field use a reinforcing breastplate was sometimes added, together with a wrapper over the upper bevor.

1 Close-helmet with field visor.

2 In England extra pieces for the tournament were known as 'double pieces', 'pieces of advantage' or 'pieces of exchange'. Pieces for the tilt include the tilt visor with narrow, low-vision-slits. The lower edge of the armet closes over a flanged edge on the collar and locks at the chin. The visor fits into the upper bevor.

3 Grandguard; the hasp on the right attaches on the wearer's left side of the helmet, while the hole on the left of the face-guard fits over the pierced lug on the upper bevor and secures with a split pin. Slots on the chest fit over a staple.

4 The pasguard is secured to the elbow by a split pin through a pierced lug on the couter below. A strap on the grandguard secures the upper half.

5 The manifer straps over the gauntlet, while a strap from the pasguard is buckled through a slot in the cuff. For the tourney a reinforcing breast, wrapper and also a visor reinforce and a locking gauntlet might be worn. For the foot tournament the field armour was given a right pauldron that mirrored the left one rather than being cut away for a lance-rest; leg-armour was removed and a wrapper fitted.

6 One of four matching vamplates for lances.

7 Demi-shaffron to protect the upper part of the horse's head.

8 Matching saddle steels; en suite stirrups were also provided.

9 Cuisse, poleyn, greave and sabaton of a contemporary armour for Sir Henry Lee. The laminated strips around the ankle are a feature of some Greenwich armours. The spur is a fixture.

10 Fastenings.

(Graham Turner © Osprey Publishing)

233

Brigandine of c.1540, probably Italian, in the Metropolitan Museum of Art, New York. Lined with small overlapping plates, men of rank covered the front with rich material such as silk or satin, while the rivet heads were of tinned iron or gilt latten. At first it was fastened down the front (or sides) and over the shoulders, by straps and buckles or lacing; some were laced down the front and sides. By the second quarter of the century side and shoulder fastenings were usual. (Author's collection)

Two cuts in the covering below the mouth allowed smaller scabbards to be inserted that held one or more by-knives and a bodkin. These seem to have sometimes been worn on the inner side or could instead be set in the dagger sheath. The bodkin may have been used to pierce eyelet holes for points. Perhaps in the second quarter of the 16th century a transverse rib developed below the knives, to stop the scabbard sliding through the hanger.

From 1575 the baldric became an alternative way to carry the sword when worn with armour, but it was advisable to wear a waist sash to stop the sword swinging about. In the 1550s and 1560s it was fashionable to wear a matching cloth pouch on the right side, with a metal mount at the mouth, to which was attached the suspension loop. If worn with armour a flap was buttoned over the mouth and the mount discarded.

By the end of the 15th century a sword was increasingly worn with civilian costume and was common after 1530. It now became popular for duelling. The latter had been a way of settling disputes for centuries, but for men of rank it had usually been done in full armour in the lists. Now duels on foot between men in civilian dress became more popular: a way to settle disputes without resorting to expensive equipment. The duelling sword did not need to be as sturdy as a military weapon, since it would be used against an unarmoured opponent; therefore the blade was lighter and grips developed to guard the unprotected hand. The early rapier was simply a long civilian sword whose edged blade might be wider than that of a tuck. It was not until mid-century that the word came to refer to a purely thrusting sword. This move, as opposed to the cut, was now favoured and promoted by Italian fencing masters, where the science of duelling had developed. Those wishing to learn might also consult the manuals such masters produced, and the skill was later also taken up by Spanish masters.

Unlike the military sword, civilian weapons did follow European fashion in developing a more complicated hilt, partly because duellists were unarmoured. Hilts were sometimes simply bright steel, or could be blued by heat treatment or fire-gilt. They might be inlaid with silver plates decorated in relief or with strips along the guards, chiselled or pierced. Engraved silver plates might also be riveted on. The steel could be decorated by chiselling; in the first part of the century a roped design and animal heads were the usual styles. Damascening was sometimes used but counterfeit damascening (inlaying the wire into hatching) was far more common. Encrusting (like damascening but with the precious metal left proud and then engraved or chiselled) first appeared on chiselled hilts mid-century and was the commonest decoration by 1600. Occasionally enamel was employed.

Perhaps the most famous fencing master in England in the later 16th century was the London master, George Silver, who published a treatise entitled *Paradoxes of Defence* in 1599. Silver notes that Italian teachers maintained the English would not hook their forefinger over the cross nor lay the thumb on the blade or the hand on the pommel, because the English hilts lacked protective finger rings; therefore they could not thrust straight. They probably did hook the finger if using an Italian style of hilt.

A Greenwich close-helmet, c.1540, now in the Victoria & Albert Museum, London. A sprung stud locks the visor. (Author's collection)

The opponent's blade might be warded by the left hand or with the cloak wrapped round the arm, which could also be used to envelope the blade. By mid-century, however, a dagger was often carried in the left hand specifically to engage an opponent's sword. A weapon popular during the reign of Henry VIII was the Holbein dagger in fashionable Swiss style. This had a hilt that was shaped like an 'I' made from cast metal and decorated with strapwork and faces. The sheath was of ornamented metal, sometimes of intricate pierced design. By about 1550 a Scottish style of dagger was reportedly popular. A matching sword and dagger might be ordered by wealthier men, the dagger with simple cross-guard and a ring-guard – or, in the second half of the century, a shell – on the outside. Daggers were carried in a sheath on the right side, two staples on the locket attaching to the waist belt. After about 1560 the dagger was usually worn well back. In some cases the locket had a ring either side for two cords with a tassel, 'a venecian tassel of sylke' as Thomas Becon calls it mid-century. Robert Dudley, Earl of Leicester, had cords of silver and gold, blue and gold, black and gold, and crimson silk and gold with matching tassels. Chains, ribbons or a large bow were also seen. Some lockets were also made to take by-knives and a bodkin. False scabbards were common, being leather cases made to cover a sword or rapier scabbard tightly but did not enclose the hilt itself.

The Rapier

When in civilian dress, knights now sometimes wore a rapier. Much ink was spilt at the time in assessing whether the traditional sword or the English tuck was better than these weapons. Sir John Smythe wrote *Instructions, Observations and Orders Mylitarie* in 1591, published four years later. In it he points out that the rapier is too long for a footsoldier to draw in the press of battle or a horseman to draw unless he lets his rein fall, and is not therefore a military weapon. Moreover, the blade was so hard and narrow that it broke when it struck armour. Tucks, however, with their foursquare thrusting blades, he notes as sometimes worn on horseback by men-at-arms and demi-lances, under their thighs in the Hungarian or Turkish manner.

George Silver disliked rapiers, referring to them as 'bird-spits' and, echoing Smythe, he lists all the things they cannot do in battle: pierce a corselet with the point, unlace a helmet, unbuckle armour or cut through pikes. He considers them unsuitable for cutting, excessively long and with inadequate guards. He says that many skilled men using them are wounded because they cannot uncross the weapon without stepping back. Nevertheless, rapiers were becoming popular for wear with civilian dress and their owners had to be trained in their use. For this they went to the foreign fencing masters who were setting up schools in London and who may have provided a further reason for Silver's hostility to the new weapon.

The Articles for the due execution of the *Statutes of Apparell*, of 6 May 1562, was based on a proclamation of 1557. Nobody under the rank of knight was to wear gilt spurs or damascened or gilt sword, rapier or dagger, upon pain of forfeiture and imprisonment and fine. It also stated that no man was to wear a sword, rapier or other weapon over 'one yard and halfe a quarter of blade, at the vttermost: neither any Dagger aboue the length of xii inches in blade: neither any Buckler, with a sharpe point, or with any point aboue two ynches of length'. Forfeiture, imprisonment and fine were the penalty. Officers were empowered to cut down blades exceeding permitted lengths and might be stationed at town gates; in 1580 they nearly caused a diplomatic incident when they stopped the French ambassador at the bars at Smithfield, to the fury of the queen.

Elizabethan Hunting Scene

Hunts were good exercise and provided extra meat. They might be carefully planned to drive the game down to where the huntsmen were waiting, armed with crossbows, bows or wheellocks. Small crossbows were sometimes carried in the saddle; the cord could be drawn back by a cranequin (the handle cranking a ratchet that engaged teeth on the drawing bar to wind it back) or a goat's-foot lever. Crossbows were sometimes even combined with a wheellock. Some small game was killed by blunt heads that prevented the bolt penetrating and literally blowing it apart, although many preferred to hunt birds and small game with falcons and hawks. The most dangerous animal was the wild boar, at the time increasingly rare in England and destined to become extinct during the 17th century. Large mastiffs or alaunts were used to seize the animal by the ears. It could be attacked with a boar-spear furnished with a lug either side of the blade socket to prevent the animal running up the shaft; boar-swords (rare in England) similarly had blades with a bar fitted through a slot near the point. Deer were hunted with greyhounds in couples, or deerhounds. Breaking (cutting up) a deer was a skill and men of good birth would be taught how to dismember a kill as part of their training. Rarely, a trousse might be carried, a kit containing a knife with a cleaver-like blade and various eviscerating implements in slits in the sheath.

(Graham Turner © Osprey Publishing)

Other Weapons

The hand-and-a-half-sword, or bastard sword, continued in use but now even longer weapons were becoming more common. The fearsome-looking two-hand sword was largely designed for infantry use in cutting through ranks of pike shafts to allow those following to break into the enemy formation. The base of the blade might be furnished with two lugs to stop an enemy weapon sliding down, this portion often covered in leather to provide a grip.

The horseman's hammer now often had a steel shaft to prevent cutting, fitted with a hammer-head backed by a diamond-sectioned spike. Maces were more rare, fitted with triangular or curved tubular flanges. Richer examples might be decorated, for example with silver or gold damascening on a blued or russeted ground.

The two royal bodyguards, the Gentlemen-at-Arms and the Yeomen of the Guard, carried pollaxes and partisans respectively on State occasions.

Firearms

The principal gun used by the gentry was the wheellock, which used the spinning action of an abrasive wheel against a piece of iron pyrites to create sparks. The great advantage of the wheellock was that it could be wound up ready for action so that the pistol could be discharged swiftly. For military use a pair of pistols was carried in leather holsters at the saddle bow, but a man of rank would only use these when serving as a captain of cavalry. The other form of lock was the snaphance, in which a flint struck the face of a steel mounted on a pivoted arm. This form of ignition would eventually be modified by amalgamating the pan cover with the steel, to form the flintlock. The snaphance was cheaper than the wheellock, which also had the disadvantage of having the main moving parts inside the breech, making servicing difficult in the field, especially as the parts could break if roughly handled. The English did not at first take up the idea of the cartridge, whereby the powder and ball were tied in a paper cartridge, though from mid-century it began to appear in mainland Europe.

Novelty combination weapons were very occasionally carried, such as swords fitted with a small pistol in the hilt, or horseman's hammers combined with a wheellock pistol similarly firing through the end of the grip.

Sumptuary Laws of Henry VIII

Sumptuary laws were designed to ensure that men's position in society was reflected in their dress and appearance. Henry VIII produced the following version of the laws:

None shall wear … cloth of gold or silver, or silk of purple colour … except … Earls, all above that rank, and Knights of the King (and then only in their mantles). None shall wear … cloth of gold or silver, tinselled satin, silk, cloth mixed or embroidered with gold or silver, or foreign woollen cloth … except … Barons, all above that rank, Knights of the Garter, and Privy Councillors. None shall wear … any lace of gold or silver, lace mixed with gold or silver, silk, spurs, swords, rapiers, daggers, buckles, or studs with gold, silver or gilt … except … Baron's Sons, all above that rank, Gentlemen attending the Queen, Knights and Captains. None shall wear … velvet in gowns, cloaks, coats, or upper garments, or embroidery with silk, or hose of silk … except … Knights, all above that rank, and their heirs apparent. None shall wear … velvet, satin, damask, taffeta, or grosgrain in gowns, cloaks, coats, or upper garments, or velvet in their jerkins, hose or doublets … except … Knight's Eldest Sons and all above that rank.

Horses

Henry VII had banned the sale of good stock abroad in 1495, blaming the Yorkists for this and so causing a shortage of good mounts. At the beginning of the 16th century horses bred for war were similar to those of the previous century, stallions that were deep-chested for good windage, with solid quarters and a thick neck yet still reasonably nimble. They were not especially large by today's standards: one look at the armour made in about 1515 for a horse of Henry VIII confirms that in height it was no more than a hunter. In order to highlight his importance in foreign eyes especially, Henry VIII sent men to find horses in Italy. For the Field of Cloth of Gold in 1520 Henry chose a Neapolitan, but his stables also contained a Frieslander bay from the Duke of Mantua, a horse of the breed of Isabella, Duchess of Milan, from the Duke of Ferrara and 25 Spanish mounts from Emperor Charles V.

Acts were passed to force every owner of an enclosed park to keep two mares in it, each at least of 13 hands (1535), to forbid any stallion less than 15 hands and over the

Opposite:
Brass of Sir Ralph Verney, 1547, now in Aldbury, Herts. He wears a loose heraldic tabard over his armour. (Author's collection)

age of two from being placed in areas where mares and fillies were kept (1540) and to force the nobility to keep specific quotas of horses (1541–42). These latter acts included archbishops and dukes (seven trotting horses for the saddle, each at least three years old and 14 hands high); marquesses, earls and bishops with an income of £1,000 or more (five of these trotting horses); viscounts and barons with an income of £1,000 (three trotting horses); and those with incomes of 500 marks (two trotting horses). Anyone with an income of £100 per year, whose wife wore a silk gown or any French hood or bonnet of velvet, 'with any habiliment, paste, or egg of gold, pearl or stone, or any chain of gold about their neck or in their partlets, or in any apparel of their body' also had to maintain such a trotting horse. The Gentlemen Pensioners created by Henry also had to keep studs, and many received parks taken from dissolved monasteries. Sir Nicholas Arnold received such a park at Highnam, seized from Gloucester, where he maintained Neapolitan warhorses and animals from Flanders. Maintaining a stud was not cheap, not least because fencing, gates and walls had to be maintained to ensure that only desired stallions covered the mares.

Several of the Pensioners wrote treatises on horse breeding and management that reveal Italian ways of thinking that were themselves based on Xenophon's *Hippike*. Other men of position also favoured Italian methods to manage their horses – Robert Dudley, Earl of Leicester, imported a Pavian riding-master, Claudio Corte, during his time as Master of Horse (1558–81) and one Pensioner, Sir Thomas Bedingfield, translated Corte's work. Federigo Grisone published his *Rules of Horsemanship* in Naples (1550); this was translated in England and presented to Dudley. However, Elizabeth railed against poor horse breeding and issued several proclamations.

The new ideas of less powerful but more agile horses for war were gaining ground but never in the 16th century ousted the traditional warhorse that carried fully armoured men, especially in the tilt. More emphasis was now placed on teaching movements such as the

A Greenwich garniture for Henry Herbert, Earl of Pembroke, made 1550–57. The cuirass has an anime breastplate and he wears a close-helmet of burgonet form. This is the most complete Greenwich garniture to survive. Originally the steel was bright, being decorated with etching and gilding. (Glasgow City Council [Museums])

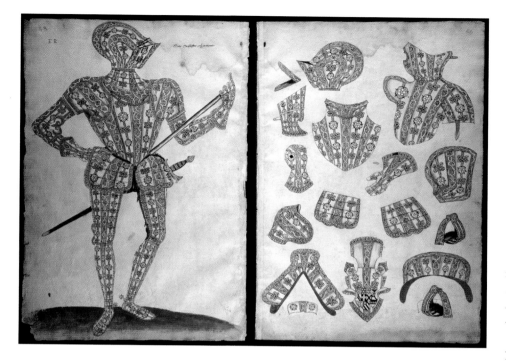

Armour for Sir Christopher Hatton, from the Jacob Album, which contains some 30 design drawings and is named after Jacob Halder, master armourer at Greenwich (1567–1607). This highly decorated garniture could be made up for the tilt using the reinforcing pieces seen on the right. On the left of this second page are a locking-gauntlet and matching pauldron, for the foot tourney; at the bottom are saddle steels and a demi-shaffron complete with coat-of-arms. (Victoria & Albert Museum)

croupade where the back kick is performed when the animal has jumped into the air. This new 'management' was increasingly popular; Corte advocated the use of rings to train and exercise horses: 'for skirmish, for battell, and for combate, either offending or defending. It is also a comelie sight in the rider, and standeth him in steed for the exercise of the turneie, and all other feates of armes.' Veterinary medicine was now making progress in England, largely thanks to the enquiring mind of an illiterate groom in the service of gentlemen, Christopher Clifford, who wrote (one assumes with help) *The Schoole of Horsemanship*, published in 1585. By the end of the century Arabs, Barbs or Spanish jennets were increasingly used in European studs to produce elegant yet swift, strong mounts.

Life on Campaign

Abroad

Knights and lords could find themselves campaigning in several theatres: in 1511 Thomas, Lord Darcy, was sent with about 1,500 archers to assist Ferdinand against the Moors of Barbary (a waste of time). The experienced Sir Edward Poynings, Warden of the Cinque Ports and former Lord Deputy of Ireland, did well when ordered to assist Margaret of Savoy (Maximilian's daughter) against the Duke of Guelders. Men of rank might also be contracted for special duties: Willoughby in 1512 was primarily nominated to be Master of the Ordnance and Artillery. Knights also led scouting parties of cavalry, as in 1513 when Sir John Neville espied the French gathering to launch a relief attempt during the siege of Thérouanne, their company being blundered into by the Earl of Essex and Sir John Peachy while Neville was reporting his findings. In Mary's reign a force under William Herbert, first Earl of Pembroke, was sent to aid the Spanish against a French army. The force included such men as Lord Bray, Ambrose and Robert Dudley, Sir Nicholas Throckmorton, the second Earl of Bedford and Sir Peter Carew, but was too late for the battle of St Quentin on 10 August 1557, when the French were defeated. However, this force played a significant role in the siege of the city that followed. In 1586 Sir Philip Sidney, appointed by Elizabeth to be governor of Flushing in the Netherlands, died of a musket wound in the thigh received at a skirmish against the Spanish at Zutphen.

On the March

Roger Williams in his *Briefe Discourse* says that few captains would force men to march over 15 miles without a break. Troops marched in various formations but it is difficult to know if the flank guards marched in line abreast or in column. Certainly the three wards, van, middle and rear, were used even when transporting the army across the Channel. It made it easier to unload large numbers of men from one ward and have them move off before the next batch of ships arrived. In open country three regiments followed one another, preceded by shot, flanked by archers and columns of artillery, while cavalry screened the army. If a retreat was necessary, Audley's advice was to face the enemy. Turning and running was asking to be cut up without being able to defend oneself.

Experiences in the field depended on forward planning and the stamp of the leaders. Thomas Grey, Marquess of Dorset, sent by Henry to join Ferdinand's troops in the invasion of Guienne (1511), was incompetent: food and pay were lacking and there was near mutiny (also because Ferdinand changed his mind). At the inquest the leaders were kept on their knees until they begged to stand, and were proved guilty.

Armour of a demi-lance, a three-quarter harness made for the Earl of Pembroke, at Greenwich in about 1555. (The Board of Trustees of the Armouries, II.137)

Rations and Supply

The army's rations highlighted differences in rank. The ordinary soldiers ate the hardest bread, multi-coloured butter and flyblown meat. The knights and lords ate the finer white bread and fresher butter and meat. While they might drink fine wines, the rank and file were sustained on daily rations of beer and ale, safer to drink than water. However, over-imbibing in Spain led to a revolt by men under Dorset while on an expedition in 1512. The armies that invaded the Continent were too large to live off the land alone and thus supply trains were a necessity. Men of rank found themselves in charge of escorting these vital parts of Henry's military machine, and not without incident, for the French chose to target them instead of risking pitched battle. In 1513 daily convoys from Calais supplied the English van and rear camped near Thérouanne, as they waited for the arrival of the middle ward, one of which convoys was seized.

In Elizabeth's reign food supply remained a problem. Keeping garrisons fed in Ireland or the Netherlands was difficult. As soon as Leicester arrived in the Low Countries he sent to England for rations so that food was available in case there were weather problems later with short notice requests.

Replacing deserters, or sick or deceased soldiers, was a headache for captains. Short campaigns were less of a problem than areas in permanent occupation, such as Ireland or the Netherlands, where levies had to be sent from England. Francis Walsingham reckoned that about 1,000 men could be found by recruiting English volunteers from Dutch regiments. In 1594 the Privy Council ruled that the captain should be responsible for immediate replacement of anyone leaving the company. Funding for a new man was provided as a man's pay for a month and came from fines taken for deficiencies of equipment. However, this replacement had to take place within two months and the recruit be notified to the muster master. The uniform allowance for the lost soldier was also provided (gauged at the beginning of the season to his departure date) to pay for equipment and arms. Wherever possible this money was only paid out once the new man was with the company. In Ireland civilians were offered enrolment so numbers were not a problem, except that the companies lacked English soldiers.

The defences of Berwick, rebuilt during Mary's reign. Low, thick earth banks faced with stone walls absorbed cannonballs; they were set with broad arrow bastions allowing guns to criss-cross their fire and rake the ditches. (Author's collection)

Clothing of levies depended partly on the lord lieutenant. The white coats of Henry VIII's time gave way to uniforms of many hues; costs and provision of coats were down to the county. In the Netherlands officers had a doublet of Milan fustian faced with taffeta, a pair of broadcloth Venetians trimmed with silk and lined with cotton and linen, and worsted stockings. For winter wear there was a broadcloth cassock lined with baize

The Battle of the Spurs, 16 August 1513

The army of Henry VIII was besieging the French town of Thérouanne when a French force hoping to relieve it found itself facing the main English army. Rebuffed by artillery, it then found the English heavy horse bearing down on it, and decided the best course lay in a fast retreat across the fields near Guingate, thus giving the battle its name. It was asserted that this was a ploy to lure the English into a trap but no ambush was forthcoming. The knights of both sides wear armets and close-helmets and colourful cloth bases around their waists. In this period decorative horse caparisons often concealed steel armour. (Graham Turner © Osprey Publishing)

and faced with taffeta. Buckhurst thought that only colonels and above should be allowed silk and lace; captains should make do with fustian, cloth and canvas and spend on arms rather than clothing. Digges and Cecil commented adversely on the captains' love of silks and jewels. Early in Elizabeth's reign 'coat money' was paid for uniform and 'conduct money' for expenses from point of assembly to point of embarkation. Corruption was noted in many places – some captains purloined clothing allowances. Eventually they were stopped from being involved in uniform distribution.

Corruption in the Army

Corruption was the biggest drawback to making Elizabeth's army noteworthy; it was found from the highest to the lowest levels, but was endemic among the officers, including men of rank. The Council did increasingly monitor local authorities, particularly after 1585 and Elizabeth's entry into the war in Europe. Tougher demands were balanced by more concern for ordinary soldiers. Musters gave captains opportunities for selling releases. Lords lieutenant organized musters but where there were none commissioners were deferred to, selected from justices of the peace and other prominent gentlemen and commissioned by the Queen with a detailed set of instructions. Unfortunately captains used their time to enrich themselves and made it hard for any honest muster-master. It was for service in Ireland that deception was greatest. After levying in Chester and once clear of the area, a captain exacted payments from the new recruits and left them with their equipment (also probably paid for); he now had their conduct money as well. He then briefly hired the correct number of 'soldiers' from local civilians in order to pass muster; the equipment was returned to await the next muster. The captain then went to Ireland and could try for passage money as well; shortfalls – every place in a company in some cases – were covered up for musters by drawing on other companies or engaging native Irishmen. Pay, known as imprests, was also in the captain's hands, given weekly as a proportion that was made up every six months. The trouble was that the old feudal idea of men in control of their contingents had not been shaken off, despite re-organization in the army where the state was in charge of recruitment and wages. Corruption went to high levels: Sir George

Carey was dabbling in fraud in Ireland, while Sir Henry Sidney was arranging for a number of new servants to be paid out of the concordatum fund that was designed for unexpected payments but not of the type Sir Henry had in mind.

The corruptions of captains and others were on the agenda in the 1589 Normandy campaign, with strict penalties for those caught. However, the brisk muster by Lord Buckhurst came to nought when the troops found themselves stuck in camp because the embarkation was postponed. Then there was the farcical argument by Captain Cosbie that the men should all look similarly smart with new Spanish morions instead of the

Walter Devereux, first Earl of Essex (dated 1572), wearing a German armour. The pauldrons, now attached to the vambraces, are buckled to the collar. Leather tabs called pickadils can be seen around the edges. (The Print Collector/HIP/ TopFoto)

Italian form with high crest while – even more shocking – some were black while others were not. The pikemen, moreover, had not been supplied with peascod breastplates. So indignant was he that he had the troops throw away their arm-defences and only carry helmet and cuirass. Cosbie even moaned about the lack of stockings in Sussex.

Discipline in Tudor Armies

Discipline was quite high in the Tudor army of 1513. The penalties for misdemeanours such as falling asleep on duty were usually simple fines, however, and nothing like the torture and execution that appear in Elizabeth's reign. Much of the trouble seemed to stem from the German troops under Henry's command. On 15 August there was a riot in the camp near Aire-sur-Lys that resulted in many men dead on both sides. It would have been worse had not the senior officers charged in to break it up, an act for which they were commended by Maximilian.

At first the king simply looked at the last disciplinary code and, after discussion with his commanders, made any necessary alterations, with no oath of obedience necessary from the soldiery. There is no code known for the expedition to Scotland in 1560. By the second quarter of the century company commanders were expected to swear in each man. Issuing such codes meant they could be tailored to the occasion. Leicester's code of 1585 for service in the Netherlands is one of the most imposing, beginning with a demand that every man receiving pay be bound by the articles. Discipline was usually the responsibility of the high marshal and provost marshal, and their greatest problem was desertion. Even hanging deserters as an example did not stop the rot. Matters were compounded by captains wanting leave; though the general or garrison commander would sign a pass for pressing matters at home, where no such need was apparent the captains simply went anyway. Shortage and irregularities in pay sparked off mutinies: in Ireland it was simmering almost non-stop. The mutiny in Ostend in 1588 even involved the gentlemen volunteers, and their grievances included ghastly victuals and bad quarters. They seized the governor, Sir John Conway, and despite royal sympathy Conway eventually brought in new troops and hanged one man from each of the nine companies involved.

Arguments and duels of honour marked out the men of rank. Two of Willoughby's colonels, Sir William Drury and Sir John Burgh, disagreed over precedence in the parade before King Henry. Two further arguments finally led to a duel in which Drury was seriously wounded in the arm. It was amputated and he died two days later.

Field Medicine

The great English medical humanist was Thomas Linacre, founder of the Royal College of Physicians and physician to Henry VII and Henry VIII. He translated the works of Galen and others; Renaissance medical learning began to appear in England. If barbed arrowheads were used they had to be flattened with pincers before extraction. If deeply embedded in a wound the head might be pushed right out the other end and snapped off. Gunshot wounds were probed to locate a ball before slender pincers were inserted to grasp it; tatters of clothing also had to be removed. Bullets were thought to poison a wound, and so it was cleansed by pouring boiling elder oil into it. This caused terrible pain and often resulted in fever and inflammation. The great French surgeon, Ambroise Paré ran out of oil on one occasion and instead resorted to the old method of egg yolk and turpentine; he discovered this had far better effects, but his methods were slow to catch on everywhere. Boiling oil seems sometimes to have been used to cleanse other wounds as well. Cannonballs and bullets could smash a bone, so amputation was a general answer. The operation might be swift, with screws used to compress blood vessels above the site of the operation, but there was little knowledge of cleanliness and none of bacteria. In order to remove a leg, the patient might sit on a chair with the limb laid on a bench. A surgeon's assistant might hold the patient from behind while another sat astride the leg to hold it above the site of operation; a third held the lower part of the limb up slightly clear of the bench. Paré also switched from the practice of using hot irons to seal bleeding arteries, instead tying them with ligatures. Where possible, broken limbs could be set between wooden splints. Dislocations were treated in much the same way as today. Pain might be numbed by pressing the nerve in the neck, administering poppy juice or even giving a strong drink of liquor.

A close-helmet of c.1570 probably evolving from a 'sparrow's-beak' form. Both were to be found in English churches and suggest English work under Italian influence. Staples and sneck hooks are generally used to secure movable pieces. (Author's collection)

The Knight in Battle

In the early 16th century warfare was waged in much the same way as it had been in the previous century. When knights remained mounted they served as the shock troops of the army, using their heavy horses and lances to punch a hole through enemy ranks. However, light cavalry was also used for scouting and skirmishing, with a light spear that was not couched under the arm. The number of men of knightly rank should not be exaggerated. At Flodden in 1513 only one of the Earl of Surrey's 500 retainers was a man-at-arms. The rest of the infantry was made up of missile troops, hedges of pikemen and billmen. Henry VIII insisted that men practise regularly with the bow but it was really a losing battle. Groups of handgunners were increasing in number, armed with either heavy muskets or lighter calivers.

In Audley's opinion, the bigger the army, the less shot (archers and handgunners) was required. These should be set around the other infantry three, four or five deep, two archers and two handgunners if four, but an extra archer if five. Having been harangued by the king and reminded of the plentiful coffers by the treasurer-at-war, the soldiers were roused by their captains, given food and drink and reminded that God was on their side. The council of war would presumably decide the order of battle: a square (the 'just square'), a rectangle (the 'broad rectangle') or more complex, such as the 'saw-tooth'. It is not certain how commands passed down the ranks but perhaps the sergeant was becoming a useful link in that chain of command. One formation placed wings of handgunners to filter the enemy on to the main body, as archers had done in the 14th century.

p.252:
The Greenwich garniture of Robert Dudley, Earl of Leicester, c.1575. It is embossed with the ragged staff badge of Warwick, which, together with the etched borders, was originally gilded. The horse's shaffron has a bear and ragged staff on the central plate. The armour is already fitted with a tilt visor and a manifer to reinforce the left hand; not illustrated are the grandguard and pasguard for the tilt. (The Board of Trustees of the Armouries II.81/HIP/TopFoto)

France

Supplying the army on campaign resulted in a number of clashes with varying outcomes. On 27 June 1513 the English supply train bound for the camp at Thérouanne, having reached Guines safely, set off under the eyes of Sir Edward Belknap and 300 men. It was joined by Sir Nicholas Vaux, captain of Guines castle, with a further 24 horse and 36 foot. Near Ardres the cavalry stopped behind to drink and the infantry became more ragged, little knowing a French force, concealed in the woods, was watching. Choosing their moment they fell on the hapless wagons; the carters cut the traces and fled on the carthorses. The English cavalry made a hopeless effort but the archers used the cover of the wagons to hold off the enemy until their arrows ran out. Sir Nicholas failed in his attempt to rally the foot and both knights had to beat a retreat towards Guines, leaving many dead behind them, not to mention the entire supply train. Sir Rees ap Thomas set out from Thérouanne with his light horse but too late – the French had removed the wagons. Henry's commanders learned a bitter lesson: discipline was stepped up and numbers increased significantly, though attacks continued. The battle of the Spurs, however, (so-named from the fact that the French cavalry soon decided to quit the field, with the English horse in hot pursuit) resulted from a French attempt to resupply

The battle of the Spurs, 1513. The English cavalry charge is depicted on the left, with beleaguered Thérouanne and siege camp behind. (Topham Picturepoint/TopFoto)

The Bataile of Spurs anno·

Thérouanne. Henry VIII (at this engagement surrounded by a bodyguard of mounted archers rather than gentlemen) took Maximilian's advice and placed light artillery pieces along a hill to guard the English mounted scouts. The English archers appear to have begun the French debacle but the cavalry sent them into full retreat. Cruickshank suggested that the panic might have been caused by a general fear of the English. The Venetian ambassador said of the Earl of Shrewsbury that he came from the family of Talbot and to that day the French still threatened crying babies with the Talbots.

Scotland

In Scotland the English faced pikemen trained by French captains. Flodden in 1513 was the last major battle in Britain in which the longbow would take any great part. At Flodden the English cannon were hurried into position with commendable speed after marching round a bog. The damage done by the artillery on either side was not convincing, although it seems to have helped unsettle the Borderers and Huntly's Highlanders on the Scottish left, for they moved from their elevated position to launch the first charge. The English archers made some inroads on lightly armed Scots on the left and right of the line, but others were more heavily armoured and thus took fewer casualties. It was the disciplined stand of the English columns that told most on the Scots, since the latter had always had a tendency to break if unsuccessful in the first rush. They were helped by the Scottish pikes, which might hold off horsemen but English billmen on foot hacked a way through by slicing the tops from the unwieldy pikes. Stanley's column may have displayed an early example of fire and movement – keeping enough troops to occupy the Highlanders' front while slipping the rest round to hit their flank.

The battle of Pinkie Cleuch in 1547 has been called the first modern battle in Britain, since both sides used large numbers of pikemen and handgunners. The English also backed their army with an accompanying fleet, which bombarded the left of the Scots position from the Firth of Forth. Now archers, handgunners and artillery combined to stop and reverse the oncoming pike formations once the English cavalry had been repulsed. Spanish horse also galloped along and poured fire into their position. Such was the destruction that some 6,000 Scots were killed as opposed to 800 Englishmen. The victory allowed Somerset to establish garrisons in many places, but the cost of maintaining them was high and their presence alienated the natives. French pressure finally forced their abandonment in 1549. These defeats show that the disparate elements of the Scottish armies made cohesion difficult. Some, like the Highlanders and Borderers at Flodden, lacked the discipline to stand under fire and threw away their advantage in a wild charge.

With so few of knightly rank present it may be thought there was little work for such people, but many knights still led from the front. At Flodden the flight of the Cheshire contingent left gaps that were exploited by the Scottish pikes, but knights such as Sir William FitzWilliam and Sir John Lawrence stood with their men and died to keep the enemy at bay. Edmund Howard was unhorsed twice or possibly more as he tried to reach his brother the Lord Admiral. Several knights were captured, including Sir Henry Grey. At Pinkie the English heavy horse and demi-lancers crashed into the Scottish pikes. Lord Arthur Grey of Wilton had led the cavalry and came out with a pike wound in the mouth and throat. Sir Andrew Flammach just managed to hold on to the royal standard, assisted by Sir Ralph Coppinger, a Gentleman Pensioner, although the snapped staff was seized by the Scots.

Religious Conflict, Ineptitude and Rebellion

Religious unrest provided much of the exercise for English armies in the 16th century. Under Henry VIII this was largely due to the dissolution of the monasteries, which sparked the Pilgrimage of Grace in 1536–37.

In 1549 John Kett's rebels were slaughtered at Dussindale by the Earl of Warwick. The 1549 southern revolts were a reaction to the spread of Protestantism, while in Elizabeth's reign the flight to England of Mary, Queen of Scots, saw the Northern Rebellion in 1569. Alarming as these were, the rebels lacked the calibre and the equipment of the men sent against them. The English nobility did not generally back the rebellions.

War in Elizabeth's reign was somewhat hampered by the queen's natural tendency to hold back from committing her troops even after ordering an advance. This stemmed from her belief that battles could be lost and the consequences might then be infinitely worse. It stopped her commanders from being given free rein to capitalize on a promising situation. Elizabeth was not wholly to blame for lacklustre performance – indecision and bickering pervaded the entire hierarchy of command, while few of her generals showed any great aptitude in prosecuting war. One such episode took place during the invasion of Scotland in 1560, itself held up for three months, though the lapse was used to prop up the Scottish rebels and boost supplies for the English. At the siege of Leith, French forces came out and challenged the English during truce negotiations, but were successfully pushed back first by artillery and then by heavy horse. However, Lord Grey made no attempt to draw the whole force further out and cut off its retreat; only some French footsoldiers were accidentally caught out after chasing their enemies too far. The assault on the defences was worse: artillery failed to create wide enough breaches and flanking fire had not been dealt with adequately; all this occurred after Sir Ralph Saddler, Sir James Crofts and Kirkaldy of Grange had viewed the breach and advised Grey of the futility of an attack. To make matters worse, wall heights had been misjudged so that scaling ladders used against undamaged sections of wall were far too short. Grey blamed the Duke of Norfolk, a lacklustre self-promoter, who readjusted the facts to clear himself, though both men were to blame. Grey had actually suggested at one point that Edinburgh was an easier target, though an attack would have jeopardized the regent and friendly Scots there.

In 1569 the earls of Northumberland and Westmorland raised a northern rebellion in favour of Mary, Queen of Scots. It was crushed when Lord Clinton and Robert Dudley, Earl of Leicester, marched to support the Earl of Sussex in York. Lord Hunsdon quelled a smaller rebellion in 1570. The Earl of Sussex invaded Scotland that year to chase the Borderers who had aided the Northern Rebellion and to back anti-French feeling.

Foreign Assistance

In 1572, 300 volunteers crossed to the Low Countries, soon aided by Sir Humphrey Gilbert with 1,200 additional volunteer troops, to block Spanish occupation of the country. Further foreign adventures occurred, beginning in 1585 when the Earl of Leicester was sent to the Netherlands to assist the Dutch against the Spanish. In 1589 Peregrine Bertie, Lord Willoughby, an able soldier who had proved his ability in the Netherlands, was sent to assist the Protestant Henry of Navarre to keep the French throne. The expedition should have been called off in late September when help was no longer required but Willoughby, with thoughts of honour in a glorious expedition, ignored the message from Sir Edward Stafford and set sail. Once in France the English troops joined those of Henry IV of France and set out on 11 October; in 40 days and with full kit they marched 227 miles in cold, wet weather with muddy roads, little rest and sniping from French country folk who prevented attempts to leave in search of food. The suburbs of Paris fell but the king refused to seize the city itself for fear of damage and loss of good will; of 20 towns invested only four put up any resistance. Vendome fell to artillery fire that breached the walls. Le Mans fell to barrage, Willoughby ordering bridges of barrels lashed to ladders to take his men over the river on their side.

A woodcut from Derricke's *Image of Ireland* shows an English force with demi-lancers in three-quarter armour, pikemen and caliver men. (British Library)

At Alençon, Willoughby and his marshal made a special engine to pull down the drawbridge, enabling the fort to be seized, though their machine was lost the night before it could be employed on the town drawbridge. Although the king's troops were repulsed from the walls the garrison surrendered. The final stronghold, Falaise, was bombarded until two breaches were made, both so dangerous that a few enemy soldiers could hold them. Yet the French, together with English officers and gentlemen (their main force being some miles away), seized them and opened the gates. A lone musketeer carried on firing until five cannon blasted his tower into the moat, from which he escaped, albeit a prisoner. The success for Henry was little owed to the English and Willoughby had lost more men from illness and hostile peasants than from battle. It is doubtful if the once-feared name of the English soldiery still had much impact.

Peregrine Bertie, Lord Willoughby d'Eresby, resting in a Greenwich armour. A later copy. (The Board of Trustees of the Armouries I.67/HIP/TopFoto)

The only real battle in which Elizabethan troops were involved took place at Nieuport, Holland, on 2 July 1600. Sir Francis Vere had brought over an English regiment to assist Prince Maurice of Nassau and acquitted himself well on 24 January 1598, when he pursued the Spanish invaders. Having ordered Dutch musketeers to keep up fire along the trees, he skirmished with the enemy squares. When the prince's cavalry arrived Vere charged the rear of the squares while the prince took the flanks. The Spanish musketeers fled and the allies got among the pikes. The Dutch cavalry chased after the retreating Spaniards but Vere held his horsemen to check the counterattack he knew would come. Sure enough, Spanish horse came after the Dutchmen but turned back when they saw Vere. In July 1600 a major clash occurred by the dunes near the sea, nine miles from Ostend. Vere held two ridges with his advanced guard to wear down the Spaniards but as things grew hot the reinforcements did not arrive and some 1,600 English troops found themselves holding back the whole Spanish army. Wounded twice in the leg, Vere encouraged his men but was forced to withdraw. When word finally reached the rear, counterattacks were launched that caught the tired Spaniards and broke them.

Three large naval and military expeditions also took place. In 1589 Sir Francis Drake and Sir John Norreys went to Portugal to annoy the Spanish and perhaps seize it back for the pretender Don Antonio. In 1596 the Earl of Essex and Lord Howard (the Lord Admiral of Armada fame) landed at Cadiz. It was an opportunity to make large amounts from plunder, not just for the nobles (indeed, Essex and Howard mainly funded it with this reimbursement in mind) but also for the ordinary soldiers. The target was decided as Cadiz and Sir Francis Vere, the veteran commander in the Netherlands, withdrew 2,000 tried troops from there to provide experience in the force destined for Spain. Vere was desperate to go in first at dawn and even cut his cable when the anchor jammed in order to beat Sir Walter Raleigh. Essex and Vere landed to survey the beachhead before ordering in the first wave (of the better fighting men). Sir Conyers Clifford was sent to seize the narrow eastern peninsula and block Spanish help. A Spanish body attacked the assault force but retreated back, clambering over the rampart. This advertisement of entry was not lost and English troops followed and gained the wall top. Essex then joined them, to be confronted by a 20ft drop, but luckily Vere had sent men round to find and force a gate, which they did. The message being lost he charged the main gates with his main force and broke in. Essex, having arrived by this less precipitous route, then impetuously charged into the market place with only 30 or so men, but luck prevailed and the methodical Vere who called in his own soldiers as he advanced was then able to scatter opposition and join up with Essex and capture the town and castle within a day.

Field Medicine, 1522

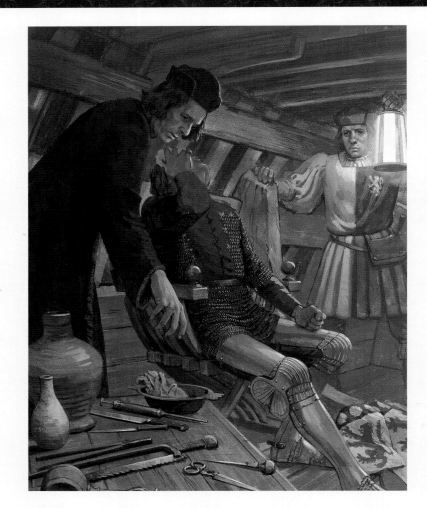

In 1522 John Russell, gentleman, landed with an English raiding party on the coast of Brittany and attacked the town of Morlaix. A culverin shattered the gate and the English made a rush that broke through into the streets beyond. During the attack John was wounded by an arrow and lost the sight in his right eye. However the town was captured and, on returning to his ship, he and several others were knighted by the admiral, Sir John Howard. This scene shows him being treated on board ship by a surgeon, with his equipment on the table. Sir John Russell would subsequently become first Earl of Bedford in 1550 under instructions left in the will of Henry VIII, for services to the crown. (Graham Turner ©️ Osprey Publishing)

Conflict in Ireland

In Ireland the English experience differed from that in mainland Europe. English troops stationed there from Elizabeth's early reign faced Shane O'Neill's uprising in 1567 and the Desmond War of 1579–83. At first Irish soldiers were equipped with close-combat weapons together with bows and javelins. However, later in the century Hugh O'Neill, Earl of Tyrone, had welded together a force equipped with muskets and calivers and including many men trained in Spain; not only were the Irish well drilled in pikes and musketry but they used the boggy, woody terrain to advantage. In 1594 the Nine Years War broke out and the tactics were put to good use. At the Ford of the Biscuits near Enniskillen the English were defeated, as they were next year at Clontibret and Curlew Hills. In 1598 O'Neill ambushed another English force on the march at Yellow Ford and caused heavy casualties by both musketry and close combat. Provoked, the Earl of Essex arrived with another army in 1599, but O'Neill had the good sense to bide his time and wait. Next year Essex was replaced by Lord Mountjoy, who thought brutality was an effective weapon. He also tried to pen the cattle and so starve the Irish rebels but his move on Ulster on 2 October 1600 was defeated at Moyry Pass by fire from O'Neill's musketeers protected behind field fortifications. Mountjoy moved to confront a Spanish force of 3,500 men that landed at Kinsale in September 1601 and, weakened by sickness, would have fared badly if O'Neill's relief force had blockaded him when it arrived. However, although not in the kind of terrain that suited Celtic fighting, O'Neill decided to take the offensive. He bungled a night march against the English camp and Mountjoy reacted swiftly. The cavalry chased the Irish horse from the field while the Irish infantry, ordered into Spanish squares by O'Neill, could not cope efficiently. O'Neill's change to the tactical defensive, as opposed to the strategic defence of Ulster and the tactical offensive, had been more than his men could achieve; one defeat had broken the spell of O'Neill's victories. Two years later he surrendered. This folly, together with poor command structure, had come up against a powerful royal army backed by naval support.

Chivalry

The code of chivalry was still alive. Fighting for honour and for the good, to protect women and the poor, had always been an ethos that some knights aspired to and others ignored. Battlefields were now largely the preserve of professional soldiers, with even less room for knights to display chivalry, partly because there were fewer knights involved in active warfare. In the Middle Ages no self-respecting knight used a bow or crossbow in battle as a matter of course; by the later 16th century Sir John Smythe was being depicted in the Jacob Album with pistol in hand, hardly a weapon for close combat. Those men of the rank of knight still felt part of an elite group but it included many ranks of society, from the king down through his dukes and earls to lesser landowners and men from mercantile backgrounds who had done good service. Wealth and position in society no longer devolved purely from landholding. Knights were at first still made by other knights, such as when Charles Brandon dubbed John Dudley in 1523 for his valour at the crossing of the Somme. But knights finally lost this right during the reign of Elizabeth, when all applications had to be passed to the Privy Council for vetting.

The panoply of chivalry continued in its most sensationalist form at the meeting of Henry VIII and Francis I of France at the celebrated Field of Cloth of Gold near Calais, in 1520. Lavish banquets, fountains of wine, tournaments, archery and even wrestling between the two kings made a magnificent pageant that attempted to offer the idea of friendship. Chivalry could also be seen in the field – in 1589 the Earl of Essex rammed his pike into the gates of Lisbon to offer single combat on behalf of his mistress. Bravado could be lethal, however – at Zutphen in 1586, Sir Philip Sidney's decision to follow the new thinking and leave off limb-defences resulted in his death. Sir John Smythe felt that, had Sidney worn his cuisses, the musket ball would have been sufficiently slowed down and not broken his thighbone.

Royal prisoners, dukes, lieutenants general, great constables etc. belonged to Henry and it was a capital offence for anyone else to hold them for ransom or free them. They must be taken to the king or commander immediately in return for a reward. The notion of chivalric behaviour survived most noticeably in siege warfare. A herald would formally demand surrender and, if refused, would appear once more before the siege began in earnest. The garrison at Thérouanne was allowed to march out (23 August 1513) although this could have been also because of their strong position. Jousts between six gentlemen on both sides were run under the walls of Thérouanne in 1534, on the invitation of Sir John Wallop whose troops were moving through the area destroying the countryside.

William Caxton had printed Raimon Llull's *The Book of the Ordre of Chyvalry or Knyghthode* in about 1484, and in 1485 printed Sir Thomas Malory's eight romances under the title *Le Morte d'Arthur*. In 1523 John Bourchier, Lord Berners, under the command of Henry VIII himself, translated the works of Froissart with a similar aim: to inspire valiant deeds. These books gave the hope that chivalry could be revived as

Greenwich burgonet with octagonal skull, c.1590, with a barred face-guard hinged at the brow. (The Board of Trustees of the Armouries/HIP/TopFoto)

it had once been; indeed such medieval works managed in England to survive the Renaissance, even though its classical leanings spelled the end of chivalric literature across the Channel in France. Already in a newly Protestant England Roger Ascham in *The Scholemaster* regretted the day when Malory's work was read in the court at the expense of the Bible, and linked the Middle Ages with Catholicism, when chivalric works came from idle monks and wanton canons. By the time Edmund Spenser published his *Faerie Queene* (1590–96) chivalry was a reminder of 'antique times', now becoming a memory. In Spain, Cervantes' *Don Quixote* of 1605 was the greatest literary knock to the ideals of chivalry, which would also soon disappear from 17th-century Puritan England, until revived in the 19th century.

The End of the Knight

Knighthood is alive and well. Through the 400 years covered by this book it had gone from a social rank held by hard riding warriors to one held by men versed in court etiquette, many of whom never saw real action. The image posed by the literary figures of the time might be inspirational but there were many who ignored chivalric ideals unless dealing with men of equal rank and sometimes not even then.

The very ethos of the armoured man on horseback with his lance had, over the centuries, come crashing into ignominious failure time and again across Europe. The French were plagued by English arrows at numerous encounters and soon realised that charging longbowmen head on with mounted knights was madness. Ordinary Flemish footmen crushed mounted French knights at Courtrai with their fearful maces. The hedgehogs of Scottish and Flemish pikemen proved a formidable obstacle to mounted men but the latter could be a useful cover for their own horsemen. The Swiss had made a name for themselves with their pikes and lethal halberds, creating a form of warfare which was taken up by Germans and soon became widespread across Europe. Added to that, the technology of guns and gunpowder was improving and would prove a significant addition to the battlefield. The German knights were flayed by artillery and handguns during the Hussite Wars of the 15th century. Bullet-proof armour could be worn, but it was heavier than normal armour as the metal had to be thickened or given extra layers. The weight meant that it tended to be reserved for the protection of vital areas. Bullets might still punch through limb armour and cause severe wounds, while mobile field guns on the battlefield could do more damage: one such caused the Earl of Arundel to lose a foot and subsequently die. Moreover the knightly lance could not get through the

Elizabeth I is taken to Whitehall. Painting of c.1580, attributed to Robert Peake. (akg-images)

Robert Radcliffe, Earl of Sussex, c.1590, wearing armour for foot combat over the barrier. The right pauldron is not cut away for a lance and there is no lance-rest. Leg-armour is discarded since blows below the barrier are forbidden. Note the elaborate helmet plume. He holds a pike, while his sword scabbard has the side-piece attached to the broad hanger, which in turn has been unhooked from its ring at his belt. (The Board of Trustees of the Armouries I.36/HIP/TopFoto)

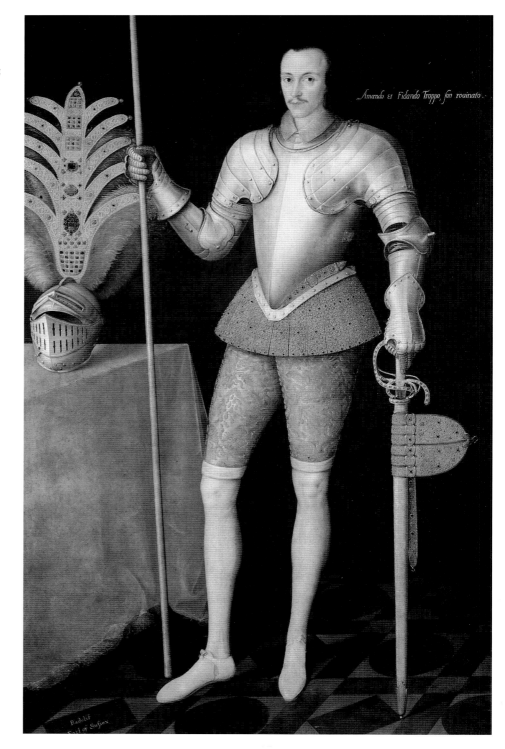

Amando et Fidando Troppo son rouinato.

massed ranks of even longer pikes. Vulnerable to gunfire, ineffective against the massed pikeheads, the *raison d'être* of the knight on the battlefield was placed in question. As the 17th century dawned the armoured knight also faced lighter, pistol-wielding cavalry. By the opening battle of the English Civil Wars the heavily armoured horsemen, not necessarily knights, were seen to be a relic of the past and bowed out from the scene. It was obvious that the title itself now meant little in warfare except to denote a man of breeding and training, usually one of the officers in the army. Already in the mid-15th century Jean de Bueil in *Le Jouvencel* saw that the training and efficiency of the soldier was the key to military success, not some chivalric glory. The knight as the great armoured steam-roller scything through infantry was a memory.

Similarly, the knight's traditional home, the castle, declined in importance during the 14th and 15th centuries. The defensive qualities of a fortress such as Bodiam in Sussex, for example, have been questioned and few castles played a major part in the Wars of the Roses. Even when gunpowder arrived in the 14th century, English castles showed little in the way of major development, unlike those seen in some Continental countries. The more stable conditions in England contributed to the decline of the castle in the later Middle Ages, with knights increasingly preferring to live most of the time in their private houses.

Critics had always pointed the finger at knighthood for failing to live up to the ideals of chivalry. Cruelty and brutality were evident even among princes of chivalry, against those people who were not members of the 'club', the ordinary men, women and children of a defeated populace. Tempers frayed during long sieges, too. In the 15th century the older ideal of courtly love had essentially been replaced by the view that love prevented the knight from doing his job. When peace descended, knighting itself might be waived; the unrest of the Hundred Years' War in France tempted knights to take advantage of the weak. In Germany many knights were poor and similarly turned to robbery, also citing their right to private war. Despite the best efforts of the church, chivalry was a concept that sat more easily on some shoulders than on others. Various writers strove to inspire the fighting elite with stirring tales such as Thomas Malory's *Le Morte d'Arthur*, where the emphasis lay on moral values. Increasingly men aspiring to knighthood might not have lineage going back generations, which in some areas of Europe had been a prerequisite. Some now hailed from free peasant stock, such as Sir John Paston, grandson of a peasant educated so well in law that he had become a justiciar. Castiglione's *The Book of the Courtier*, published in 1528, was a study of the new gentleman, a man no longer interested in chivalry but who wanted to know how to make a good life for himself. Though Italian,

p.267:
The three-quarter armour of the third Earl of Southampton, made in France c.1598. The blued steel is decorated with an all-over etched and gilt design of laurels, snakes, birds and insects.
(The Board of Trustees of the Armouries II.360/HIP/TopFoto)

265

Knight, c.1590

This figure is wearing a three-quarter Greenwich armour based on that of Sir James Scudamore in the Metropolitan Museum of Art, New York. It is fitted with a burgonet and falling-buffe. This is a medium field armour, the type worn by a demi-lance; the lighter lance meant that no lance-rest was needed.

1 Burgonet with falling-buffe, from a Greenwich armour of Sir Henry Lee. The buffe slots over a rectangular lug each side of the burgonet and a hook on the hasp fits through a pierced lug on the burgonet.

2 Burgonet of Lord Buckhurst fitted with face grille, c.1590.

3 Target, from the design for an armour for Sir Henry Lee. Targets were inspired by Spanish shields and were sometimes carried before an officer. In battle they could be used to deflect pikeheads.

4 Rapier, probably English, c.1600, the hilt encrusted with silver. The scabbard is fitted to receive a by-knife and a bodkin, the latter perhaps for piercing eyelets for points.

5 Left-hand dagger, probably English, c.1600.

6 Fencing with sword and dagger.

7 Wheellock pistol, late 16th century. This uses the spinning action of an abrasive wheel against a piece of iron pyrites to create sparks and touch off the powder in the priming pan, which then flashes through a hole into the barrel to ignite the main charge. A spanner winds up the wheel, and winds a small chain round the axle that connects to a now-tensed spring. Pressing the trigger releases the spring that pulls on the chain, so unwinding it and spinning the wheel. The iron pyrites is held in the jaws of a pivoting cock that rests on top of a pan cover. As the wheel spins, a cam swings the pan cover open to reveal the priming powder in the pan. As the pyrites falls against the spinning wheel the sparks set off the charge.

8 English snaphance pistol, dated 1593. A flint attached to the jaws of a cock is forced back against a spring and swung down when the trigger releases the spring. The flint strikes the face of a steel mounted on a pivoted arm above the pan of priming powder, producing sparks in much the same way as striking a flint to light a fire. Some snaphances were fitted with manual pan covers, others were opened automatically as on wheellocks.

9 Powder flask.

(Graham Turner © Osprey Publishing)

Castiglione's work was read widely. The new men learned about art and found a calling not on the battlefield but at court, working for the now rising state.

The rank of knight never died out, of course, any more than did that of esquire. The old connection with the 'shield bearer' (the literal translation of the latter) was long gone but the 'country squire' still denoted a man of standing in the community. The word itself, however, was increasingly debased until it became no more than a courtesy title given to all and sundry, as seen on personal correspondence today. By contrast, the title of knight retained its message of standing and service. It was Elizabeth I who ended the tradition that any knight could create another and made it solely the preserve of the monarch, which it has remained. Now the rank is awarded for service to one's country, yet the ritual dubbing with a sword, which replaced the original buffet, must still be done to seal the contract. Ranks of knighthood vary, from the knight bachelor to the prestigious Orders such as the Garter, founded in 1348, or the Bath, that was revived under Queen Victoria. The bestowal of knighthood does not now rely on a person's background status nor technically on his wealth, rather it is a public declamation of his achievements; the great horse may have gone but the rank still proclaims the man.

Glossary

Ahlespiess	A staff weapon for thrusting, consisting of a quadrangular-sectioned spike with a *rondel* to guard the hand.
Aiglet	A conical metal finial attached to the end of a point to prevent fraying and to ease passage through an eyelet.
Ailette	A small board of wood or parchment worn at the shoulder and usually painted with heraldic arms.
Aketon	A padded coat, usually quilted vertically, which was worn beneath mail to absorb blows, or on its own by ordinary soldiers. Also called *pourpoint*.
Alwite	Plate armour that is not faced with material.
Anime	*Cuirass* made from several horizontal lames.
Arçons	The *bow* and *cantle* of a saddle.
Armet	An Italian closed helmet with cheek-pieces that opened outwards to allow it to be put on.
Arming cap	A padded and quilted cap, sometimes worn under the helmet and always worn by lesser soldiers if a mail hood was still used.
Arming doublet	Lightly padded doublet worn beneath armour. It had gussets of mail attached to guard exposed parts and arming points to attach pieces of armour.
Arming partlet	Quilted collar worn below a plate collar.
Arming point	A flax, twine or buckskin lace used to attach armour.
Arming sword	The main fighting sword of a knight.
Arquebus	Longarm, usually a *matchlock* of varying bore.
Attainder	The loss of civil rights following a sentence of death or outlawry for treason or felony.
Aventail	Mail neck-defence attached to the lower edge of a *basinet*; smaller versions were attached to *armets*. In France referred to as a camail.

Backplate	Plate armour for the back.
Baleyn	Whalebone. The name refers to the baleen plates in the mouths of some species, which act as filters.
Baldric	Belt worn diagonally across the shoulder.
Ballock knife	A knife or dagger whose hilt has two swellings at the base next to the blade. Also called a kidney dagger by Victorians.
Banneret	A knight entitled to bring vassals onto the field under his own banner.
Barbut	A deep Italian helmet with a 'T'-shaped face-opening.
Bard	Full plate armour for a horse.
Base	Skirt, either of cloth or steel.
Baselard	A long civilian dagger or short sword, with an 'H'-shaped hilt.
Basinet	Conical or globular open-faced helmet that extended down at the sides and back. Also used to describe the *cervellière*.
Bastard sword	A sword capable of being wielded in one or both hands.
Baudekin	A silk cloth with a warp of gold thread. Also called siclaton.
Bec-de-faucon	A staff weapon consisting of an axe- or hammer-head backed by a beak like that of a falcon.
Behourd	A less formal version of the *tournament*.
Besagew	Roundel suspended to protect the armpit.
Bevor	Plate throat-defence used in conjunction with a *sallet*.
Bill	A staff weapon derived from a hedging bill, consisting of a broad convex hooked blade with a spike at the top and rear.
Boar-spear	Broad-bladed spear with two lugs below the blade to prevent a boar running up the shaft.
Bodkin	A long arrow-head without barbs, for piercing armour, especially mail.
Bow	The front of the saddle.
Braies	Loose linen drawers tied with a running string.
Brases	Carrying straps fitted inside a shield.
Breastplate	Plate armour for the chest and stomach.
Breaths	Holes in a helmet for ventilation and increased vision.
Brigandine	Body armour consisting of a canvas jacket inside which were riveted many small plates. The outside was usually faced with cloth or leather.
Broad-head	A wide barbed arrow-head with long cutting edges, used for hunting or maiming warhorses.
Burgonet	Open helmet with neck-defence, peak and cheek-pieces.

Burnet	A brown cloth.
Buskins	Boots made from soft leather or velvet.
By-knife	Small knife carried in a scabbard or dagger-sheath.
Byssine	A fine cotton or flax material.
Caliver	Longarm of medium–regular bore.
Canions	Cloth extension down the thigh.
Cannon	Tubular or gutter-shaped plate defence for the upper or lower arm. Also the term for a gun so large that it needed to be supported on a bed or carriage.
Cantle	The rear part of a saddle.
Cap-à-pied	Fully armed, literally 'head to foot'.
Caparison	Cloth, or occasionally mail, covering or housing for a horse, the former often used to carry the owner's coat-of-arms.
Celata	An open-faced Italian sallet.
Cervellière	A small hemispherical steel skull-cap.
Chape	A metal terminal fitted over the tip of a scabbard or sheath to protect it.
Chappe	A small leather rain-guard fitted over the sword cross to protect the blade in the scabbard.
Chausses	Stockings, either of cloth or mail.
Chevauchée	An armed expedition into enemy territory.
Close-helmet	Helmet covering the head that opens by pivoting the front and back halves.
Coat of plates	Body armour consisting of a canvas jacket inside which plates are riveted. The outside is usually faced with cloth or leather. Occasionally the uncovered plates are worn over a fabric lining. Also called pair of plates, hauberk of plates, cote à plates or plates.
Codpiece	Plate defence for the genitals. Also a similar cloth covering for civilian wear.
Coif	A mail hood. Also a cloth cap secured under the chin with ties. See also *arming cap*.
Conroi	A unit of cavalry, often in multiples of ten.
Constabularia	A unit of men, probably ten.
Coronel	A small crown of points used instead of a single sharp head on lances for jousts of peace. The use of several points helped spread the impact of the blow.
Cote	The tunic.
Cote-hardie	A front-fastening jacket worn over the doublet.
Courser	A warhorse.
Couter	Plate defence for the elbow.

Cranequin	Spanning device for crossbows consisting of a ratchet and winder.
Crinet	Plate defence for a horse's neck.
Crupper	Plate defence for a horse's rump.
Cuirass	Armour for the torso, usually denoting the *breast* and *backplates*, *fauld* and *culet*.
Cuir bouilli	Hardened leather that has been boiled or soaked before shaping.
Cuirie	Solid body armour, presumably of leather, sometimes reinforced by circular plates.
Cuisse	Plate defence for the thigh.
Culet	Plate defence below the *backplate*.
Destrier	The largest, strongest and most expensive war-horse.
Dubbing	The light blow with a hand or sword that made a man a knight.
Enarmes	Carrying straps fitted inside a shield. See *brases*.
Estoc	A thrusting sword with a long, stiff blade. Also called a tuck in England.
Falchion	A cleaver-like single-edged short sword.
Falling-buffe	Defence for the lower face, made from *lames* that can be lowered over one another.
Fauchard	A staff weapon consisting of a long cleaver-like blade, with a *rondel* to guard the hand. It was popular with French infantry.
Fauld	The hooped skirt that hung from the *breastplate* to guard the lower abdomen.
Fitchet	A vertical slit made in *super-tunics* with no side opening, allowing access to keys or purse hung from the tunic girdle.
Flanchard	Plate defence for a horse's flank.
Frog-mouthed helm	A helm whose lower front plate below the vision-slit is extended forward to deflect a blow. Also known as a tilting helm, and used largely for *jousts of peace*.
Frounce	Flounce.
Fuller	Groove running down a sword blade to lighten it.
Gadling	A proud metal stud on the knuckle or finger joint of a *gauntlet*.
Gaignepain	*Gauntlet*, probably of leather, worn on the right hand with armours for jousts of peace.
Galoches	Clogs.
Gambeson	A padded coat usually quilted vertically. The term generally refers to a coat worn over the armour rather than beneath it.
Gamboised cuisse	A padded and quilted tubular thigh-defence, sometimes richly decorated.
Gardbrace	A reinforcing plate worn over the *pauldron* on Italian and some west European armours.

Garde-corps	Long garment with wide tubular sleeves provided with slits for the arms to pass through. Also called *herygoud*.
Garnache	A beltless garment cut like the *tabard* but with shoulder line wide enough to cover the elbows.
Garniture	A set of matching pieces that allowed armours to be made up for several types of combat.
Gauntlet	Defence for the hand and wrist.
Genouillier	Plate defences for the knee.
Gisarme	Also called *guisarme*. A staff weapon consisting of a convex axe-head with the lowest point attached to the shaft.
Glaive	A staff weapon with a long convex cutting edge. See also *fauchard*.
Gorget	A plate collar to guard the throat.
Grandguard	Reinforce worn over the shoulder and upper chest in *jousts*.
Graper	A metal or leather stop nailed round the lance behind the grip.
Great basinet	A *basinet* with plate throat- and neck-defences attached.
Greave	Plate armour for the lower leg.
Guard-chain	A chain attached to the waist belt or breastplate and fixed by a toggle to the helm, sword or dagger to prevent loss.
Guard-of-the-vambrace	A reinforcing plate worn over the front of the *couter* on Italian and some west European armours.
Guige	The strap for suspending the shield from the neck or for hanging from a peg.
Guisarme	See *gisarme*.
Hackney	A riding horse.
Halberd	Staff weapon consisting of an axe blade backed by a hook and topped by a spike.
Hand-and-a-half sword	See *bastard sword*.
Hanger	Wide, shield-shaped sling to carry the scabbard.
Hauberk	A mail coat.
Haubergeon	A shorter version of the *hauberk*.
Haute-piece	An upstanding flange on a *pauldron*.
Helm	A large helmet enclosing the entire head.
Herald	An official employed by a king or nobleman, and who wore his arms. Heralds delivered messages and identified coats-of-arms.
Herygoud	See *garde-corps*.
Hounskull	The name sometimes given to the pointed visor worn with the *basinet*. Such a combination also gave rise to the Victorian term: 'pig-faced' basinet.

Houppelande	A front-fastening gown often worn over the doublet.
Hure	A cap.
Impresa	Decorative tournament shield designed for display only.
Jack	A quilted jacket made from many layers of linen or two layers stuffed with tow.
Jack of plate	Defence for ordinary soldiers consisting of a jacket enclosing small plates secured by twine.
Jamber	Defence for the lower leg.
Jousts	Contest between two mounted opponents with lances.
Jousts of peace	Contest between two mounted opponents using blunted lances.
Jousts of war	Contest between two mounted opponents using sharp lances.
Jupon	Also spelt 'gipoun'. A cloth coat worn over the tunic and buttoned or laced down the front. The term also refers to a similar style of *surcoat* worn over armour, occasionally fastened at the sides or rear.
Kettle hat	Open-faced helmet with a broad brim.
King-of-arms	The rank above that of *herald*.
Klappvisier	A visor attached at the brow of the helmet instead of the sides.
Lame	A strip or plate of steel, sometimes used to provide articulation in armour.
Lance	A long spear used on horseback.
Lance-rest	A bracket attached to the wearer's right side of the *breastplate* against which the *graper* was rammed to stop a lance running back when a strike was made. It derives from the French word '*Arrête*' meaning stop.
Langet	A metal strip attached to the head of a staff weapon, nailed to the shaft to provide a more secure fixture and to help prevent the wood from being cut.
Latten	Copper alloy very like brass, used for decorating some plate armour.
Left-hand gauntlet	*Gauntlet*, often of mail, used to grasp an opponent's blade.
Lists	The *tournament* arena where combats took place.
Livery	Robes worn by a lord's followers, bearing his badge and colours.
Locket	A metal mount to protect the mouth of a scabbard or sheath.
Locking-gauntlet	*Gauntlet* for the right hand that can be secured in the closed position to prevent loss of a weapon in the *tourney*.
Mail	Armour made from interlinked iron rings. Most were riveted but sometimes alternate lines of riveted and welded rings were used.
Manifer	Reinforce worn over the left *gauntlet* and lower arm-defences in the *jousts*.
Matchlock	A gun fired by lowering a glowing slow match onto gunpowder.
Morion	An open helmet with high comb, wide brim and cheek-pieces.

Morris pike	A pike, probably a corruption of 'Moorish pike'.
Muffler	A mail mitten.
Musket	A heavy longarm usually fired from a rest.
Nasal	The noseguard on a helmet.
Palfrey	A good riding horse.
Pantoffles	Leather overshoes; also cloth slippers.
Partisan	Staff weapon consisting of a long tapering blade furnished with two flukes at its base.
Pasguard	Reinforce worn over the *couter* in *jousts*.
Pauldron	Plate shoulder-defence that overlaps the chest and back.
Peascod	Fashionable style of drawn-down waist for doublet or *breastplate*.
Pelisson	A *super-tunic* lined with fur.
Petronel	Longarm with shortened barrel and curved stock to fire from chest, for use on horseback.
Peytral	Plate, or occasionally mail, defence for a horse's chest.
Pickadils	Leather or fabric tabs decorating the main edges of pieces of armour.
Pieces of advantage	Reinforces worn during certain *tournament* events.
Pike	A long spear used by infantry.
Plackart	Plate stomach-defence.
Poire	A pear-shaped wooden or leather buffer hung behind the shield on the *breastplate* of some west European armours for *jousts of peace*.
Polder-mitten	Lower cannon with a large, shell-like plate covering the outside of the elbow, the joint and part of the upper arm, worn on the right arm in *jousts of peace*.
Poleyn	Plate defence for the knee.
Pollaxe	Staff weapon consisting of an axe-blade backed by a hammer or a fluke and topped by a spike. Some have a hammer backed by a fluke.
Pommel	The piece on the end of a sword hilt to counterbalance the blade. Also the front board of a saddle.
Poulaine	A shoe with pierced decoration.
Pourpoint	See *aketon*.
Pursuivant	The rank below that of *herald*, identified by wearing the *tabard* sideways.
Quintain	Dummy used for weapon practice.
Rapier	Long, narrow-bladed thrusting sword with elaborate hilt.
Rebated	A weapon point or edge that has been blunted, for use in *tournament* contests.

Ricasso	The blunt portion of a sword blade beyond the hilt to allow a finger to be hooked over it.
Rondel	A disc attached to some staff weapons to guard the hand, and behind an *armet* to guard the strap holding the *wrapper*.
Rondel dagger	A dagger with a disc at each end of the hilt to guard the hand.
Rouncey	A horse suitable only for casual riding.
Rump-guard	A single plate that hung from the *culet*.
Sabaton	Plate armour for the foot.
Sallet	A helmet drawn out to a tail at the rear. Some were open faced, others protected the face.
Scale	Armour made from overlapping scales secured to a backing.
Scallops	Decorative edging made by slitting.
Schynbald	A solid plate shin-defence.
Shaffron	Plate defence for a horse's head.
Siclaton	See *baudekin*.
Side-piece	The diagonal strap attaching the scabbard to the front of the belt.
Side wing	A plate extending from the *couter* to guard the inside of the elbow or from the *poleyn* to guard the outside of the knee.
Skull	The main part of a helmet covering the top and sides of the head above the ears. Also a simple metal cap.
Slow match	Length of cord soaked in saltpetre.
Snaphance	Gun in which ignition is caused by sparks from a flint striking a steel.
Sneck hook	Small pivoting hook for securing through a pierced stud.
Spanish morion	Open helmet with tall skull, wide brim and cheek-pieces.
Spaudler	A plate shoulder-defence.
Standard	Mail neck-defence, usually with an upstanding collar of mail links.
Stop-rib	A raised strip of steel riveted to a plate to guide weapon points away.
Sumpter	A pack horse or mule.
Super-tunic	A garment worn over the tunic. Also called a *surcoat*.
Surcoat	In military parlance, a cloth garment worn over armour, usually lined and mostly sleeveless. In civilian parlance, a *super-tunic*, sometimes similar to the military version.
Tabard	A loose surcoat, usually open at the sides, which was put on over the head. It had wide elbow-length sleeves, and was used to display the wearer's arms. *Heralds* wore a similar coat with their master's arms.

Tang	The continuation of a sword blade that passes through the hilt.
Targe	Circular shield carried on foot.
Tasset	Plate defence for the thigh, attached to the *fauld*.
Testier	A padded defence for a horse's head and neck.
Tilt	The barrier separating two contestants in the *jousts*, usually in *jousts of peace*. Also known as a toile, it was originally of cloth but was soon replaced by a wooden barrier. It was also the term for *jousts* over the barrier.
Tilt visor	Visor with very narrow sights, used in the *jousts* over a barrier.
Tonlet	Deep laminated plate skirt.
Touch box	Container for carrying priming powder for a firearm.
Tournament	Originally a contest between two teams but later used to embrace the developed form in which jousting and foot combat also took place.
Tourney	A term used to denote the mounted team event during a *tournament*, to distinguish it from other events.
Trapper	See *caparison*.
Trousse	Set of hunting implements.
Tuck	English thrusting sword. The English name for an estoc.
Turner	The upper part of an upper *cannon*, which turns independently to aid arm movement.
Two-hand sword	Large sword designed for use in both hands.
Upper and lower stocks	The hose divided into two parts.
Vambrace	Plate defence for the arm.
Vamplate	A circular plate attached over the lance to guard the hand.
Venetians	Trunks fastening below the knee.
Ventail	Flap of mail worn across the chin and sometimes also covering the mouth.
Volant-piece	Brow reinforce.
Wambais	See *Aketon*.
War-hammer	A horseman's weapon consisting of a short staff with a hammer-head. The horseman's pick was a form backed by a fluke.
Wheellock	Gun in which ignition is caused by sparks from iron pyrites pressed against a spinning abrasive wheel.
Wrapper	A reinforce for the *bevor*. A prow-shaped plate strapped over the lower part of an *armet*.

Bibliography

Ayton, Andrew, *Knights and Warhorses: Military Service and the English Aristoricracy under Edward III* (Boydell & Brewer Ltd, Suffolk, 1994)

Barber, Richard, *The Knight and Chivalry* (Longman Group Ltd, London, 1970)

Barber, Richard, *The Reign of Chivalry* (Boydell & Brewer Ltd, Suffolk, 2005)

Barber, Richard, and Barker, Juliet, *Tournaments: Jousts Chivalry and Pageants in the Middle Ages* (The Boydell Press, Woodbridge, 1989)

Barker, Juliet, *The Tournament in England* (Boydell & Brewer Ltd, Suffolk, 2003)

Bellamy, J. G., *Bastard Feudalism and the Law* (Routledge, London, 1989)

Blair, Claude, *European Armour* (B. T. Batsford Ltd, London, 1958)

Boardman, Andrew W., *The Medieval Soldier in the Wars of the Roses* (Sutton Publishing Ltd, Stroud, 1998)

Boccia, Linello Giorgio, *Le Armature di S. Maria delle Grazie di Curtatone di Mantova e L'Armatura Lombarda del '400*, Bramante Editrice (Busto Arsizio, 1982)

Boulton, D'A. J. D., *The Knights of the Crown, The Monarchical Orders of Knighthood in Later Medieval Europe, 1325–1520* (Boydell & Brewer Ltd, Suffolk, 1987)

Boynton, L., *The Elizabethan Militia 1558–1638* (Routledge & Kegan Paul, London, 1967)

Bradbury, J., *The Medieval Archer* (The Boydell Press, Woodbridge, 1985)

Bradbury, J., *The Medieval Siege* (The Boydell Press, Woodbridge, 1992)

Burgess, E. Martin, 'Further Research into the Construction of Mail Garments', *Antiquaries Journal* XXXIII (1953), pp.193–202

Burgess, M., 'The Mail-Maker's Technique', *Antiquaries Journal* XXXII (1953), pp.48–55

Contamine, Philippe (trans. Michael Jones), *War in the Middle Ages* (Basil Blackwell, Oxford, 1984)

Cornish, Paul, *Henry VIII's Army* (Osprey Publishing Ltd, London, 1987)

Coss, Peter, *The Knight in Medieval England 1000–1400* (Alan Sutton Publishing Ltd, Stroud, 1993)

Cruickshank, G. C., *Elizabeth's Army*, (2nd ed.) (Oxford University Press, London, 1966)

Cruickshank, G. C., *Army Royal* (Oxford University Press, London, 1969)

Cunnington, C. Willet and Phillis, *Handbook of English Mediaeval Costume* (Faber & Faber Ltd, London, 1969)

Curry, Anne, and Hughes, Michael (ed.), *Arms, Armour and Fortifications in the Hundred Years War* (The Boydell Press, Woodbridge, 1994)

Davis, R. H. C., *The Medieval Warhorse* (Thames & Hudson Ltd, London, 1989)

Dillon, The Viscount, 'Tilting in Tudor Times', *Archaeological Journal* (1898)

Dufty, R., and Read, W., *European Armour in the Tower of London* (HMSO, London, 1968)

Duggan, Anne J. (ed.), *Nobles and Nobility in Medieval Europe* (Boydell & Brewer Ltd, Suffolk, 2002)

Eaves, Ian, 'On the Remains of a Jack of Plate Excavated from Beeston Castle in Cheshire', *The Journal of the Arms & Armour Society*, (vol. XIII, 2 Sept. 1989)

Eaves, Ian, 'The Tournament Armours of King Henry VIII of England', *Livrustkammaren* 1993 (Stockholm, 1994)

Eaves, Ian, 'The Greenwich Armour and Locking-Gauntlet of Sir Henry Lee in the Collection of the Worshipful Company of Armourers and Brasiers', *The Journal of the Arms & Armour Society* (vol. XVI, 3 Sept. 1999)

Eaves, Ian, *Catalogue of European Armour in the Fitzwilliam Museum* (Boydell & Brewer Ltd, Suffolk, 2002)

Edge, David, and Paddock, John Miles, *Arms and Armour of the Medieval Knight* (Bison Books Ltd, London, 1988)

Embleton, Gerry, *Medieval Military Costume* (The Crowood Press Ltd, Ramsbury, 2000)

Embleton, Gerry, and Howe, John, *The Medieval Soldier* (Windrow & Greene Ltd, London, 1994)

Ferguson, Arthur B., 'The Indian Summer of English Chivalry', *Studies in the Decline and Transformation of Chivalric Idealism* (Durham, NC, 1960)

Fiorato, Veronica, Boylton, Anthea, and Knüsel, Christopher, *Blood Red Roses* (Oxbow Books, Oxford, 2000)

Foss, Michael, *Chivalry* (Michael Joseph Ltd, London, 1975)

Gies, Frances, *The Knight in History* (Robert Hale Ltd, London, 1986)

Gravett, Christopher, and Breckon, Brett, *The World of the Medieval Knight* (MacDonald Young Books, Hove, 1996)

Gruffudd, Elis (trans. M. B. Davies), 'Suffolk's Expedition to Montdidier 1523', *Bulletin of the Faculty of Arts* (Fouad I University, vol. vii, 1944)

Gruffudd, Elis (trans. M. B. Davies), 'The Enterprises of Paris and Boulogne', *Bulletin of the Faculty of Arts* (Fouad I University, vol. xi, 1949)

Gruffudd, Elis (trans. M. B. Davies), 'Boulogne and Calais from 1545 to 1550', *Bulletin of the Faculty of Arts* (Fouad I University, vol. xii, 1950)

Haigh, P. A., *The Military Campaigns of the Wars of the Roses* (Sutton Publishing Ltd, Stroud, 1995)

Hooker, J. R., 'The Organization and Supply of the Tudor Military under Henry VII', *Huntington Library Quarterly* (vol. 23)

Jones, Terry, *Chaucer's Knight* (Methuen London Ltd, London, 1985)

Karcheski, Walter J. Jnr, and Richardson, Thom, *The Medieval Armour from Rhodes* (Boydell & Brewer Ltd, Suffolk, 2003)

Kelly, Francis M., and Schwabe, Randolph, *A Short History of Costume and Armour, 1066–1800* (David & Charles Reprints, Newton Abbot, 1972)

Keegan, J., *The Face of Battle* (Pimlico, 1991)

Keen, Maurice, *Chivalry* (Yale University Press, London, 1984)

Keen, Maurice (ed.), *Medieval Warfare* (Oxford University Press, Oxford, 1999)

Koch, H. W., *Medieval Warfare* (Bison Books Ltd, London, 1978)

Lander, J. R., *The Wars of the Roses* (Secker & Warburg, London, 1965)

Mann, Sir James, *Wallace Collection Catalogues. European Arms and Armour*, 2 vols (The Trustees of the Wallace Collection, London, 1962)

Morris, J. E., *The Welsh Wars of Edward I* (OUP, Oxford, 1901)

Munby, Julian, Barber, Richard and Brown, Richard, *Edward III's Round Table at Windsor* (Boydell & Brewer Ltd, Suffolk, 2007)

Myers, R. A., *The Household of Edward IV* (Manchester University Press, Manchester, 1959)

Nicolas, Sir Harris, *Wardrobe Accounts of Edward IV* (W. Pickering, London, 1830)

Nicolas, Sir Harris, *The History of the Battle of Agincourt* (Facsimile of 1833 edition) (H. Pordes, London, 1971)

Nicolle, David, *Medieval Warfare Source Book*, 2 vols (Arms and Armour Press, London, 1995, 1996)

Nicolle, David, *Arms & Armour of the Crusading Era 1050–1350* (Greenhill Books, London, 1999)

Norman, A. V. B., *The Rapier and Small Sword, 1460–1820* (Arms and Armour Press, London, 1980)

Norman, A. V. B., *Wallace Collection Catalogues, European Arms and Armour Supplement* (The Trustees of the Wallace Collection, London, 1986)

Norman, A.V.B., and Pottinger, Don, *Warrior to Soldier 449–1660* (Weidenfeld & Nicolson Ltd, London, 1966)

Norman A. V. B., and Pottinger, Don, *English Weapons and Warfare 449–1660* (Arms & Armour Press, London, 1979)

Norris, Herbert, *Tudor Costume and Fashion* (Dover Publications, 1997)

Oakeshott, R. Ewart, *The Sword in the Age of Chivalry* (Lutterworth Press, London, 1964)

Oman, Sir Charles, *A History of the Art of War in the Sixteenth Century* (London, 1937)

Pfaffenbichler, M., *Armourers* (British Museum Press, London, 1992)

Phyrr, Stuart W., La Rocca, Donald J., and Breiding, Dirk H., *The Armored Horse in Europe, 1480–1620* (Metropolitan Museum of Art, New York, 2005)

Prestwich, M., *Armies and Warfare in the Middle Ages* (Yale University Press, London, 1996)

Richardson, Thom, *The Armour and Arms of Henry VIII* (Trustees of the Royal Armouries, Leeds, 2002)

Rogers, Clifford J., *War Cruel and Sharp: English Strategy under Edward III 1327–1360* (Boydell & Brewer Ltd, Suffolk, 2000)

Rudorff, Raymond, *The Knights and their World* (Cassell & Company Ltd, London, 1974)

Stenton, Doris, *English Society in the Early Middle Ages*, The Pelican History of England 3, (Penguin Books Ltd, Harmondsworth, 1965)

Sutcliffe, Matthew, *The practice, proceedings and lawes of armes* (London, 1593)

Thompson, M. W., *The Decline of the Castle* (Cambridge University Press, Cambridge, 1987)

Thompson, M. W., *The Rise of the Castle* (Cambridge University Press, Cambridge, 1991)

Tincey, John, *The Armada Campaign 1588* (Osprey Publishing Ltd, London, 1988)

Turnbull, Stephen, *The Book of the Medieval Knight* (Cassell and Company Ltd, London, 1985)

Verbruggen, J. F., *The Art of Warfare in Western Europe during the Middle Ages* (The Boydell Press, Suffolk, 1997)

Walden, Howard de, *Some Feudal Lords and their Seals* (1903, reprinted by Crécy Books, Clifton, 1984)

Watts, Karen, 'Henry VIII and the Pageantry of the Tudor Tournament', *Livrustkammaren* (1994)

Williams, Alan, and Reuck, Anthony de, *The Royal Armoury at Greenwich 1515–1649 – A History of its Technology* (Royal Armouries Monographs, London, 1995)

Young, Alan, *Tudor and Jacobean Tournaments* (George Philip, London, 1987)

Index